GENESIS
OF THE JET

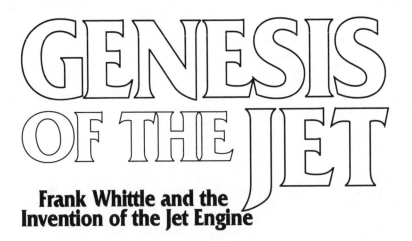

GENESIS OF THE JET

**Frank Whittle and the
Invention of the Jet Engine**

John Golley

in association with
SIR FRANK WHITTLE, OM, KBE, CB

Technical Editor
BILL GUNSTON

Airlife
England

Copyright © 1996 John Golley, Bill Gunston

First published in the UK in 1987 under the title *Whittle: the true story*
This edition published in the UK in 1996
by Airlife Publishing Ltd

4th impression 1999

British Library Cataloguing-in-Publication Data
  A catalogue record for this book
  is available from the British Library

ISBN 1 85310 860 X

Printed in England by Livesey Ltd, Shrewsbury.

Airlife Publishing Ltd

101 Longden Road, Shrewsbury SY3 9EB, England
Email: airlife@airlifebooks.com
www.airlifebooks.com

Contents

Preface

This is the human and dramatic story of a very great Englishman. By creating and giving birth to the turbojet, Sir Frank Whittle became one of the greatest inventors of all time, and his name is 'immortalised' in the annals of aviation technology. His superhuman fight to establish and develop his project is the theme of this book, which is the result of long research and collaboration with the inventor.

Working with a genius is a privilege and an unforgettable experience for any writer. Sir Frank's unfailing good humour and his willingness to discuss his traumatic life in the most intimate detail reveals the strength of his character and his moral courage. His words are quoted throughout, whenever possible. Thus, this is his story in association with him.

I have also had the privilege of working with Bill Gunston, who is an author of many aviation books and a walking encyclopaedia of aeronautical history. Bill's encouragement and professionalism have been of enormous help throughout.

I would like to thank the Prime Minister, the Rt Hon Margaret Thatcher PC MP, for her generous appreciation of Sir Frank's life and work. Also Lord Kings Norton, Chancellor of the Cranfield Institute of Technology and past President of the Royal Aeronautical Society and of the Royal Institution of Great Britain, who has kindly written the foreword and given me much help. My thanks to Sir Arnold Hall, formerly Director of RAE and Chairman of the Hawker Siddeley Group, and to Sir Rolf and Lady Dudley-Williams, Reg Voysey, Group Captain J. H. McC. Reynolds, Michael Daunt, and Andrew Stevens. Finally, to Roy and Eileen Fowkes for their hospitality, introductions and back-up.

John Golley

It was in 1984 that Sir Frank asked me whether I would assist him in writing his definitive story. I considered the first thing to do was to contact publishers in the UK and USA, and this wasted more than a year. I soon felt that I was letting Sir Frank down — something that does not bear contemplation — and I judged that I needed a co-author. Picking John Golley was a singularly happy choice. In the event John wrote almost the whole book, apart from one or two bits of background and the appendices and captions. I have been only too glad to stand behind him in setting down a story of technical discovery which for excitement and importance is hard to equal.

Bill Gunston

Foreword

by Lord Kings Norton

In AD 60, or thereabouts, Hero of Alexandria designed, and, just possibly, constructed, his aeolipile, which was a simple form of turbine driven by jet propulsion.

In 1794, John Barber of Nuneaton designed and patented an apparatus recognizable as a gas turbine.

In 1930, Frank Whittle, of the Royal Air Force, patented his design of an aircraft engine in which a gas turbine provided a powerful propulsive jet. This, the so-called jet propulsion engine, started one of the great engineering developments of the century.

For me, this book is in two parts. First there is the development, from humble beginnings, of a major personality. Second, there is the struggle of this extraordinary man not only to convince what we call the Establishment of the value of his brainchild, but to overcome political and bureaucratic frustrations which should never have been allowed to occur. He triumphed, but by the time his technological victory was complete, control of development had passed into other hands. But also, appreciation of his tremendous contribution to technological advance had begun to develop and now his reputation as one of the great men of the 20th century is secure.

The part I played in the saga of the Whittle engines is clear from this book. I was always on the side of the angels, of whom there were too few in high places. Fortunately, I was given the opportunity in 1947 to appraise the Whittle achievement in a letter which reached the Royal Commission on Awards to Inventors. It was, I believe, instrumental in significantly augmenting the Commission's award to Whittle. That letter is reproduced near the end of this book. Had I not written it, something very like it would have been included in this foreword. Such differences as there might have been, the result of the revolution in civil and military aviation that has occurred since I wrote in 1947, would have been to rate still higher the magnitude of Whittle's contribution to technological progress. Last year, the highest possible recognition of what he did came from the Queen to my old and distinguished friend. He received the Order of Merit.

Kings Norton

Introduction

Captain 'Monty' Burton glanced down his list of passengers who would be flying with him on BA Flight 189 from Heathrow to Dulles International Airport at Washington. Usually he carried two or three VIPs, plus people who had been successful in a variety of walks of life. Today, it appeared that most of his passengers were wealthy Americans going home; then his eye caught one particular name, that of Sir Frank Whittle who with Lady Whittle would be occupying two seats up front behind the flight deck.

He had recently met Sir Frank, who had given an unforgettable after-dinner speech at their Concorde crew dinner in the Royal Air Force Club. Sir Frank's talk about his life and work with the jet engine had made a deep impression, and his great sense of humour had got them all going — especially as most of them, like Sir Frank, had RAF backgrounds. It had been a splendid show, and most moving when Whittle, in his very direct way, had related his struggles with the powers that be during the thirties and forties when he was fighting desperately to prove his invention. Monty had thought at the time that there was just a trace of bitterness in Whittle's voice, but it had been an evening which no one in the audience was ever likely to forget.

Thinking about it, Monty concluded that among all the passengers he had carried or would carry before he retired, Frank Whittle, for him, would always be the most memorable. With two million supersonic miles under his belt and six years operating with the Concorde fleet, he had been in regular contact with high society and the affluent but, in his opinion, the small, stocky jet pioneer stood head and shoulders above them all. He couldn't help thinking that way because of the enormous difference that Frank Whittle had made to his own life.

Ninety per cent of Monty Burton's flying career had been spent on jet aircraft since he had learned most of his jet flying in the early fifties on the Meteor Mark 3. The simple and immensely reliable Derwent engine powering the Meteor was an offshoot of Whittle's first jet engine which had revolutionised the entire aviation industry. After the Meteor, the jet engines of the Canberra had taken him up to 47,000 feet — an unbelievable height in those days in an aircraft without rocket assistance.

Those same Canberra engines had jetted him safely through nuclear explosions in Australia, when Britain was carrying out atom bomb tests. Four times he had flown through the dark swirling masses of radioactive cloud collecting data, and received over fifty times the maximum allowable dose of radiation. Nine Röntgens, he thought, was the limit. But that was over thirty years ago and yet here he was, still with ten fingers, ten toes and other essentials!

His life had been conditioned by the jet engine. He had had sixteen happy years flying 707s across the world and only two jet failures during that time, both of which had been easily contained — a remarkable record by any standard! And then, Concorde! Six years of supersonic flight during which he had broken world records to Auckland, New Zealand. Now, he'd only got two years of supersonic flying left before they retired him at 55. He knew perfectly well that he was capable of flying Concorde until he was sixty, but there was nothing that he could do about it — not so for Sir Frank, he thought, who was jetting all over the world, still in the forefront of jet technology and giving lectures in his late seventies.

Now he had the privilege of carrying this incredible man across the Atlantic, and he was looking forward to chatting with him on the flight deck. As the crew's transport drew up alongside Concorde G-BOAD, his first officer, Chris Norris, nudged him. "A bit thoughtful this morning, Monty", he said. Monty smiled and nodded without saying anything. Getting out, Monty looked up at the weather which was always a pilot's natural reaction before a flight. The Sun was shining through light fluffy clouds, and its rays were sparkling on the sharp supersonic nose of the aircraft. A day like this in late October, he thought, was going to give the passengers a great start.

The latter were assembling and relaxing in the special Concorde lounge, some sipping champagne. Groups of Americans were gazing out of the picture windows watching the activity around the aircraft. She stood aloof on stand Juliet 2, towering above the white-overalled figures attending her, with her sharp nose looking like the predatory beak of some giant bird of prey. Her nose dominated even her dart-like fuselage with its elegant and graceful curved-back wings carrying underneath the four mighty Olympus engines. The impression she gave was that of an aeronautical aristocrat looking disdainfully at her more prosaic relations.

Sir Frank Whittle was sitting benignly and contentedly reading *The Times*. Other passengers never gave him a glance because they had no idea who he was. When a British Airways executive came over to have a few words with him a few heads turned in their direction, but that was all. Beaming, Sir Frank stood up to shake hands, a short, cobby figure smartly dressed in a dark suit with waistcoat and wearing an Old Cranwellian tie. Having been a regular RAF officer for many years, retiring in 1948 as an Air Commodore, he was always on parade in public.

Only his white, wavy hair indicated that he was getting on in years. He was 76 at the time but his vibrant personality and erect bearing belied the fact. There was nothing in his strong face and genial manner to suggest the mental and physical torture he had endured in driving his invention through to reality. Or the aftermath which had left him totally drained in mind and spirit.

Now living alongside the shores of a lake in Maryland, about one hour out of Washington, he had just completed one of his regular hectic trips to the Old Country. He had been guest of honour at several official functions, given lectures to aeronautical and engineering associations, met captains of industry and old friends, and visited his family. Now he was on his way home with his American wife, 'Tommie', a petite, smart and charming lady — a one-time air hostess and US Navy nurse.

As he walked through the tunnel and entered the slim, luxurious interior his eyes had taken in everything going on around him. He had flown in Concorde across the Atlantic and back many times, and having been a flying instructor and test pilot he loved aeroplanes. Especially this one which was the ultimate in civil aviation and the crowning product of his achievement.

In his favourite seat up front Sir Frank had a clear view of the Marilake passenger screen displaying flight statistics. On this trip he was going to log the climb in his diary, recording time, Mach number, altitude, speed in mph, and outside centigrade temperature from the digital read-out system. Recording statistics and making calculations had been a lifetime occupation, and he enjoyed checking Concorde's progress throughout the supersonic climb up to 60,000 feet and comparing notes with previous recordings.

Captain Monty Burton and his crew had been carrying out their before start check list, involving amongst other detail, altimeters, inertial navigation systems, and the shifting and balancing of fuel for take-off. Precisely three minutes before moving off stand Juliet 2, the ground crew, using compressed air, started up number three inboard Olympus engine. With a high-pitched whine and a thunderous roar the huge jet engine blasted into action, feeding high-pressure fluid into the arteries leading to the flying controls, bringing Concorde to life.

The second inboard engine was started, and with two engines running she was towed clear of the parking area. Then the outboard engines were started, the tractor and towbar unhitched, and the communication with the ground engineer cast off before she commenced taxiing towards the runway.

All the final pre-flight checks had been completed when Captain Burton received clearance for take-off from the tower at Heathrow. Lining up Concorde on to the centre of the runway and with reheat switched on for maximum power, Monty Burton opened up the throttles, watching the centreline rushing beneath him as Concorde rapidly gathered speed. He called out "speed building" and then "one hundred knots". The engineer replied, "power checks" as Burton called "Vee one" and moved his hand from the throttles to the control column — they had then passed the point of no return. On the word "rotate" the control column came back, rotating the machine to an angle of 13 degrees above the horizontal.

At 217 knots she unstuck, "Vee two" is called — a safe climbing speed in the event of engine failure. Then Burton asked for "Positive rate of climb" having at least twenty feet between his main wheels and the ground. "Gear up", he ordered and the First Officer selected it up. At 240 knots the nose-up pitch attitude was increased from 13 degrees to 20 degrees, as Concorde climbed up and away at 4,000 feet per minute at a steady 240 knots.

Sir Frank had recorded 13.30 — take off in his neat clear hand and, having heard the thuds as the landing gears came up, he was waiting for the reheat, or afterburners, to be switched off to reduce engine noise. Reheat was one of the many inventions on which he had worked almost half a century earlier. Exactly 72 seconds from take-off he heard the change of jet engine noise, and recorded the time in his diary with the words reheat off.

He knew that they switched off the afterburners to cut down the jet roar as part of air traffic control regulations. He had recently been involved in discussions on both sides of the Atlantic regarding a more efficient and quieter engine to power a Phase Two supersonic jetliner which could carry more passengers. Turbine blade technology had improved since the design of the Olympus, and research was being carried out by Rolls-Royce and American firms to develop an engine silencer as part of an engine noise suppressor programme.

Thinking about turbine blades took his mind back to an astonishing discovery he had made nearly fifty years ago. British Thomson-Houston of Rugby, who were then producing turbine blades for his first engine, had failed to allow for a most important phenomenon: the radial pressure gradient which must exist in the whirling flow from a ring of nozzle blades. He had discovered this fact during a series of calculations, and according to his theory twice as much twist on the turbine blading was needed as had been provided by BTH in the company's original design. He remembered that, much to his surprise, he had made a fundamental discovery in turbine design.

Monty Burton had reduced power and eased the control column forward to reduce pitch to 12 degrees from the horizontal in order to cut back the rate of climb from 4,000 to 1,200 feet per minute whilst maintaining an indicated airspeed of 250 knots. Having crossed the radio beacon close to Reading and cleared the great urban areas surrounding London, the nose and vizor had been raised and Concorde accelerated to 300 knots.

She had shot through a pattern of cloudlets sailing like an armada of tinted orange, brown, grey and white powder-puffs into a blue umbrella sky dominated by the orb of the Sun. The uplifting of her nose and vizor restored her clean, pure pencil-like shape for supersonic flight, and freed her from aerodynamic buffeting, which made the flight much smoother.

When she started her supersonic climb — restricted to avoid sonic boom overland — from 28,000 feet up to 55,000 feet, the throttles were fully opened and the computers instantly signalled the engines for maximum power. Concorde responded by picking up her skirts and she was away. Sir Frank sensed a surge of power flowing through the airframe, and felt the acceleration as the inboard reheats ignited, closely followed by the outboard adding about twenty per cent more thrust to the engines.

Climbing on full power, Whittle estimated that she must be burning over forty-four tonnes of fuel per hour. He had been told that Captain Burton had taken on 93 tonnes for a journey lasting three hours-and-forty-five minutes! Thinking about it took his mind back to a thesis he had written in 1929 when he had come to the general conclusion that, if very high speeds were to be combined with long range, it would be necessary to fly at great heights where the very low air density would greatly reduce resistance in proportion to speed. He had been an officer cadet at RAF Cranwell then. At the time he had been working on his theory, the maximum speed of RAF fighters was rather less than 150 mph, and their service ceiling about 20,000 feet.

Monty Burton watched his Mach number climb until it passed Mach one. As it did so he noticed a fluctuation on his pressure instruments, especially the vertical speed indicator, and he knew that a shock wave had shot past the static pressure-ports on the side of the fuselage. Within seconds Mach 1.01 was recorded on the Marilake indicators in the cabin, and the passengers could see for themselves that Concorde had gone supersonic.

When Concorde had accelerated through the sound barrier, the centre of lift began to move to the rear of the aircraft. Fuel was then pumped into a previously empty tank at the tail to restore the aircraft's balance.

Sir Frank had recorded a Mach number of 1.3 at 37,000 feet at an outside temperature of minus 50 degrees centigrade. At Mach 1.3, he knew instinctively that the Olympus engines would then be taking full advantage of the shock waves as the varible ramps inside the engine air intakes had come into operation. These ramps slow down the air to subsonic speed at the entry to the engine compressor for good engine efficiency, which was a subject close to his heart.

As she had gone supersonic he was reminded of his first flight in Concorde, which had been one of the proving flights out into mid-Atlantic and back. Apart from experiencing her breathtaking performance, he had been fascinated by the Sun. They had taken off from Heathrow at sunset, and as they flew west towards the setting Sun it appeared to be rising. Their speed was so great that they were overtaking the Sun, giving them an apparent sunrise or a sunset in reverse, as he liked to call it.

Conversely, as they flew east at these latitudes the Sun had set in the west at three times its normal rate, casting, as it did so, a vast curved shadow of the Earth, up and ahead of the aircraft.

Back in 1936, when he was working on the design of his experimental engine, he had never foreseen that one day he would be crossing the Atlantic in three-and-a-half hours — though his notebook of that year recorded engine calculations for up to 1,500 mph. Sitting comfortably in Concorde, accelerating in the climb to Mach 2 or twice the speed of sound, reminded him of jet engine development since 1948 when the Olympus engine was orginally designed. He knew of no other engine in the aircraft industry that had been developed like the Olympus, but was convinced that they could get more thrust out of it yet.

He had done a lot of paperwork on gas turbine engine requirements for a new generation of supersonic transports. A speed of Mach 2.3 was visualised in his calculations so far, for an aircraft carrying 300 passengers with a range as far as San Francisco to Tokyo non-stop. He believed that any Phase Two project of this nature could come about only by a combined effort between America, Great Britain and France. Development costs were so high that he doubted whether any one country could go it alone. He had talked at great length to leading aircraft and engine companies in the three countries concerned. Acting as a catalyst, he had done his best to interest them in forming a common consortium, in which the firms concerned would become sub-contractors of the main international company, but though getting mainly positive responses he hadn't succeeded, as yet.

He thoroughly enjoyed his gourmet lunch flying at some 59,000 feet, or at twice the height of Mount Everest, as the Captain described it. Looking out of his window he had seen the curvature of the Earth, and the dark blue sky leading into the blackness of infinite space. He was musing over the fact that she was travelling at a speed of over 1,300 mph but using less than half the fuel she had consumed at lower altitudes, when he received the Captain's invitation to visit the flight deck.

Monty Burton found him charming and interested in everything that was happening in the cockpit, although Sir Frank must have seen it all before. There was a genuine warmth about him which transmitted itself to the crew. He listened patiently while Monty gave him a brief summary of their current position, and flight details, pointing to specific instruments. Sir Frank, naturally, was particularly interested in the Flight Engineer's panel, which displayed the fuel management system, and recorded all its intricate detail. Studying the vast array of dials, knobs and switches he asked the Flight Engineer a number of highly technical questions about fuel flow, revs, temperatures, back-up systems and air inlet controls.

Monty watched him peering intently at the dials on the panel, taking off his glasses and pointing to a particular reading which had interested him. Then Whittle cracked a joke with the Flight Engineer which caused a great deal of amusement. It was amazing, Monty thought, that Whittle at the age of 76 should be thinking and planning ahead for the next twenty years of jetliner development, while he would be forced to retire as a Concorde Captain at the age of only 55.

After they landed at Dulles International Airport, outside Washington, Monty Burton addressed his passengers;

"Ladies and gentlemen", he said, "welcome to Washington on this fine autumn afternoon. We have covered the 3,900 miles from London to Washington in 3 hours 37 minutes, giving us an average speed of well over 1,000 miles per hour. The maximum speed that we achieved was 1,340 miles per hour, and our maximum height was 60,000 feet, eleven miles above the surface of the Earth.

"Today, we have the great honour indeed of carrying Sir Frank Whittle who invented the jet engine which made all this possible".

There was a great round of applause and a bit of cheering which was a most unusual occurrence from Concorde passengers. When Monty Burton got out of the aircraft an American passenger came up to him and said,

"You know, Captain, you've really put the icing on the cake for me. To travel in Concorde as a fellow passenger with Sir Frank Whittle is something I can relate to my grandchildren".

Chapter 1
Humble Beginnings

1907, the height of the Edwardian era, neared the end of an age of tranquillity and elegance, an age in which Britain's might was unchallenged round the world. Gentlemen wore frock coats and top hats; their tight-waisted ladies would never be seen without gloves, and in summer sported a straw boater and parasol. Everyone was excited to learn that the Wright brothers really had made a flying machine that actually worked. In November, an Englishman (later naturalized Frenchman) by the name of Henry Farman became the first European to remain in the air for longer than 59 seconds, having completed a circuit in 1 minute and 14 seconds. Onlookers threw their hats in the air.

There was no Edwardian elegance about the life and background into which Frank Whittle was born on June 1st of that year. His parents had broken away from the family tradition of working in the cotton mills of Lancashire to settle in a typical working-class house in the Earlsdon district of Coventry. There his father, Moses Whittle, worked as a foreman in a factory manufacturing machine tools.

Frank's parents were Lancashire born, and members of large families. Their upbringing had been haunted by the shadow of poverty and conditioned by a very hard life. Each had had to start part-time work in the mills about the age of ten or eleven and had been reared in a strict Wesleyan tradition. It was shortly after their marriage that they moved to Coventry where Frank was born.

Moses Whittle was a skilful mechanic and a very prolific inventor who was unable to process sound ideas because of his lack of technical education. Therefore, young Frank was lucky to grow up in an atmosphere of invention which was to dominate his life. One of the few things he remembers at the tender age of four was being given a toy aeroplane: "Its propeller was driven by clockwork and it was much too heavy for a flying model, but it could be suspended from the bracket of the gas mantle by a length of string and it would perform a circle in the brief interval before the spring ran down. Whether that toy was the starting point of my interest in aircraft I don't remember, but it is linked in my mind with memories of occasional flights over Coventry at about that time by one or two early aviators".

He began his education at the Earlsdon Council School at the age of five: ". . . a street urchin on six days of the week and a carefully washed and carefully dressed little boy on Sunday". On that day he was often a very unwilling member of the chapel congregation, sitting through interminable prayers and sermons which he didn't understand at all. But there were compensations because Sundays seemed to be his father's favourite day for an enthusiastic outburst of drawing, so that at an early age he became familiar with the drawing board, T-square and other implements of the draughtsman's trade.

Discipline was strict at home, his father used the razor strop on him when necessary, and the Wesleyan churchgoers were very strait-laced and unrelenting. Despite his rigid upbringing, young Frank was a mischievous lad and already showed signs of cocking a snook at the Establishment. The First World War broke out when he was seven years old, and he began to take an interest in aeroplanes. He was to see them being manufactured at the Standard Works outside Coventry and occasionally flying over the area. The greatest event in his life as a small boy happened when an aircraft force-landed a few hundred yards from his home. It was the first time that he had ever seen one at such close quarters and the event remained a life-long memory especially as, when it took off, it nearly removed his head: his cap had to be fished out of a gorse bush.

His father was ambitious and had been saving up to buy a small engineering company. In 1916, when Frank was nine, Moses Whittle borrowed enough money to buy the Leamington Valve and Piston Ring Company and the family moved to Leamington Spa. The little factory was far less imposing than its name, housing only a few lathes and other machine tools, all powered by a single-cylinder gas engine.

The Whittle family, growing in number, had had the courage to go it alone, and for a time things went well. The Great War was providing plenty of work for small engineering companies in the Midlands complex, and the Whittle enterprise was no exception. Moses discarded his push bike and invested £5 in an ancient two-seater Talbot-Darracq. To be seen in a motor car in those days was a sign of opulence as young Frank discovered: ". . . One day, while I was playing with a number of companions, I saw this contraption come sailing down Dale Street [Leamington Spa] with my parents perched high in its bucket seats — my father looking as proud as a Rajah riding an elephant. I acted as though I did not belong to them — but it was no good — my companions had watched the proceedings with great glee and teased me unmercifully".

This happened about the time when his mother tried to send him to a small school which she believed to be a little superior to an elementary school — the curriculum included French and there was a small charge of sixpence a week. In the event, he only stuck it out for one morning and refused to go back because he had had rather a rough time as a new boy. His mother relented and he went to Milverton Council School instead.

Frank was a very small boy and sensitive, but not lacking in physical courage. At Milverton he showed the first signs of becoming a brain when he won a scholarship to Leamington College, and it was here that he first became aware of class distinction and divided loyalties. The College boys were identified by a yellow gore in their caps, which the locals called 'Tuppenny Custards', and these promoted fights amongst the two factions. He frequently had to run the gauntlet of groups of jeering young toughs.

He had been acquiring his first practical experience of some manufacturing processes in his father's workshop. Moses gave him small sums on a piecework basis for drilling valve stems and doing lathe work. Thus, from an age of ten or eleven, he had begun to use machine tools and absorb the atmosphere of the workshop floor.

Having started in the 'A' stream at Leamington College, he did so badly in his first term that he was demoted from IIIA to IIIB. This made him sit up and take notice: ". . . The disgrace provoked me out of a natural laziness into becoming top of the form in the succeeding term — the only time I was to be top of my form throughout my school career".

The First World War was then reaching its final, dramatic stages. Young Whittle had spent almost a third of his eleven years under its shadow but had not been greatly affected by it. One of his father's brothers was lost at sea, and one of his mother's brothers had lost an eye in the Dardanelles campaign.

Searchlights had probed the night sky, and there was the odd Zeppelin raid, but, apart from seeing troops on the march and the effect of rationing, the war was a comparatively distant thing. His interest in aeroplanes, however, was growing all the time and the flying VCs, such as Captain Albert Ball, Billy Bishop, McCudden and the like, became his heroes.

Moses Whittle's small business had expanded during the Great War and there had been an improvement in the family's financial position. This modest prosperity came to an end in the immediate post-war period when: ". . . My parents found it increasingly difficult to make both ends meet, and to these troubles were added others. Because my father had failed to have a certain agreement recorded in writing, we were turned out of the house we then occupied, and for a few days were homeless. We all slept on mattresses in the loft of the workshop. For a time after this the family occupied two small rooms in one of the poorer districts of Leamington".

Before this dismal event young Frank, who had been working conscientiously, gained another scholarship which gave him the choice between going to a grammar school or a money grant of £10 a year. But his parents simply could not afford the cost in clothing and travelling to send him to grammar school, and elected to take the money grant to help out with school books and clothing while he was at Leamington College.

It is impossible to say what effect a grammer school education might have had on young Whittle at this stage. He could not escape from his working-class background and the poverty-stricken situation facing his family. Yet he longed to lift himself out of his social class, and to that end went to some trouble to rid himself of his Lancashire accent. While at Leamington College, which he regarded as a rather miserable period in his life, he recalled that: ". . . I was costing my parents nothing in school fees, and my other school expenses were covered by the scholarship grant, but nevertheless, my parents found it very difficult to provide me with clothes appropriate to the status of the school, and I was probably one of the shabbiest members of it".

As he grew up, certain facets of his character and attitude became evident. Generally speaking, he could be described in his early teens as being a small, somewhat sensitive youth who was a bit of a rebel, but had brains when he wanted to use them. In fact, there was much more to Whittle's character than the "could do better if he paid more attention to homework" remark on his reports.

He had a very strongly developed sense of curiosity and spent a great deal of time, when he should have been doing his homework, in Leamington Spa Reference Library reading subjects which intrigued him: ". . . The one subject I was particularly interested in at school was chemistry, but outside school I was a voracious reader of popular science books, and acquired a fairly wide knowledge (for my age) of astronomy, physiology, engineering (particularly aircraft engineering) and a wide range of other subjects, shorthand, comparative religion, etc.".

During his school days he first became acquainted with Stodola's 'Steam and Gas Turbines', and although the text was way above his head, he learned something about the construction of turbines. He was also studying aircraft theory to such an extent that he was quite confident that he could step into the cockpit and fly an aeroplane.

This intense interest in science and engineering subjects which he had developed at such an early age was quite remarkable. Later in life he reflected that: ". . . Had the headmaster and his colleagues realised what a useful amount of knowledge I was acquiring out of school, they might have been more lenient about the results of my official studies". In the School .Certificate examinations he obtained six credits but no distinctions — not even in his favourite subject, chemistry, and he failed to matriculate!

His schoolmasters, however, began to recognise that he had something special. During his last two years, they had allowed him to work in the laboratory on his own instead of being on the playing field. This enabled him to get well ahead of the practical chemistry laboratory programme, and allowed him time for unauthorised attempts to make explosives. On one occasion he had four official quantitative analysis experiments going simultaneously, and also attempted to make sodium picrate — an explosive which readily detonates:

". . . I dissolved a considerable quantity of picric acid in a strong solution of caustic soda. I then allowed the solution to cool and filtered off the crystals of sodium picrate which had formed and then put the beaker with the solution back on the sand tray, with the object of obtaining a second crystallization. Within a few seconds of doing so it exploded. Fortunately for me

I must have blinked at the very instant of the explosion because, though my face was bright yellow, none went into my eyes. My other four experiments were, of course, ruined, and my heart sank when I saw the mess in the laboratory. I was profoundly astonished that anything in water could blow up and spent a laborious two hours wiping bottles, etc.".

Although young Whittle spent a great deal of his spare time reading books, his image was not that of a 'swot'. His punishment record was one of the best in the school, and he confessed to a fairly extensive record of undetected crime including forging his mother's signature to explain his absence when he had played truant or his failure to do his homework. He had also achieved a reputation amongst his set as being rather a daredevil, and was always willing to go one better in such activities as running along bridge parapets, bicycle stunts, and climbing trees. Anything, in fact, which required wiriness, strong nerve, and a good sense of balance.

The annual school sports appealed to him even less than organised games. Everybody was obliged to enter for at least two events, and he selected the two which called for the least effort, e.g., the hundred yards and the long jump. Despite his attitude, he was a good sprinter and won medals for it. It seemed that he was ready to take on anything, providing he wasn't compelled to do it. An example of this was the marathon: ". . . It was purely voluntary and did not count as one of the two compulsory events, otherwise, in all probability, it would have been the last thing I would have done. It was the height of optimism to enter for this event in any case, because of my size. Nevertheless, I came in fourth, but in such a state of exhaustion that I vowed that I would never do it again". But stroppy Whittle had two more goes in succeeding years, and came in fourth on both occasions.

He had made up his mind when he was about fourteen to join the Royal Air Force as a boy apprentice. The minimum age was fifteen, and his parents agreed that he could go after his fifteenth birthday at the end of the Christmas term, 1922. This left him with a short spell in the VIth form where he elected to take physics, chemistry and mathematics. He had badly wanted the dignity of the Sixth but, to his great chagrin, he was not made a prefect as were all the other sixth formers.

In due course, he entered and passed the written examination for entry as an aircraft apprentice at Royal Air Force, Halton. He came through with flying colours, feeling very confident that it would only be a matter of time before he qualified as a pilot achieving his boyhood dream. All the books he had read about the theory of flight, aircraft engineering and science, he thought, would now stand him in good stead — the forthcoming medical examination would be only a formality.

In January 1923, together with 600 other young enthusiasts, he was taken by special train from Baker Street to Wendover and thence to Halton Camp. Two days later he was on his way home, having failed the medical examination. Poor physique was the explanation given, but after making further enquiries he discovered that it meant that he was under-sized, being only five feet tall with a correspondingly small chest measurement.

He was bitterly disappointed, and before leaving Halton made unsuccessful attempts to have his case reconsidered: ". . . My persistence, however, was not entirely wasted. A service policeman took me along to see a physical training instructor, Sergeant Holmes, who also took pity on me. He gave me a list of Maxalding exercises, and showed me how to do them. In addition, he wrote out a diet sheet for me, and when I returned to Leamington I carried out his instructions to the letter".

For six months Whittle did his exercises and stuck to his diet, drinking daily doses of olive oil which never became an acquired taste! But the treatment was effective, and he added three inches to his height and another three to his chest measurement. Once again he applied to take the medical examination but was turned down. It seemed to be a case of once rejected, always rejected.

This bureaucratic attitude would have knocked the stuffing out of most hopefuls, but not Whittle. He went through the whole procedure again as though he had never applied before and got away with it! He passed the written examination once more, but this time found himself reporting at Cranwell in September 1923. There he passed the medical without difficulty and got himself into the Royal Air Force at last, although in a sense, under false pretences.

Chapter 2
RAF Cranwell 1923-1926

Full of enthusiasm and dedicated to becoming a pilot, 364365 Boy Whittle, F, arrived at No 4 Apprentices Wing RAF Cranwell to start training as a fitter. He was just sixteen years old. The Apprentices School had been set up only four years previously as part of Lord Trenchard's basic development programme for the RAF. Its function was to ensure a flow of skilled technicians, without whom the RAF could not operate. Cranwell was also the home for the new RAF Cadet College which had been instituted to provide a regular supply of qualified officers to the permanent force. Young Whittle was to spend the first five years of his RAF service within this environment.

He soon developed an intense hatred for the tough, uncompromising, and rigid atmosphere surrounding him. His dream of becoming a pilot quickly faded on the parade ground and in the workshops, where his basic training involved spending long hours chipping and filing away at chunks of cast iron or steel. Although he regarded this as being a rather meaningless and time-wasting exercise, it wasn't his major concern. The RAF was then a very young service, and many of the NCOs were old sweats from the Army. Their coarse and obscene comments and belief that in the Service one was not paid to think but to be a blindly obedient automaton cut right across his Wesleyan upbringing and intelligence.

By comparison to the rest of the training programme, school was a pleasant change; ". . . the education officers were civilians who treated us quite differently from the NCO instructors of the workshops and parade ground. In school we were accepted as human beings rather than as mere numbers. Major G. Lees, OBE, who took classes in structures and mechanical drawing became one of my closest colleagues in later life".

The training syllabus was intensive, and the time was mostly divided between workshops and school with a number of hours each week on parade-ground drills and hard physical training. After the first year Whittle began training as a fitter/rigger directed mainly to the repair and maintenance of the then recently introduced metal airframes. The work became more specialized and varied, and he spent more time in the coppersmith's shop, on pattern making, in the foundry, in the machine shops, in the blacksmith's shop, and in the fabric-working shop (the days of the metal-skinned aeroplane had not yet arrived and so the metal structure was at that time still covered by doped fabric).

Apprentices were paid five shillings a week, which was increased to ten shillings (£0.50) when they became eighteen years old. This was a good sum in those days bearing in mind that an agricultural labourer, who had a family to maintain, earned rather less than £1 a week. The dislike which most of them had for the routine at Cranwell made them appreciate life at home which they had previously taken for granted. They received three leave periods each year totalling six weeks, and ". . . needless to say, we looked forward to these breaks with intense longing and we were never happy to return to Cranwell".

During the three years which Whittle trained as a boy apprentice he remembered that ". . . The chief thing which preserved me from complete misery was the Model Aircraft Society in which I spent practically every spare minute. This Society had the double merit of satisfying a deep interest and of serving as an acceptable alternative in the eyes of authority to attendance at organised games".

Whittle's attitude to a life of strict discipline caused him to be in a lot of trouble and more often than the average boy. Fortunately, during his three years as an apprentice, he escaped punishment which could have been entered on his crime sheet and ruined his chances of a cadetship. He received many extra fatigues for getting into mischief, but was skilful enough to complete his apprenticeship with a fair list of undetected crimes, as he had done at school.

At one stage he confessed that; ". . . there was one time when I seriously contemplated desertion. I was driven to this pitch of desperation by a combination of circumstances. My life was being made a misery by the hostility of one of the Leading Boys, news from home had distressed me, I was in trouble in various other ways, but above all, I had come to feel that there was no hope of attaining the object for which I had joined the RAF, namely to become a pilot".

Whittle and an accomplice planned to steal an aeroplane, take off and fly to France. He had noticed that quite frequently a Bristol Fighter was left unattended outside a hangar with its engine ticking over. They both considered it a practical scheme, although neither had ever flown before. Whittle had convinced his chum that he was fully capable of flying the machine, and the chap trusted him — or did he? Fortunately for the RAF and the aviation industry, this wild scheme came to nothing because Whittle's friend suddenly took French leave and vanished, having decided that a push bike was safer than a Biff[1] piloted by FW!

Despite his strong dislike for the strict discipline and coarse barrack-room life, there were compensations which were to be of great benefit to him. In school subjects he was doing very well, partly because of his extra year in the sixth form at Leamington, which had given him a head start over his contemporaries, and also because his attitude to school had changed; ". . . I had a very real interest in nearly every subject covered, perhaps because it was easier to discern the practical application of the knowledge which was imparted, for example, the mathematics was clearly relevant to the kind of engineering in which I was interested".

He may not have appreciated it at the time, but those three years as an apprentice were giving him a good basic knowledge of engineering. Also, he was acquiring considerable skill with basic fitting tools and, in fact, undergoing a first-class training. One cannot tell if the hard life at the Apprentice School was instrumental in forming his determined character, or whether it had always been part of his mental make-up. Despite being temperamentally unsuited to a strictly disciplined environment, he never gave up but fought his way through the long three-year course. He never wavered in his life's ambition to become a pilot, and this undoubtedly was his driving force throughout.

He had his first taste of the air shortly after his first year at Cranwell. The officer in charge of the Model Aircraft Society took various members up for short trips. Whittle was taken up in an old Avro 504 and remembered that he had no sensation of speed — just a great rush of wind and the ground hardly seeming to move. It was a wonderful experience and very different from what he had imagined. He had no fear, only an overwhelming desire to do it over and over again. Having read so many

[1]Biff — Bristol Fighter.

aeroplane magazines and studied the theory of flight in the reference library, long before he became an apprentice, he really believed that he could have flown the machine himself without an instructor to help him.

His work with the Model Aircraft Society, which made life pleasurable, was to have a profound influence on his subsequent career. Through his association with it he became better known to the CO than many of the boys, because Wing Commander Barton and other officers took a considerable interest in its activities. VIPs visiting the Wing would also include the Society in the itinerary. Making a model aircraft had become more than a serious hobby for Whittle. For him, model-making was no fad or craze, but represented a world of total dedication. Creating an aeroplane from the drawing board, constructing it, carrying out flight tests, and doing the inevitable repair work fascinated him.

The climax of his model-making at Cranwell came when he headed a small team which embarked on a very ambitious project — a large model of 10 ft 6 in wingspan powered by a two-stroke petrol engine. He was responsible for the drawings and made the wooden jigs for the construction of the delicate ribs and other parts of the structure, and he also did most of the fabric work. Some of the officers would drop in from time to time to see how things were going, and Whittle, being the head of the show, was the chap who explained everything. These informal discussions gave him a priceless opportunity to reveal the depth of knowledge he had acquired by private study, and his grasp of calculations and theory.

Whittle made such an impact on the establishment with his model-making that the CO turned a blind eye on one particular visit he made to the Society, knowing perfectly well that Whittle should have been in the workshops. When the CO talked to him Whittle did his best to conceal his agitation, knowing that he ought not to have been there. Later the CO confirmed this to his associates, but explained that at the time he had felt it better to let it pass because he considered that Whittle was getting greater benefit from the work he was doing on the model than he would have got from extra technical training!

It came as a considerable surprise to him to learn that he had been recommended for a cadetship, because he had never been a Leading Boy. In the past, only Leading Boys had been on the list; ". . . the first indication that I might be in the running came when I was detailed to act as CO's orderly. This meant wearing one's smartest uniform and accompanying the CO throughout the day. We all knew the real purpose of it, namely, to give the CO a better opportunity to examine one's bearing and fitness for officer status than he could obtain from his normal contacts with us".

In the final passing-out results Whittle was placed 6th. He commented much later that; "I owed this position partly to having done very well in school subjects, but also, undoubtedly, to efficiency marks which could be awarded at the CO's discretion . . . . I have much reason to be grateful to Barton and to others who backed his judgement such as R. A. George, my Squadron Commander, and H. A. Cox, the Senior Education Officer. It is not for me to comment on the quality of Robert Barton's judgement beyond stating the fact that four of the five he selected passed out in the first seven from the RAF College, and all except one, who was killed, have since attained high rank".

In the event, in 1926 only five cadetships were awarded, and Whittle thought that he had just missed the boat. However, he was sent up to London in company with the first five for the very stiff medical examination required for flying duties. Fortunately for him, the apprentice who had passed out top failed the medical and Whittle got his recommendation after all. He learned later that it had been a very narrow squeak, and Wing Commander Barton had fought very hard indeed for him. So hard, in fact, that Marshal of the Royal Air Force, Lord Trenchard, had concluded a meeting with words to the effect "If you have made a mistake, Barton, I will never forgive you".

Whittle's cup of joy was overflowing when he went home for a few weeks' leave. He could hardly believe that, at last, his boyhood dream of becoming a pilot was approaching reality. It transcended everything else, even his becoming an officer and having social status for the first time in his life. While on his leave he had formed a strong affection for a girl called Dorothy Mary Lee who came from a middle-class family — although, he said, there was not a trace of snobbery in her. Coming from a working-class family he had been acutely aware of the sharp contrast in their backgrounds, both in home comforts and social habits. Now he had strong personal reasons for bridging that gap, and becoming an officer would help him to do so.

Thinking back over his good fortune, Whittle began to realise that luck had played a vital part in his progress. When he had finally applied to be accepted as an apprentice he had been extremely lucky that somebody in the RAF hadn't discovered his previous rejection papers. Yet, it was due to that rejection on medical grounds that he had had an extra year in the 6th form at Leamington which had enabled him to have such a head start over the others. In the final analysis it was against all the odds, he thought, that the top apprentice should have failed the medical.

They say that it is better to be born lucky than rich, and the young Whittle had certainly had his fair share; but that was only part of the story. It wasn't being lucky that placed him sixth out of some 600 apprentices, or singled him out as a potential mathematical genius, as Barton described him to Trenchard. He had earned a Cadetship with his brains, aggressiveness and drive, in spite of living and working in an atmosphere which was foreign to his nature. Talking about the Apprentices' Wing, much later in life, he said that; '. . . we received a first-class training during our three years which was to stand me in very good stead later on, however much I may have disliked parts of it at the time".

The magnitude of the social step-up associated with the award of a Cadetship was perhaps best illustrated by a small incident a few hours before he went on leave for the last time from the Apprentices' Wing; ". . . I passed the Squadron Sergeant Major who gave me a look which it would be hard to describe, and said, 'I suppose the next time I see you I shall have to stand to attention and say, "Sir"!' I deemed it wise to make no comment and just responded with a happy grin. Fortunately, such a situation, which would have been mutually embarrassing, never arose".

*   *   *

After his three-years' apprenticeship was over, Whittle was promoted to Leading Aircraftman and he went on leave as such. At the end of his leave he was, by custom, formally discharged from the RAF and joined the RAF College at Cranwell, as though from civilian life, as a Flight Cadet. He soon found himself in a public school atmosphere with its deep-rooted customs.

As a First-Termer he was the lowest of the low, an object to be ragged and kicked around by members of senior terms who would exert their authority on the slightest breach of etiquette. While the military tailors were making his uniform of officer pattern, his family had to raise the money to have him kitted out in a dark lounge suit and bowler hat, pending completion of his uniform — the symbol of junior status. Their bowler hats naturally received special attention from members of the senior terms. It was not unusual to see the slightly ludicrous spectacle of the First Term marching, heads up, swinging their arms, chests out, but with battered bowler hats, some with their crowns almost detached and flopping up and down in rhythm with the step.

As an apprentice, Whittle had been used to marching to the dining hall carrying his knife, fork, and spoon, and eating his meal off a bare deal table. Now at dinner he was dressed up in a boiled shirt and bow tie, seated at a mess table covered with spotless linen and adorned with a shining array of cutlery. On his first night at dinner he was quite confused about which implement to use, but was saved by a kindly steward who whispered in his ear.

Whittle soon began to realise what a terrific jump it was from the working class into the kind of class represented by the Cadet Wing. But it was this upper-class society which he wanted to enter and which he was determined to emulate and outdo at the same time, saying that; ". . . I wanted to be an officer and a gentleman, as the expression was, and beat them all in flying".

During the First Term he was to find this social transition period very difficult because he was an ex-apprentice amongst a great majority of ex-public schoolboys. Although his apprenticeship training had given him certain advantages, particularly in the workshops, the social gap was as wide as the Gulf of Mexico! He proceeded to overcome this problem in the only way he knew how, and that was to get his head down and outdo them.

This proved to be a formidable task. In the first place he was physically small and actively disliked team games. Furthermore, he pursued the cult of the individual and preferred to remain as inconspicuous as possible. Hardly the sort of chap who would appeal to the more flamboyant and team-spirited public school fraternity!

Frequently on guest nights beat ups were held by the Third Term, and cadets of the First Term (and, sometimes, the Second Term) were singled out individually. On one occasion Whittle, who was lying in bed after lights out, heard approaching footsteps and was told to report to Hut 22, which he did with all possible speed hoping that promptness might be in his favour; "On arrival", he said, "I found the whole of the Third Term sitting in rows facing a table. "Get on that table", I was ordered, and then standing to attention in pyjamas, I learned that I had been walking about as though I owned the place and that it was time that I had the bounce knocked out of me. I was then ordered to leap off the table and bend over a chair to receive one swipe from every member of the court with whatever implement took their fancy. It was most important not to make a sound during this procedure, though this was extremely difficult when some of the more sadistic members took their turn. I received perhaps twenty blows — though quite a few of them from some of the softer-hearted members of the court were comparatively gentle.

Nobody was more surprised than I was to learn that I had been walking about as though I owned the place, because I supposed I had been creeping about as inconspicuously as possible, not only acutely conscious of the fact that I was a First Termer but also one of the few ex-apprentices".

The RAF College in the mid-twenties was fairly primitive, and not the imposing block of buildings which it became later. Flight Cadets were housed in a series of temporary huts of First World War vintage with the inevitable stove for heating. Each hut comprised a sleeping room for five Cadets, sitting room, bathroom, lavatory and a room for a batman. The hut commander was a Third Termer and the three other new Cadets quartered with Whittle were N. E. Tindal-Carill-Worsley, J. A. C. Stratton and Rolf Dudley Williams. (This early association with Williams was to prove of key importance in the development of the jet.)

The First Term, which lasted for six months, was a breaking-in period during which the RAF firmly stamped its mark on each Cadet and in which flying training began. Going through such an intensive doctrination, Cadets hardly had time to take breath or to think for themselves, such was the system. Even so, Flight Cadet Whittle, F. gained a reputation for asking awkward questions.

The course lasted for two years and there were new entries every six months. The training syllabus was designed to turn out General Duties officers, and therefore the curriculum covered a very wide range of subjects of which flying was the core. Such subjects included humanistics, such as English literature and history; and science subjects, comprising physics, mathematics, mechanics and theory of flight. Apart from school and workshops, Cadets attended lecture courses on navigation, signals, meteorology, Air Force Law, armament, and organisation. Drill instruction, physical training, arms practice, and compulsory games ensured that their bodies were in good shape and sharpened their reflexes. It was a very full life!

Cadets had to record their sporting activities and PT in their games log books. Whittle, who disliked team games, satisfied the requirement by taking up fencing, and playing the occasional game of tennis. He said that; ". . . I really enjoyed fencing and became moderately proficient with the foil, sabre and épée, but though I was several times selected as a member of the College team, I did not succeed in getting my colours, chiefly I think because, in matches, I failed to perform in accordance with my normal standard. As soon as it became important to win it had an inhibiting effect, and I was afflicted with a kind of stage fright which caused me to become self-conscious and over-anxious".

Chapter 3
Pilot and Prodigy

Every Flight Cadet at Cranwell accepted the fact that he had to get his head down at school, slog through the workshops, attend endless lectures, and sweat it out on the sports fields and parade ground, but with one objective in mind which transcended everything: to fly.

The exploits of fighter aces of The Great War had created images and made a profound impression upon them. Whittle's heroes as a young boy were the VCs[1], who had achieved immortality during the great air battles over the Western Front. Cinema, radio, press and magazines portrayed war pilots as flamboyant, cavalier characters, and in so doing had presented flying as the ultimate challenge to young men with guts and a spirit of adventure. The Royal Air Force provided the major platform from which these young enthusiasts could leap into the sky.

When they arrived at Cranwell, most Cadets expected to be able to jump into a cockpit and take off, but the flying programme in those days was less intense than it is today. After their period of initiation when they started flying training, it was only for two or three sessions of one-and-a-half hour periods for each Set of pupils. Alas, flying was often washed out because of the weather and, much to their disgust, they found themselves back in the workshops or practising buzzing (Morse).

Whittle received only five-and-a-half hours of dual instruction on an Avro 504K during his First Term, and finally went solo after a total of eight hours early in his Second Term. This was a good performance, bearing in mind that his tuition had been spread over so long a period. It must be remembered that when Whittle was learning to fly, in 1926, the aeroplane was in its very early stages of development, as was the motor car! In the public's eye it was a dangerous contraption of dope, fabric, wood, and wires, which only a lunatic or daredevil would venture up in. The

[1]VC — Victoria Cross: Britain's highest military decoration.

sight of a biplane chugging through the sky was a novelty for the vast majority, who would gaze upwards until it disappeared from view.

During Whittle's Second Term the 1918-vintage Avro 504K trainer was replaced by the Avro 504N. The two biplanes were very similar, but the old 504K, generally known as the 'Mono Avro', had a Monosoupape rotary engine (i.e. the whole engine rotated round a fixed crankshaft), while the 504N had a stationary Armstrong Siddeley Lynx radial engine and a more modern form of undercarriage.

A characteristic of the old Mono Avro was the strong smell of the castor oil lubricant which was ejected with the exhaust from the rotating cylinders. The engine was not controlled by a throttle in the normal sense, but by a device known as a 'fine adjustment'. In effect, it only had two speeds — Stop and Go. When descending, the engine could not be throttled back in the normal way; instead, the ignition was cut in and out at short intervals with a thumb switch (the blip switch) on top of the control column. No aircraft was fitted with brakes in those days, so that taxiing by having to use the blip switch was quite a skilful business, and failure to blip while gliding in often meant a dead stick landing.

The first real test of Whittle's capability as a pilot came after he had just completed three-and-a-half hours' solo flying, when he had total engine failure. It is an electrifying moment for any pilot when his engine coughs, bangs, splutters and fades out, and he cannot bring it back to life. Suddenly the roar from his engine gives way to the wind whistling and screaming through the struts and wires as, automatically, he looks around for a place to get her down.

On this occasion Whittle was lucky because his engine failure occurred when he was in close proximity to the North Aerodrome. He said afterwards that; "I had no difficulty in getting down without damage to the aircraft or myself". The statement betrayed just a hint of over-confidence, because any pilot — Whittle was only a fledgling then — has problems when making a dead stick landing.

A few weeks later he was to write off an aeroplane. Recalling the incident, he said; "On that occasion I got lost in conditions of rather poor visibility. After a time I was forced to the conclusion that it would be necessary to land to find out where I was, and so I selected a large flat and vivid green field and landed safely

Apprentices Whittle and Allen with 10 ft 6 in span petrol-driven flying model at the Apprentices' School at Cranwell, 1926.

RAF College, Cranwell, 1927. Flight Cadet Whittle squatting at bottom right.

become efficient.

Again the art/need for a

Turbines?

It seems that, as the turbine is the most efficient prime mover known, it is possible that it will also be developed for aircraft, especially if some means of driving a turbine by petrol could be devised. A steam turbine is quite unpracticable owing the weight of boilers, condensers etc.

A petrol driven turbine would be more efficient than a steam turbine as there need be no loss of heat through the flues, all the exhaust going via the nozzles.

The cycle for a petrol driven turbine is shown opposite.

It is a constant pressure cycle.

Air is compressed adiabatically (AB) into a chamber where it is heated at constant pressure by burning petrol (ie air enters the chamber at the same speed as it leaves the nozzles)

Crazy flying at the RAF Pageant, Hendon, with Whittle (from FTS at Digby, ex-No 111 Fighter Squadron) flying one of the 504Ns.

Cat shot of a Fairey Flycatcher fighter (S1297) at launch speed of 58 mph.

S1419, a Flycatcher float seaplane, on catapult test by Frank Whittle in 1931.

S1800, a Fairey IIIF, with floats, on special catapult trials.

S1325, the Fairey Seal used for ditching trials on 26 July 1932 ". . . though the fuselage reached a vertical position it fell back".
"I stepped into the dinghy with an immense feeling of relief, and floated away from the aircraft."

S1207, another IIIF, being recovered on the Hein mat gear after alighting at sea. Whittle and Cpl Lewis come aboard.

With Dorothy Mary Whittle after the graduation ceremony in Cambridge in summer 1936.

The original WU, with its instrument panel; sadly, the background has been eliminated. The lower diagram on page 250 is relevant.

After the second reconstruction in October 1938 the engine had ten separate combustion chambers. The 10 hp BSA car engine was still used for starting; its starting motor alone would have sufficed.

Chaps at Ladywood in 1938; Whittle can be seen in the rear at the WU (Model 3), with testers on the job.

This sums up a lot of Whittle's years of struggle, showing one of the combustion test rigs, using a barrel of 'white spirit'. Very much hand-to-mouth testing, at the BTH Ladywood Works.

enough. The aeroplane pulled up very smartly because it was a field of young wheat with very soft soil. It was raining fairly heavily. After a short interval a few children and a farm labourer came up to see what it was all about. They told me where I was and so, contrary to regulations (for a pupil), which I ought to have known but didn't, I decided to take off and so enlisted the aid of the farm labourer in starting my engine.

I went to some trouble to teach him the starting drill and then, when I thought that he had taken it all in, I climbed into the cockpit and called out, 'Switches off', and waited for him to indicate that he was ready to swing the prop by calling, 'Contact'. However, he stood for a moment or two scratching his head in a puzzled way and then compromised with, 'Be you ready to start 'er zur?'. I replied, 'Contact'. He flicked the propeller about one inch and leapt smartly out of the way. Nothing happened. After a number of repeats he got a little bolder, and at last we got the engine started.

By this time the wheels had sunk nearly to the axles in the soggy ground so that when the engine was running at full power, with the stick forward, the tail lifted in response to the slipstream on the elevators, but for a second or two there was no other effect. I kept the engine going and began to inch forward. My immediate thought was that I would not succeed in getting off at all, but it was a large field and I reasoned that as I gathered speed the wheels would begin to ride over the soft ground.

The windscreen of the open cockpit was covered with rain and so, as I attempted to take off, I had my head out of the starboard side of the cockpit anxiously watching the approaching hedge, wondering whether I would succeed in clearing it. When I realised that I would, I relaxed, but then I saw with dismay that I was heading straight for one of the very few trees in sight. It was much too late to do anything about it, and though I made an instinctive attempt to turn to the right, the whole of the port side of the wings smashed into the branches. The 504K swung round and ended up in an almost vertical position in the next field with its nose still in the tree. I was quite unhurt but, of course, very worried". The aircraft was a write-off.

Whittle had far more cause to worry later when confronted by his Flight Commander. Not only had he got himself lost but he had attempted to take off after a forced landing, which was strictly against regulations, and pranged[1] his aircraft in the process. The Flight Commander didn't mince his words, pointing

---

[1]Prang — RAF slang for crash.

out rather bluntly that apart from other things, Whittle's crabwise wheel tracks across the field showed quite clearly that he had taken off across wind. This explained why he hadn't seen the tree.

Young Whittle was very lucky that the authorities didn't throw the book at him on this occasion. This was probably due to his potential, and his first-class record in the Apprentices' Wing. He said long afterwards that, "I could have put up quite a good defence for getting lost at least, though I did not realise it at the time. It never occurred to me to point out that there was no compass in the aeroplane. In my mind's eye I can still see the screw holes in the dashboard where the compass should have been. This episode happened on the day of the annual cross-country run in which every cadet was obliged to take part. By the time I arrived back at Cranwell it was all over, and one or two of my fellows took some convincing that I had not wrecked the aeroplane to avoid this unpopular event".

This was Whittle's first major prang and although he carried it off in a light-hearted manner, in common with most pilots, it affected him more than he realised at the time. Acutely conscious that he must not blot his copybook again, he proceeded with a little more caution. Then during the next Term when he graduated from Avros to Bristol Fighters, he passed through a very strange phase in his flying career.

It began when he blacked out during a tight loop performed by his instructor. Completely unaware that this was quite normal, from the effect of high 'g', he immediately thought there was something radically wrong with him, and that he would never make the grade as a competent pilot. His sensitivity had made it impossible for him to confide in his flying instructor, whose bad temper and impatient cursing had caused him to be over-anxious in the air. These anxieties resulted in his having great difficulty in landing the Bristol Fighter. When he talked to Professor de la Bère about his problems, it started a sequence of events which led to his being temporarily grounded.

Young Frank Whittle must have gone through purgatory before he finally decided to confide in his mentor. Pupils are normally told about black outs, and know what to expect when they experience one. It is an emotional and rather frightening physical phenomenon to black out for the first time. One's body is forced down into the cockpit as if compressed by some giant weight, flesh is pulled down from the face, and arms and legs become leaden and immobile. As the 'g' forces increase, one loses consciousness and momentarily blacks out as vision disappears. A passenger will usually black out before the pilot, who knows what is coming and tenses his abdominal muscles to prevent it.

His instructor must have pulled the stick back really hard in the loop to have made Whittle black out. Maybe, he did it out of devilment or to teach young Whittle a lesson, but it reflected badly upon him. His bad temper and coarse language had made it impossible for him to engender confidence and respect from his pupil.

The Medical Officer, Wing Commander Tyrell, could find nothing physically wrong and was able to allay all Whittle's fears. He was tested on the Reid Reaction Indicator — the forerunner of the Link Trainer[1] — and the result showed that he was well above the average. This test coupled with the MO's wise counsel did the trick, and he had no further troubles of that kind. But, like many other pupils who recover from over-anxiety and loss of confidence, he then swung the other way.

This swing to becoming a daredevil got him into trouble on several occasions during his Fourth Term. The police caught him low-flying over Sleaford in a Bristol Fighter, for which he received 28 days' restrictions, during which he was confined to camp. Low flying is an exhilarating experience for any pilot, and hedge-hopping fast across an undulating landscape is as heady as champagne. Except for sweeping past clouds it is the only way one can get any real sensation of speed.

Whittle said that he was most unfortunate, "I was caught on the only occasion on which I beat up Sleaford with a Bristol Fighter because another cadet had been doing it regularly, and when the police caught me they were really lying in wait with their notebooks out and pencils licked. This other cadet happened to be the Under-Officer of my squadron, and it was he who marched me into the Squadron Commander's office to hear the charge. He told me afterwards, that as he stood there and heard the charge read out, he was for the moment quite convinced that a mistake had been made, and that he ought to be standing in my place, especially as he had been flying the same aeroplane. It was not until I admitted the charge that he realised that I was the guilty person after all — in this instance at least!".

His enthusiastic and adventurous drive was not confined to his flying. There were a few rather ancient motorcycles available for loan to Cadets and, despite the keen competition, he managed to

[1]Link Trainer — forerunner of the flight simulator.

acquire one. On the following summer Sunday he cut Church Parade and set off for Coventry for the day. By this time his family had moved from Leamington Spa to Corley Moor, a village about six miles from his girl friend's home in Coventry. His primary object was, of course, to see Dorothy Lee to whom he was abqut to become engaged.

It was a grilling hot day, and after 15 miles a piece of casing worked loose and broke the magneto driving chain. He patched it up in the blazing sun and, instead of turning back as he ought to have done, he pressed on. Between Newark and Leicester the engine seized because he had forgotten to operate the plunger of the oil pump, a necessary procedure about every five miles. After cooling down, having a cast-iron piston, the engine freed and he carried on towards Coventry.

In the evening, when he attempted the return journey to Cranwell, the case of the driving chain worked loose, causing the chain to come off. To add to his troubles, he started to be very sick from sunstroke. He was then only a mile or so from his home at Corley Moor, and his parents, who had taken an evening walk along the same road, found him in distress. His father persuaded him to return home, and wired Cranwell that he was too ill to travel.

Three days later, having succeeded in patching up his machine, he started off for Cranwell with rather dramatic results. "In Leicester", he said, "I made the stupid mistake of overtaking a tram on the offside and found my path blocked by another oncoming tram. When I also attempted to pass outside that one, I found myself heading for an oncoming bus. We collided head on, but fortunately by this time both the bus and I had slowed down to little more than a walking pace. I ended up clinging to the radiator cap of the bus but was not hurt.

My motorcycle also seemed to have escaped damage except for twisted handlebars, and so, after an exchange of addresses, I continued my journey. After a few hundred yards the licence holder fell off. I put it in my pocket and carried on, still with the handlebars on the skew. Between Leicester and Newark I became aware of an odd sensation, and on looking down saw that the whole engine was bouncing up and down. The collision had fractured the bracket linking the engine bearers to the rear part of the frame, and so the engine was supported at its lower end only by the gear chains.

By this time I was in no mood to attempt any further repairs and so continued at reduced speed and hoped for the best. Then, when only three miles from Cranwell, the driving chain case came adrift once more in such a manner that it fouled the spokes of the rear wheel and made an appalling noise. Finally, I arrived back in Camp to find many people curious about the extraordinary noise they had been hearing".

He received 7 days' Restrictions for being absent without leave, but the episode was only the beginning of his love/hate relationship with motorcycles. The Coventry escapade revealed that Whittle wasn't going to be a natural performer on two wheels but the fact that he, nominally a Wesleyan, had absented himself from Church Parade to visit Dorothy Lee was particularly significant at this time. Although he had occasionally cut Church Parade, he had once held very strong religious beliefs, but these had eroded to such an extent that he had come to regard himself as an atheist. "By degrees", he said, "I was forced to the conclusion that my beliefs were inconsistent with scientific teaching. Once the seeds of doubt were sown the whole structure of my former religious beliefs rapidly collapsed, and I swung to the other extreme".

Whittle was becoming more and more engrossed in science, and was at his best in physics, mathematics, and theory of flight. Having a naturally enquiring mind made him continually ask searching questions, sometimes making him unpopular! But Professor O. S. Sinnatt, the principal instructor in these subjects, recognised his undoubted talent and encouraged him. Each Cadet had to write a science thesis each term on a subject chosen by himself. During his first three terms, Whittle dealt with one subject in three parts entitled 'Chemistry in the Service of the RAF', a major proportion of which concerned explosives, incendiaries and gas warfare. These science theses occupied many hours of time outside the set curriculum, and Whittle took full advantage of them to prove his capabilities. His thesis in his Fourth Term was entitled 'Future Developments in Aircraft Design'. It was to change the course of his life, and sowed the seed of a revolution in aviation.

This thesis was written during the first six months of 1928. During the previous year the RAF High Speed Flight had recaptured the Schneider Trophy for Britain at an average speed of 281.65 mph. The seaplane[1], which was then just about the ultimate in aircraft design, was years away from being translated into any kind of useful operational aeroplane. Aircraft, almost all

[1]The Schneider Trophy was contested by seaplanes.

biplanes, were just beginning to go from wood to metal structures in a crude way, employing metal frames but still covered with fabric. Efforts were being made to streamline aircraft and make them more powerful but that was about all. There were, as yet, no such things as retractable undercarriages and variable-pitch propellers. Against this background Whittle wrote, ". . . the various aspects of possible aeronautical development which I attempted to cover could only be dealt with comparatively superficially. Nevertheless, in the course of its preparation I came to the general conclusion that if very high speeds were to be combined with long range, it would be necessary to fly at very great height, where the low air density would greatly reduce resistance in proportion to speed. At the time I was working on this thesis the maximum speed of RAF fighters was rather less than 150 mph, and the service ceiling was about 20,000 feet.

"I was thinking in terms of a speed of 500 mph in the stratosphere at heights where the air density was less than one quarter of its sea-level value. (I had covered the properties of the atmosphere in my earlier thesis.) It seemed to me unlikely that the conventional piston engine and propeller combination would meet the power plant needs of the kind of high speed/high altitude aircraft I had in mind, and so in my discussion of power plant I cast my net very wide and discussed the possibilities of rocket propulsion and of gas turbines driving propellers, but it did not then occur to me to use the gas turbine for jet propulsion".

His paper was the outcome of five long, hard years of experience in the workshops and at school both as an Apprentice and Flight Cadet. Professor O. S. Sinnatt, after reading his thesis, said, "I couldn't quite follow everything you have written, Whittle. But I can't find anything wrong with it" and awarded full marks.

His two years as a Flight Cadet ended in July 1928, when at the age of 21 he passed out second, receiving the Abdy Gerrard Fellowes Memorial Prize for Aeronautical Sciences. He had distinguished himself in everything he tackled, with the exception of field sports. Being small and an individualist by nature made it difficult for him. This probably accounted for his strong dislike of team games, which were of paramount importance to the Cranwellian society. He was to show that he was a better leader than follower.

Although Whittle had performed brilliantly in school subjects his prime ambition was to become an outstanding pilot. Next to the Sword of Honour, the most coveted prize at Cranwell was the R. M. Groves Memorial Prize. This was awarded to the Cadet adjudged the best pilot of his term, and Whittle was in line for it. He was one of three pilots chosen to represent 'B' Squadron, flying Armstrong Whitworth Siskin fighters, and his squadron commander, Squadron Leader (later ACM) A. Coningham, regarded him as his leading string.

Unfortunately Whittle was disqualified for dangerous flying: "I felt slightly aggrieved about this because my programme of aerobatics in the Siskin had been worked out carefully by Coningham and myself and I adhered to it. At one point when we were discussing the programme the squadron commander had remarked '. . . you should then be at about 1,200 feet — that should give you enough height for a bunt'. A bunt is the first half of an outside loop, a steepening dive which ends inverted. At the time he had not, I believed, bunted himself, and so I pointed out that bunting meant losing 1,000 feet and I thought it would be more prudent to start a little higher so we agreed that I should bunt from 1,500 feet. I believe it was this item on the agenda which caused the judges to disqualify me".

If such was the case, the disqualification was grossly unfair to Whittle, who had had his squadron commander's agreement to perform a bunt as part of his flying display. This violent and dangerous manoeuvre not only requires courage and skill but puts a great deal of pressure on the pilot. Whittle's downward bunt from a height of only 1,500 feet had to be performed with great accuracy, otherwise he might have gone straight in and made a hole in the ground.

The bunt is a most uncomfortable aerobatic. As Whittle throttled back and pushed his stick forward, so his flying speed built up in the dive. Only his harness straps, pulled hard and tight, kept him in the cockpit. Negative pressure built up and forced his blood into his head as he shot round the bottom of the loop inverted, before half-rolling out into level flight.

The bunt is most spectacular, especially when performed at low level as Whittle had done. He claimed that he was the first Cadet to do it, and might possibly have been the first to do it in other than a training type of aircraft — the Siskin was an operational fighter aircraft. That he chose to include a bunt in his display was indicative of his sheer guts and determination.

At the end of the course he was assessed as Exceptional to

Above Average on Siskins. But despite this high proficiency rating he was brought rapidly down to earth by remarks in his log book. Under 'Any special faults in flying which must be watched'. Inscribed in red ink were the words 'Over Confidence. This is most marked. He gives aerobatics too much value and has neglected accuracy. Must learn to discipline his flying. Inclined to perform to the gallery and flies too low'.

Whittle felt that his disqualification in the competition had influenced that final entry in his log book. But he had other things on his mind as he packed up to leave Cranwell for the last time. Uppermost was the thought of seeing Dorothy Lee, whom he loved, and returning home as a newly fledged Pilot Officer, elated by the wings he was at last entitled to wear.

The previous five years had been a hard slog, often harsh in the extreme, but he had become an RAF pilot and distinguished himself. At last he was an officer and a gentleman, and the future looked rosy. Thinking about it took his mind back to the old days when he was at Milverton Council School. At the age of eleven he had determined to fight his way out of the working class and to rid himself of the handicap of his Lancashire accent and, to this end, would often sit near Leamington High School girls at play listening carefully to their mode of speech.

Now, all that was behind him and he had proved that he could do better than the vast majority of his public school contemporaries both in the air and on the ground. He knew that the next four years during which he would be serving as a General Duties officer would be crucial, because after that he would have to specialise. Meanwhile, he was going to enjoy his leave and look forward to more flying when he got his posting.

*   *   *

On 27 August 1928, Whittle set forth from his home outside Coventry on a brand new motorcycle to report to No 111 Fighter Squadron based at Hornchurch in Essex. Thus began one of the most carefree periods in his whole life, and a very pleasant contrast from the rigors of the preceding five years. Except, perhaps, when he came to grief in Aylesbury on his journey south. "In this case it was definitely not my fault", he said, "an ancient car driven by an ancient and deaf man shot out of a side turning on to the main London road and I struck him amidships.

"My motorcycle stopped dead while, in obedience to the laws of Newton, I shot over the car bonnet and landed in the road several yards beyond, but with nothing worse than a shaking". Unfortunately for Whittle, this happened just outside Aylesbury Police Station, and he hadn't bothered to get a driving licence. This neglect, for which he was subsequently fined, also invalidated his claim on the insurance company.

As a brand new Pilot Officer, but with Cranwell training and tradition behind him, Whittle stepped into a more relaxed life on his arrival at Hornchurch. The intimate atmosphere of the small mess in which there were only about fifteen officers, a few of whom were married and lived in married quarters, appealed to him: "you went on colour hoisting parade at eight o'clock in the morning and you were finished for the day by four o'clock in the afternoon, unless you were Orderly Officer". There was plenty of leisure time during which he could continue his attempts to solve the problem of propulsion for high-speed high-altitude aircraft. It was possible to go on week-end leave every other week-end unless one was on official duty, and the quota of annual leave was 61 days.

Fighter Command was then a smaller formation known as Fighting Area, which formed part of the Air Defence of Great Britain. Squadron training was based on a systematic pattern which culminated in the annual ADGB exercises. During the first part of the training programme the emphasis was on individual training. This was followed by practice in flying in flight formation, after which the emphasis was transferred to the training of the whole squadron as a single fighting unit.

No 111 Squadron was equipped with Siskin IIIs, and the flying training programme was comparatively elastic so that, within limits, pilots could more or less please themselves what they did with their flying time. Whittle had two favourite pastimes — low-flying up and down the Thames and playing Chase me Charley with another pilot on days when there was plenty of cumulus cloud.

The relaxed atmosphere at Hornchurch did nothing to curb Whittle's enthusiasm for pursuing the ultimate in flying, which occasionally got him into trouble. He had been making careful fuel consumption tests on the Siskin and decided, on one particular flight, to prove a conclusion he had reached about the possible endurance of the aeroplane. In the case of this long endurance flight his Flight Commander, F/Lt A. P. Davidson, found it hard to believe that Whittle had not made an unauthorised landing somewhere. Consequently, Whittle was reprimanded for remaining in the air well beyond the official endurance of the Siskin!

Davidson also took a poor view of Whittle's attempts to do tail slides, because of the stresses imposed on the aircraft. During this unorthodox manoeuvre the pilot stalls the aircraft with the nose way up. As it drops down, the aeroplane slides back on its tail — the trick being to keep the aircraft steady and not allow it to flick out during the slide. Whittle could not convince Davidson that the aeroplane was virtually falling under gravity and was, therefore, subject to an almost negligible load. Unless the stick is held very firmly the reverse airflow tends to cause the control surfaces (elevators, ailerons, and rudder) to snatch violently, so Davidson ordered Whittle to desist forthwith.

Whittle enjoyed tempting providence in aircraft, and a flick roll at ground level was one of his specialities: "I had developed it to the point where I could just spin my wheels by touching the ground immediately before doing it. It must have been a shattering sight for anybody who witnessed it — it was, in fact, far easier and less dangerous than it looked! Long before doing it at ground level I practised it repeatedly over the level surface of stratus cloud until I got the speed just right to gain a few feet in height between the beginning and end of the manoeuvre.

"I found that at about 85 mph I would lose a few feet — at 90 mph I just maintained height, but at 95 mph I could gain 10-15 feet, and so 95 mph was the speed I used at low height. In those days I had an astonishing faith in the accuracy of the airspeed indicator. I was, so far as I know, the first young idiot to start doing this aerobatic at so low a height, but once it had been witnessed by one or two others as foolhardy as myself they soon followed suit".

Whittle misjudged his flick roll stunt once, when he only just succeeded in keeping his starboard wing tip from going into the Thames. When he first saw it performed by someone else he was petrified. The urge to perform daredevil stunts is part of any fighter pilot's make-up, but Whittle seemed to have had it to an exceptional degree. The fact that he was selected to represent the Squadron in individual and formation aerobatic displays proved that he was more skilled than most of his contemporaries, and had the right stuff in him.

Low-level beat-ups and aerobatics were all part of the fun, and there was no problem as long as they were performed in authorised areas. The Air Ministry had been taking a very serious view of anybody, reported by the police and/or public, who did them elsewhere creating a danger or annoyance. It had become a court martial offence, punishable by dismissal from the Service. The RAF, like the other Services, was fighting for money in a climate of disarmament, and could not afford the inevitable bad publicity created by irresponsible pilots of whom Whittle, in those days, was undoubtedly one.

He very nearly wrecked his career in the RAF through a low-flying escapade. He and another young officer, J. S. Pole, flew up the Thames to Canvey Island and amused themselves and the locals by performing low aerobatics just offshore. Whittle was sobered up by seeing a policeman on the beach writing in a notebook, so he chased after Pole and indicated by hand signals that there was something wrong and to return back to base at Hornchurch. After landing he told other pilots what had happened, and one of them — McGregor (later Air Marshal Sir Hector McGregor) — told him that the Canvey Island police were after him for a similar offence.

Having previously been caught and punished at Cranwell for low-flying over Sleaford, Whittle was desperately worried, and persuaded someone to take him to the Police Station on the Island that very evening. After a long talk with the police sergeant he learned that the earlier offender — McGregor — had been reported as a result of a complaint from one of the families living there. The impression he received was that if this family wished to take no further action, the police would also let the matter drop.

A day or two later, Pole and Whittle went to Canvey Island to make their peace with the Levy family: "They were quite charming to us and were horrified to learn that their original action in writing to the Air Ministry and complaining to the Police might end in wrecking the careers of three young officers. They had a married daughter living with them who was nearing her time and it was because of this that they had complained. They didn't want the child to be born with a face like a Siskin's Jaguar engine.

"Their object had merely been to stop it happening again. They said they would do all they could to help us, and so I pointed out that if it became a court-martial matter, it would at least help if they refused to give evidence. They promised to do this. Pole and

I left in a state of considerable relief and in a slight alcoholic haze from the hospitality we had received.

"When we told McGregor of the success of our expedition he also paid a visit to the Police Station on Canvey Island, to try and stop the police report on his own case from going in. It happened that by sheer coincidence, while he was flannelling the sergeant, our new CO, S/Ldr F. O. Soden, landed on Canvey Island in his own private aeroplane with Douglas Sender, the Accountant Officer, as passenger. Sender knew all about our misdeeds (but the CO did not) and also knew that at that moment McGregor was probably in the police station saying honeyed words to the sergeant.

"Sender was convulsed with mirth when another policeman came up to the aeroplane, and, not knowing to whom he was speaking, asked Soden 'wot 'e thought 'e wos a doin' of' and went on to complain that they were getting sick of low-flying aeroplanes over Canvey Island, particularly those with black stripes along their sides (the markings of 111 Squadron). So the cat was out of the bag as far as our new CO was concerned.

"The next day McGregor, Pole and I were at the receiving end of some strong comments about our stupidity. A few days later we were called into the CO's office once again to learn that a lengthy report about all three of us had been received from the Chief Constable of Essex. Soden commented, 'You lucky young devils!' (meaning it was lucky for us that the report had been sent to him and not to the Air Ministry) and dropped the report in the wastepaper basket. Had he not done so the whole course of the rest of my life would almost certainly have been altered. I have never ceased to be grateful for his leniency".

About a year later, Whittle learned that the Air Ministry had been most reluctant to drop the matter, and had tried to induce the Levys to take further action. They replied that they had no wish to do so, especially as the young officers concerned had visited them and apologised. But the Air Ministry persisted until ultimately the family dropped the A.M. letters back into the pillar box marked 'Gone Away'. Thus, Whittle's luck had held good and the three of them escaped a well deserved court-martial.

He wasn't so lucky, however, with his motorcycle, and a few weeks after his crash in Aylesbury he wrecked it again at night at a 'T' junction in the neighbourhood of Harrow. The junction was badly lit and, at the last moment, he failed to realise that he was heading for an iron rail fence until it was too late to do anything but swerve: 'I swerved right, struck the fence, and took a toss down a six foot embankment — had I swerved left instead I would probably have gone down a thirty foot embankment on to the Metropolitan railway. I was saved from anything worse than minor scratches and a severe shaking by the fact that I was wearing a Sidcot flying suit and sheepskin thigh boots which were badly torn".

Fortunately, this last prang ended Whittle's motorcycling career because the insurance company wouldn't renew, which invalidated his hire-purchase agreement. "These experiences", he recalled much later, "left me with a very strong prejudice against motorcycles in general, and possibly contributed to my prejudice against piston engines".

While he was with 111 Squadron, Whittle had to qualify in night flying. Once he became proficient, he and other pilots were detailed to carry out night-flying exercises in co-operation with the Royal Engineers' Searchlight Detachments. On 23 July 1929 he flew to RAF Manston on the north-east Kent coast to attack night bombers — the idea being to add reality to a mock bombing raid on London by attacking any bomber caught in searchlight beams.

On that particular night over the Isle of Dogs, Whittle's Siskin was picked up at 6,000 feet by one searchlight, and then everybody in the area trained their beams on him. Despite all his efforts, including looping and slow-rolling, to convince those down below that he was a fighter and not a bomber, they wouldn't let him go. So the bombers flew in undetected while he gave a display of aerobatics by searchlight!

He had found it rather odd at the time that the RE's hadn't identified him by his navigation lights, but had no idea that these had failed because of a flat battery: "This caused some commotion when I came in to land. Although I had received a green Very light in response to my own, giving me permission to land, I was not visible to the party on the flare path and there was a hurried scramble to depart when I came in very close to the first flare".

At the end of September 1929, Whittle was posted to the Central Flying School at Wittering as a pupil on the 30th Flying Instructors' Course. His total flying time was then 333 hours, mostly on Siskins.

Chapter 4
Wittering – A Chain of Events

After the effervescent and sometimes boisterous life in 111 Squadron, Whittle became a pupil once more and had to settle down in the more formal and scholastic atmosphere of a Flying Instructors' School. The aeroplane was the Avro 504N and his instructor was Flight Sergeant Marsh. When not actually receiving instruction in patter from Marsh he went up with another pupil and they practised their patter on each other.

Flying instruction was supplemented by lectures, and the three months' course provided valuable training and added to his experience — to qualify as a flying instructor was a plus for any regular officer classified as a GD (General Duties) pilot. But his time at Wittering was an important link in a chain of events which eventually determined the pattern of his life.

Whittle had had plenty of leisure time since he passed out of Cranwell, and had continued his search for a suitable type of power plant for a very high-altitude high-speed aeroplane. One scheme he had explored was that of using a conventional reciprocating engine driving a low-pressure fan instead of a propeller. The idea was that the engine and fan would be entirely enclosed within a hollow nacelle or fuselage and that the fan would draw in air through a hole in the front and, after it had been heated by the exhaust and other waste heat of the engine, expel it through a nozzle at the rear with increased velocity, thus providing a propulsive jet. He had also recognised that a big increase in the speed of the propelling jet could be obtained by burning additional fuel before expulsion from the nozzle. However, his calculations indicated that weight and fuel consumption were excessive — as the Italians were to find out in 1940 at considerable expense with their Caproni Campini scheme. But while he was at Wittering it suddenly occurred to him to substitute a turbine for the piston engine. His calculations convinced him that it would be far superior to anything he had visualised previously. Thus, in October 1929, Whittle had developed his Cranwell thesis, written fifteen months previously, into the answer he was looking for.

His calculations had led him back to the gas turbine, but this time of a totally new type which produced a propelling jet instead of driving a propeller. He realised that this change would require the compressor to have a much higher pressure ratio than the one he had visualised for his piston engine scheme. But once this idea had taken shape, he found it extraordinary that he had taken so long to arrive at a scheme which seemed so very obvious and was disarmingly simple.

The most advanced piston engine at that time was a special racing engine which powered the Schneider Trophy seaplane. It had been developed by Rolls-Royce, and was called simply the R. Rolls had based it on the Buzzard, a big 12-cylinder engine of about 800 horsepower.

A new team of brilliant engineers made the R run much faster than the Buzzard, and added a double-sided supercharger giving a boost pressure of over 12 pounds per square inch. This was far beyond the capability of ordinary fuel, but a fuel expert, Rod Banks, concocted special mixtures with high anti-knock quality. Eventually, by September 1929, the R could run at 2,900 revolutions per minute to give 1,900 horsepower. This was enough to drive Flying Officer Waghorn's Supermarine S.6B at the winning average of 328.6 mph. But the RAF could not exceed about half this speed. Their engines had to use ordinary fuel, and run for much longer than the 40 minutes of the Schneider race.

Moreover, though the thrill of seeing the sleek brightly painted little seaplanes screaming round the Solent at low level was absolutely without precedent, the aviation experts believed that there was not a lot more speed to come in future. To get quite modest increases in speed demanded disproportionate increases in power, and to get such power meant piston engines so big and unwieldly as to overburden small racers. Making allowances for the different needs of the RAF, it thus seemed doubtful that any fighter would do much better than 300 mph — ever! To Whittle, his concept offered the prospect of escape from nearly all the existing limitations. If proven, there would be no longer any obvious limit to the speeds which might be attained.

Searching into the unknown had always been an inbuilt desire as far as Whittle was concerned. That was why he chose, 'Future Developments in Aircraft Design' as his thesis at Cranwell. He enjoyed speculation, and often dreamt of new inventions which stimulated his mathematical mind. In his youth, he had been an addict of H. G. Wells and Jules Verne, amongst other writers. His calculations and theories in 1929 were seemingly pure science fiction. But there was a flying instructor at Wittering who became deeply involved in Whittle's project and was to influence the course of his life.

He was F/O W. E. P. (Pat) Johnson, known in the RAF as Johnny, and had the distinction at that time of being the only officer in the RAF qualified in instrument flying. Whittle had previously met him at Manston, and knew that he had a very strong interest in technical matters. Before joining the Service, Johnson had qualified as a patent agent and was currently serving on a Short Service Commission, having turned down a permanent commission because he wished to return to his profession.

Although Johnson was not Whittle's instructor, Whittle soon noticed that he decorated his aeroplane with wool tufts and tapes to make the airflow over the wings visible to his pupils, and decided to adopt the same practice. He could not foresee then that, ten years later, Johnson would use the same technique in a transparent model of a jet engine combustion chamber and bring to light some very important facts.

Whittle explained his scheme to Johnson, who became deeply interested and arranged for him to see Group Captain Baldwin, the Commandant. Although Baldwin was not a technical man, he was considerably impressed and undoubtedly influenced by Johnson's enthusiasm for the proposal. He agreed to bring the matter to the attention of the Air Ministry, and a few days later Whittle was instructed to report to Adastral House in London with his sketches and calculations.

This was a daunting experience for the young Pilot Officer of twenty two, who had only recently passed out from Cranwell, and Whittle could well have been totally disillusioned with the outcome and scrapped his project. He first saw Mr W. L. Tweedie, a technical officer in the Directorate of Engine Development. Tweedie told him bluntly that the Air Ministry's attitude towards the practicability of the gas turbine was coloured by a highly unfavourable report (p. 245) written a few years previously. Despite his pessimistic outlook, Tweedie took him to the Air Ministry's South Kensington Laboratory to meet Dr A. A. Griffith, who was interested in gas turbines for driving propellers.

Whittle was left to do most of the talking, and duly presented his case to Griffith and another scientific officer. The result was most discouraging. Griffith said that Whittle's assumptions were over-optimistic and that there was, at least, one important mistake in the calculations.

Griffith was a highly qualified scientist with a growing reputation in the academic world. He certainly had the knowledge to do a quick design study of Whittle's turbojet proposals. Had he done so with intellectual honesty he would inevitably have come to the conclusion that, with easily foreseeable improvements in materials and component efficiencies, a revolutionary (in every sense of the word) aircraft propulsion engine was at last within reach.

Speeds of 500 mph would be attainable at heights up to and above 40,000 ft. Though the fuel consumption might seem somewhat excessive, this would be largely compensated by the very low power plant weight. Griffith should have recognised that here was an engine of very low weight, not limited to high-grade petrol as fuel, of great simplicity and vibration free and, above all, capable of operation at heights and speeds entirely out of reach of the piston engine/propeller combination.

He was at that time far more qualified than Whittle to point out the ways in which the gas turbine as a high-speed aircraft power plant was a much more favourable proposition than a stationary gas turbine for shaft power at sea level. This was by virtue of the very favourable effect of very low air temperatures at great height, the high efficiency of that part of the compression due to ram effect at high forward speeds, and so on. Yet, seemingly, this intellectual giant failed entirely to do what he should have done. Not only then but eight years later when, after Whittle's first engine had run, Griffith wrote a report damning the project with faint praise.

It is not as though Griffith shared the view of most of the engineering world that the gas turbine was not a practical proposition, and that there had been many failures to prove it. On the contrary, Griffith himself was advocating the development of gas turbines, but driving propellers.

It was a few years before Griffith succeeded in getting Ministry support for his own proposals. One cannot say for sure that, had he given a favourable report on Whittle's jet engine, this would have resulted in Ministry backing. Whittle's proposals being far simpler than his own, it is very likely that the modest sums needed to initiate the development would have been forthcoming.

Why then did Griffith, and therefore the Ministry, damn the

project? Sheer incompetence, despite his reputation and qualifications? Professional jealousy? Intellectual dishonesty? Or a combination of these things? We shall never know!

After his interviews Whittle returned to Wittering in low spirits. However, when making a careful revision of his calculations he cheered up: "I discovered another important mistake which largely had the effect of neutralizing the first one, and so I was happy to find that my conclusions were not so very wrong after all. Nevertheless, I can well imagine that my first error may have done much to prevent the scheme from being as carefully considered as it otherwise might have been".

A little later, Whittle received a letter from the Air Ministry to the effect that the scheme he proposed was a form of gas turbine, and that as such its successful development was considered to be impracticable, because materials did not then exist capable of withstanding the combination of high stresses and high temperatures which would be necessary if a gas turbine were to have an acceptable efficiency.

This was a blow to Whittle, because he felt that the Air Ministry should have foreseen the possibility of big improvements in materials and kept the proposal on ice for potential development. Having had the thumbs down from those in high places and the door slammed in his face, Whittle was at the cross-roads and didn't quite know what to do next.

Despite the Air Ministry's rejection, his friend Johnson urged him to take out a patent and offered to help him draft it. Together, they prepared a Provisional Specification which was duly filed on 16 January 1930. In accordance with regulations, the Air Ministry was notified but expressed no official interest in the patent. Therefore, there was no suggestion that Whittle's invention should be put on the secret list. This meant that, shortly after the Complete Specification was filed and the patent granted in October 1932, the invention would be published through the world.

It seems incredible today, after years of jet travel which has changed our lives and shrunk the world, that Whittle's patent for the first turbojet engine was taken out all those years ago. His scheme was to become the most significant invention of the twentieth century, and yet nothing was done to protect his patent and he was left to plough his own furrow in a climate of hostility and derision.

At the end of the three-months course at Wittering, Whittle

became a qualified flying instructor with the category B.1 — the highest possible for a newly qualified instructor. His proficiency as a pilot was assessed as above the average. Then, to his horror, he was posted to No 4 Flying Training School in Egypt. This would have thwarted his wish to get on with his jet engine, so he put his problem to the Station Commander and managed to get his posting switched to No 2 FTS at Digby.

* * *

No 2 FTS was one of the five schools at which Short Service officers, officers entering direct from University with permanent commissions, and airmen selected to be sergeant pilots, were taught to fly.

Whittle wasn't too pleased at finding himself back in that part of Lincolnshire. Digby was only about five miles from Cranwell, and the memory of those five long and hard years on that bleak plain was still fresh in his mind. But, despite this aversion, there were moments when he began to realise how much his Cranwell training had done for him.

When he was with 111 Fighter Squadron, for example, he had been the only Old Cranwellian on the station. Cranwell, in those days, could supply only a trickle of regular officers and Old Cranwellians were few and far between. Apart from that, Whittle was also an ex-Apprentice, and so he had had the most intensive and complete training that the RAF could provide. It was only natural that his associates wanted to ask him questions about Cranwell, and this set him apart from others and gave him added status. And, shortly after his arrival at Digby his promotion to Flying Officer was gazetted — this was automatic after 18 months' service as a Pilot Officer.

At first it seemed a bit of a come down to be flying Avro 504Ns and having to teach people to fly after having been a fighter pilot and living in a squadron atmosphere. He had really enjoyed those carefree days in 111 Squadron, and liked to recall incidents which stood out in his memory. He would never forget the disbelieving look on his Flight Commander's face when he had kept a Siskin in the air for an hour longer than its official maximum endurance and they all thought that he had crashed or force-landed somewhere. Or, when, champing at the bit to go off duty, his flight commander and a few erks — ground crew — watched him from the terrace coming down from 13,000 to 3,000 feet inverted — the penalty for which was a severe rocket from his flight commander and an even more severe ache in his ears. He had realised, when he arrived at Flying Training School, that he was going to have to simmer down; but, at least, he would have time to do more calculations and be able to fly over to Wittering and see his friend Johnson. He was convinced his gas turbine project would work, and felt strongly that neither Dr Griffith nor the Air Ministry had really got down to evaluating his scheme as they should have done.

Whittle soon found that life at Digby had its compensations. Teaching people to fly proved to be a much more interesting occupation than he had expected, and was by no means without its excitements. Having suffered a bad-tempered and foul-mouthed instructor at Cranwell, whose choleric behaviour had nearly destroyed his confidence, Whittle was determined that nothing like that would happen to his own pupils.

Commenting about instructing, he said that, "many a time an instructor is faced at very short notice with the difficult decision as to whether to take over the controls or to let the pupil get himself out of some particular difficulty. If a nervous instructor takes over control before he need do, he tends to destroy the confidence of the pupil, but if he leaves it too late he may destroy both his pupil and himself".

Apart from instructing — Whittle usually had four pupils at one time — he gave lectures in theory of flight, a subject which had fascinated him since his early youth. His first two pupils were G. Silyn Roberts and R. A. McMurtrie, who became personal friends. Roberts was a University entrant with a permanent commission, and McMurtrie a Short Service Officer. McMurtrie was later selected for a permanent commission and, during the war, rose to the rank of Group Captain and won the DSO and DFC. Roberts became an Air Marshal with the AFC, so both were more successful than their instructor as far as flying decorations were concerned!

Whittle remembered that: "Roberts was nicknamed Pye — short for Pythagoras — because he had taken his MSc degree in physics at Bangor. In later years he has since reminded me that when he was my pupil I told him all about the jet engine and admits with amusement that he was a disbeliever, especially after he had discussed it with one of his professors who was also sceptical. He did his best in a tactful way to convince me that I was on a wild goose chase, and was much amused by the persistence with which I held my views".

After two months instructing and lecturing at Digby, Whittle's life became enlivened in a most dramatic fashion. He and the late F/O George E. Campbell were chosen as the competitors from No 2 FTS for the Crazy Flying event at the annual RAF display at Hendon. This turn was performed on Avro 504Ns by a pair of instructors from one of the Flying Training Schools, who were selected by competition.

The crazy-flying display was a comedy event and, in reality, required a highly specialised and precise form of flying. There were not many pilots in the RAF who were skilled at it, and Whittle was extremely lucky to have Campbell as his partner. 'Tich' Campbell was very experienced, having taken part in each of the four preceding displays. He was a brilliant pilot and in the same flight as Whittle, who found him most charming and a good friend.

Having decided to introduce some original features, he and Campbell evolved a carefully selected synchronized programme embodying several novel manoeuvres: "We started to take off together and flat-turn away from each other before our wheels left the ground. We would then turn to cross diagonally midway down the aerodrome, both throwing our aircraft violently from side to side. Then a flat turn in towards each other at the far end to join up into a crazy formation, both banked sharply over and side-slipping violently with our inner wingtips high and our outer wingtips practically sweeping the grass. Having flown the length of the field in this manner we would then swing away from each other in a violent flat turn, and so on.

"Another novelty was formation hopping. After joining up from a flat turn we traversed the field towards the spectators, performing a kind of switchback motion. We alternated — that is to say, as Campbell went up I went down and vice versa, keeping in close formation all the time with Campbell leading. The highlights of our show were two mock collisions. In the first of these, after a steep climbing turn at opposite sides of the aerodrome, we dived towards each other to pass with only a foot or two to spare between our wingtips. In the second we added a further touch by each banking sharply to starboard as we passed. The first time we ever experimented with this manoeuvre at Digby, we used the compass base as a marker. Judging from the reports of our fellow instructors afterwards, we had been very successful in creating the illusion of a certain and very spectacular head-on collision".

Practising for the crazy-flying competition, literally in front of his pupils, enhanced Whittle's status as a flying instructor and made him a cut above the others. Although he didn't do it for that purpose, nevertheless that is what happened.

A stunt pilot has to be the complete master of his aeroplane, and be able to put it in exactly the right position at the right time. He must fly his aeroplane as if he was glued to it, so that pilot and machine become one entity. Becoming part of his machine builds up a supreme confidence which enables him to fly to the ultimate limits and sometimes beyond. Skill, nerve, and sheer guts are essential qualities, and Whittle had these in abundance. His pupils at Digby admired those qualities when they watched Campbell and Whittle performing their hair-raising stunts.

Whittle had a natural desire to demonstrate his skill rather than merely call attention to himself — as some of his associates may have believed. He frequently argued that the particular skills acquired in crazy flying could be of great value as, for example, in the event of a forced landing in difficult circumstances where the ability to do steep controlled sideslips could be decisive. His enthusiasm for crazy flying was a natural progression from his previous low-flying stunts including flick rolls at ground level, low bunts and beat-ups. Apart from enjoying the excitement of low-level aerobatics, Whittle was determined to become the master of his aeroplane in all aspects of flight. However, he did not attempt highly dangerous low-level manoeuvres without carefully working them out and practising them on a blanket of cloud which simulated ground level.

The late 'Batchy' Atcherley (Air Marshal Sir Richard Atcherley), one of the best pilots in the RAF, was one of the early pioneers of crazy flying. One of his most memorable performances was at Cleveland, Ohio. There, spectators were horrified to see a bearded old gentleman, wearing a top hat and carrying an umbrella, running with coat tails flying towards an aeroplane with its engine ticking over. The old gentleman, hotly pursued by a policeman, managed to get into the aeroplane and start off before the policeman could catch him. There then followed a most hair-raising display that convinced the crowd that the man was a madman who had never flown before and was attempting to make off with the aeroplane. The onlookers had probably never heard of Batchy, whose nickname certainly proved appropriate on that occasion!

Apart from creating gasps and laughs from the crowd, crazy flying was a dangerous sport, as Whittle found out. While practising the formation hopping manoeuvre with Campbell at Digby, he wrecked his aeroplane: "I was so concentrating on keeping station and synchronizing properly, that, when Campbell went a bit too high, I went a bit too low and struck the ground very heavily. I bounced into the air again but knew I must have done some severe damage, not only because of the force of the impact and the sensation of something giving way but I could also feel an unusual slight swaying motion!

"I had no option but to bring the aeroplane down because I couldn't bale out. Though I was sitting on my parachute I was not wearing the harness, and it was not feasible to struggle into it. (Campbell and I both thought it unwise to wear our parachute harness, because normally we were never at any time at a height where a parachute could be used, and it might have hampered our escape from the cockpit in the event of an accident.)

"I climbed very gently while I pondered my situation. I thought the swaying motion I could feel might be due to a fracture of one or more of the main structural members of the fuselage, and that there was a danger of the aeroplane breaking its back completely at any moment.

"As I made a gentle circuit to get into position to land, I had the pleasure of seeing the blood wagon (the ambulance) travelling rapidly towards the aerodrome, the fire crew manning the fire tender, and officers and airmen pouring out of offices and hangars to witness the inevitable crash.

"I made a careful approach after fastening my Sutton harness as tightly as I possibly could and then, when I was still a few feet above the ground, the aeroplane suddenly decelerated and plunged its nose into the ground. Apart from a severe blow on the shin I was unhurt, and as I could hear a hissing noise as petrol dripped on to the hot engine I lost no time in getting out of the cockpit.

"My brother officers said they had never seen anybody get out of an aeroplane so fast! The aeroplane itself was a complete write-off but it did not catch fire. Its back was broken just aft of the rear cockpit. The crash had occurred a little earlier than I had expected because, unknown to me, the starboard undercarriage leg had broken away from its top joint and was swinging from the axle which, in turn, was dangling from the port undercarriage leg and this festoon of wrecked undercarriage had acted rather like an anchor. It was this wreckage swinging to and fro which no doubt accounted for the swaying sensation I had felt".

Two days later, Whittle's undercarriage collapsed on a flat-turn take-off, and his aeroplane flicked over on to its back just prior to leaving the ground. Once again, his luck held and he escaped unhurt. He lowered himself from the inverted cockpit and walked disconsolately back towards the tarmac: "I was met by a furious flight commander. Wylie Raeburn was rather hostile to the crazy flying business altogether because it dislocated normal routine, and so it may be guessed that his feelings on the subject were not improved when he saw two of his precious aeroplanes destroyed in three days.

"As I came up to him he stood there with his face flushed with rage and said furiously, 'Why don't you take all my bloody aeroplanes, make a heap of them in the middle of the aerodrome and set fire to them — it's quicker!' He then turned his back on me and stalked away, but he soon recovered his natural good humour".

A few days later the crazy-flying competition was held at Spitalgate, near Grantham, and Campbell and Whittle were adjudged the winners. Thus, Whittle had achieved his ambition to perform at the Hendon Air Pageant of June 1930 and so join the elite. These great displays, featuring crazy flying, solo and synchronized formation aerobatics, dive bombing, parachute drops and many other aspects of Service flying, always pulled in very large crowds of 100,000 or more, and had taken place every year since 1920. The huge attendances symbolised a growing national interest in the air, and in the pilots who broke records and performed breathtaking aerobatics.

Having won the competition at Grantham, Campbell and Whittle seized every opportunity at Digby for further practice. Since it was not always possible to fit it in during normal working hours they often arranged for practice in the evening, calling on volunteers from airmen of their flight to handle the aeroplanes. This was unpaid overtime as far as the airmen were concerned, who cheerfully and willingly backed them up so that they always had a more than adequate response.

In May 1930 their crazy-flying practice was interrupted by a very important event in Whittle's life — he was married on the

24th of that month to Dorothy Mary Lee in Coventry — a few days before his 23rd birthday.

Whittle's proposal to get married was not looked upon at all kindly by his CO, whose permission he had to obtain beforehand. The RAF's view at that time was that an officer should not get married until he was 30 (below which age he did not quality for a marriage allowance) or had reached the rank of squadron leader, which in normal circumstances was highly unlikely.

When his CO, Group Captain 'Crasher' Smith, stressed the Service view, Whittle relied on the fact that Smith was a very religious man who held strong moral views: "So I put it to him that it was unreasonable to expect any young man to remain celibate until he was 30. I pointed out to him that the alternative was immorality and that, though I had remained celibate up till then, it was asking too much that I should continue to do so".

Whittle's argument put his CO in a difficulty and so Smith reluctantly gave his consent, remarking that he supposed that Whittle and his wife were going to live like pigs like the rest of them — this was a reference to the fact that, owing to the lack of accommodation in the area, several married officers and their families were driven to living in shabby digs, lacking adequate toilet facilities, in nearby villages.

His CO was not the only one who disapproved, as his intention to marry had led to a breach with his parents. Although he was never quite clear why they had objected, he thought that being too young, having a fiancée three years older, and marrying out of his class were contributory factors. His parents were not present at the wedding, and it was some time before the breach was healed. But his fellow instructors gave him a good send-off for his wedding in true RAF style, flying him to Whitley aerodrome outside Coventry with an escort of ten Avros.

On his return to Digby, he and Campbell continued their practice for the RAF Pageant. Since winning the crazy-flying competition they had further embellished their performance, and were able to produce some strange noises at appropriate moments. Campbell had replaced one of the sparking plugs of his engine by a device which made a curious twittering noise when he pulled a string. Whittle, not to be outdone, had fitted a four-note car hooter to one of the exhaust pipes of the engine of his Avro J9691, operated by a length of string from the cockpit, so that, when Campbell twittered, he moaned.

When they learned that their two men had won the

competition, and would perform at Hendon, the entire station at Digby sensed an uplift. At the actual display their performance was great, and went down very well indeed — though an old lady was heard to tell an excited small boy, "There's nothing to get excited about — they haven't got far to fall!"

A few days after the display Whittle received the following letter from the AOC of No 23 Group (which comprised the Flying Training Schools in Britain):

Dear Whittle,
You will see published in Orders an appreciation by the CAS of the work done by all officers to make the Display a success.

I want to add my personal congratulations on the excellent show put up by you. The crowd appreciated your evolutions very much indeed . . .
Yours sincerely,
P. B. Joubert.

After the 1930 Display the return to normal routine of instruction at Digby seemed a little dull, but it had its lighter moments. There was a rule that nobody was allowed to walk across the aerodrome during flying hours. One day when Whittle was about to take off with a pupil he saw two figures making a short cut from the hangars to the armoury and, on the spur of the moment, decided to teach them a lesson. He headed straight towards them and having reached flying speed held the aircraft down. They saw him hurtling towards them and one, wearing a greatcoat, turned and ran back towards the hangars. The other, wearing a Sidcot suit, broke into a brisk run towards the armoury: "I turned after the one making for the hangar and saw him give a hunted look over his shoulder and hurl himself face down on to the ground. I roared with laughter and continued to chuckle at intervals for the rest of my 20 minutes' instruction".

After Whittle had landed and sent his pupil off solo, he walked into the flight office grinning broadly. The grin was wiped off his face abruptly as his glance passed from George Campbell, sitting at the side of the room, his face red with smothered laughter, to Wylie Raeburn, his flight commander, sitting behind his desk with a face purple with rage and the front of his greatcoat smothered in clay.

Wylie stood up and said, "You're coming with me to the Chief Flying Instructor, my lad". He was then marched up to the office of S/Ldr Hugh Pughe Lloyd who, after hearing Wylie's complaint, uttered a few words of rebuke and then told Whittle to get out. Apparently, Lloyd had not been able to keep a straight face. When Wylie recovered his composure he was as ready to laugh at the incident as anybody, and often referred to it as the day when Whittle made him clap his clock[1] in the clay.

By far the greater part of his flying during the year at Digby was on the Avro 504N. He did manage occasional flights on other types, but the only new types he managed to add in his log book were the Armstrong Whitworth Atlas and Vickers Vimy. On 26 November 1930 he flew a DH9a, J8471, from Digby to Hawkinge to be broken up, and understood that this aircraft was the last one in the RAF.

Throughout his time at Digby he continued to develop his ideas on the turbojet engine, and kept in touch with Johnson at Wittering. They liaised over the drafting of the Complete Specification, and made the first of several attempts to interest commercial firms in the project. Johnson had got to know S/Ldr Reid, of the instrument makers Reid & Sigrist, by virtue of his connection with blind flying. On 4 October 1930 Whittle and Johnson took off in Avro K1242 from Wittering and landed at Brooklands in Surrey to have a talk with Reid, thinking that there was a chance that he might back the invention. Reid took a very sympathetic interest in the scheme and said he thought it was sound, but that it would require far more money for development than he could possibly find. He advised them to find sponsors with much greater resources, and wished them luck. This was the first time that Whittle had dipped his toe into the whirlpool of commerce, and Reid's response was encouraging.

That particular flight to Brooklands was to stand out in Whittle's memory: "We flew over Cardington where the R.101 was riding at its mooring mast. Little did we realise that a few hours later this enormous airship was to be a mass of blazing wreckage on a hill near Beauvais in France. This was the tragic end of an attempt to fly to India, and in it the then Secretary of State for Air, Lord Thompson, and several distinguished aviation personalities including Sir Sefton Brancker, lost their lives.

"Shortly after passing Cardington we ran into some of the weather that was to contribute to the disaster, and it was fortunate for us that Johnson was an expert in blind flying because low cloud and rain very seriously reduced visibility. Had

[1] A north country colloquialism.

I been on my own I would undoubtedly have turned back, but Johnson, having complete faith in his blind-flying instruments carried on. This flight impressed very deeply upon me the value of skill in instrument flying and of the gyroscopic instruments which made it possible".

Towards the end of the year, Johnson was once again primarily responsible for the chain of events which led to a meeting in the British Thomson-Houston Company factory at Rugby. Johnson's brother was a Housemaster at Rugby School, and knew the BTH Chief Engineer. Whittle and Johnson talked his brother into procuring an interview for Whittle with F. Samuelson, the Chief Turbine Engineer, and his deputy R. H. Collingham.

BTH was an old-established company which manufactured industrial turbines on a custom-built basis. Whittle's interview took place on 24 October 1930, when the industrial depression was at its worst and the unemployed numbered over three million. He had a long talk with them and showed them his sketches and calculations which they did not question. Their attitude was that an engine of the kind he proposed would cost about £60,000 to develop. BTH could not contemplate experimental expenditure of that magnitude in the current industrial climate. They were fully aware of the difficulties in the way of successful gas turbine development, and pointed out that his proposed engine was applicable only to aircraft, and was not really appropriate to their field of activity.

Whittle privately thought that the time was ripe for ambitious experimental work, because there was so much labour available and the country needed to be in the forefront of any new technology. Their reaction was disappointing, but he did not condemn them for short-sightedness: "If anything, I was surprised that they gave such a patient hearing to a young man of 23 with no academic qualifications".

In the event, BTH's reaction did prove to be short-sighted. Seven years later, when BTH were doing sub-contract work for him producing turbine blades, Whittle made an astonishing and fundamental discovery in turbine blade design, as related earlier. Moreover, the engineers at BTH were not at all pleased to be told that they had been designing blades wrong from the word go!

Towards the end of 1930 Whittle asked his CO for a posting. He could not recollect the exact reason, but contributing factors were the fact that his wife was pregnant, he had ruffled a few feathers of those in high places including the Chief Flying Instructor, instructing was becoming less exciting, and he needed a change of style and a more demanding challenge. The CO indicated that there was little hope of a posting, so it came as a great surprise when at the end of the year he received notification that he was posted to the Marine Aircraft Experimental Establishment at Felixstowe as a floatplane test pilot.

For young Frank Whittle, 1930 had been a dramatic year. On the 16 January he had filed the Provisional Specification for his turbojet engine, on 24 May he got married in Coventry and on 24 June he had joined the élite performing at the RAF Pageant at Hendon. He was also upgraded as an A2 instructor.

Chapter 5
Test Pilot and Engineer

Whittle considered himself to be extremely fortunate to escape from training duties after only a year, and to receive an appointment as test pilot on floatplanes after a total of 609 hours flying, entirely on landplanes. He felt at the time that: "Unless somebody had stuck a pin into the Air Force List at the Air Ministry, it was at least an indication that my skill as a pilot was considered to be well above the average".

He had a strong interest in naval strategy, and while at Cranwell, in an essay entitled *Sea Power in the Pacific*, he had suggested the possibility of a surprise Japanese attack on Pearl Harbor! His only association with the sea, however, had been four seaside holidays, and he was unable to swim! When he first arrived at Felixstowe some of the junior officers believed that he was destined for the High-Speed Flight, which would have suited his style, but events were to prove otherwise.

After two flights, totalling 30 minutes as a passenger in the rear cockpit of a Fairey IIIF with floats, he was sent off solo. As he taxied out into Felixstowe harbour he noticed that the piers were crowded with officer and airmen spectators, and sensed that he might be the victim of a mild conspiracy and was expected to make an exhibition of himself. He did!

His first mistake was to forget to disconnect the water rudders on take-off, causing his machine to swing steadily to starboard. His second mistake was to ease the control column forward to lift the tail as soon as possible as was usual with landplanes: "I found myself ploughing steadily up the River Orwell with little sign of attaining take-off speed, and swinging slowly to starboard until I was practically heading for the river bank. In desperation I pulled the stick back and this did the trick, and I staggered off the water about 45 degrees out of wind".

This was hardly an auspicious start for a potential member of the High-Speed Flight, but worse was to follow. In an attempt to restore his amour propre, he did some low-flying around the harbour before finally trying to settle his floatplane gently on the water: "I still had a considerable audience and once more they were not disappointed. I used my habitual technique for achieving a three-point landing, but this was anything but successful. I could scarcely help it — it was practically instinctive, especially as for the past year I had been repeating over and over again to pupils 'Stick back — back — back — right back' ".

When the heels of his floats touched the water the aircraft lurched forward in a most disconcerting manner and he thought that this was due to having misjudged his height. He took off again — this time more successfully, and tried another landing. The same thing happened, and continued to happen on each successive attempt and he had no idea what was causing the problem.

Finally, when he decided to go into the slipway his troubles were not over: "I made insufficient allowance for the tide and was nearly swept into one of the piers". If ever Whittle had been destined for the High-Speed Flight, he had, by then, succeeded in disqualifying himself. He was not really resentful that the high-speed boys, who had their own union, had set him up. But when F/O Leonard S. Snaith was posted to Felixstowe as a floatplane test pilot a few weeks later, Whittle told him what happened to him and warned him accordingly. Snaith was, in fact, attached to the High-Speed Flight a short time afterwards, so Snaith, who also had never flown floatplanes before, must have found the advice of some value!

Once the initial atmosphere surrounding Whittle as a new boy had evaporated, he settled down happily enough at Felixstowe and enjoyed the life. Test flying offered plenty of scope for him to indulge in his technical interests. He was not content simply to perform the tests specified and hand over the readings to the civilian technical and scientific officers, as was the case with most test pilots. He wanted to delve into the problems and, more often than not, corrected and plotted his readings and discussed them with the scientific officers concerned. This proved useful on one occasion when he and his flight commander, F/Lt Pickering, had each done partial climbs on a Fairey IIIF. They got very different results. This would normally have meant at least three repeats of a very boring operation, but Whittle noted that on Pickering's flight the air temperature dropped 3 degrees per thousand feet which meant an unstable atmosphere and this disqualified Pickering's readings.

At first he and his wife had rooms in a boarding house, but later they managed to rent a furnished house on the seafront near to the station. In May 1931 his first son, Francis David, was born. Whittle soon found that it was very difficult indeed to make both ends meet on Flying Officer's pay and single allowances. He had to meet heavy medical expenses then and subsequently, which meant that they had to live as economically as possible.

One of his first flying jobs was to do tests in connection with the spinning characteristics of the Fairey IIIF. For these Mr Woodward-Nutt, a scientific officer, flew with him as observer. When he went on leave his part in these trials was taken over by F/Lt Pickering. He was astonished to read in his newspaper on the second day of his leave that Pickering and Woodward-Nutt had had to bale out. Both escaped without injury; the aircraft had gone into a flat spin from which it refused to recover.

His main, and by far most interesting, task was catapult test work. He was sent down to Farnborough for practice launches towards the end of February 1931: "The Farnborough catapult on which I experienced my first launches was mounted in a circular pit, with the wheels of the aircraft about six inches above ground level. The length of the stroke was about 50 feet and in this distance the aircraft was accelerated to just under 60 mph.

"This meant an acceleration of about two-and-a-half times the force of gravity so that, immediately before the launch, it was necessary to have one's head firmly back against the headrest. At first the sensation produced by this tremendous acceleration was very odd, but one soon got used to it".

A month after the practice launches at Farnborough, Whittle completed his first set of catapult trials from the Admiralty experimental ship HMS *Pegasus* at Lee-on-Solent. This ship was a 10,000-ton tramp converted to a seaplane tender in which capacity it featured in the Dardanelles operations of the First World War. The experimental catapult was mounted on the foredeck just for'r'ard of the large opening to the section of the hold which comprised the hangar. Two steam cranes were mounted between the hangar hatch and the catapult turntable, by means of which the aircraft were hoisted out of the hangar and placed on the catapult.

For these first trials the catapult to be tested was the Farnborough Light type (FIL) and the aeroplane was a Fairey Flycatcher, a single-seat fighter. This catapult had a telescopic ram divided into sections which slid one into another. The movement of the ram was communicated to the launching trolley by a system of pulley wheels and wire cables. The ram was operated by the firing of a slow-burning cordite charge in a breech mechanism similar to that of a 6-inch gun.

Before Whittle was fired for the first time a dummy was launched as a preliminary test. The dummy was a scrap aeroplane, and after the launch it plunged into the sea and was lost. The duration of the launch was just over one second.

Because of the roughness of the sea, Whittle was told to set down in the lee of the shore, so he had to taxi two miles or so back to the ship: "I found that getting back to the ship was by far the most unpleasant part of the proceedings. The Flycatcher had flat and rather short floats and so, after riding the crest of a wave, it would lurch into the succeeding trough with a jerk throwing up masses of water into the propeller, much of which the propeller then threw back on me.

"When near the ship I was taken in tow by a small tender. For this purpose I had to switch off the engine, climb down and, kneeling on the flat top of the float, unclip the towing gear attached to the float structure and then catch a light line thrown from the boat. With this I would haul in the tow rope and make it fast to the towing gear. Throughout this performance the float would be rising and falling in a most sick-making manner, and by the time I was eventually towed below the crane hook I was feeling anything but comfortable. I was very thankful when I was finally hoisted out of the water".

Whittle did three catapult launches before lunch, by which time the sight of soup swaying gently back and forth in his plate was sufficient to send him to his cabin. However, he received little sympathy from the ship's company, and had to complete three more in the afternoon. His six catapult launches were of very short duration. The entries in his log book for 25 March 1931 recorded the following times — 15 min, 15, 20, 10, 10, and 30, giving him a total flying time for the day of 1 hr 40 min. It appears from the remarks column in his log that, on at least a couple of occasions, he couldn't resist doing some aerobatics in between!

While his test flying at Felixstowe was proving to be an exciting and educational occupation, Whittle's thoughts were never far away from his proposed turbojet engine, and he continued his efforts to interest commercial firms. He went to see the managing director of a well-known firm which specialized in compressor manufacture, but was told that the depression precluded the company from embarking on any ambitious project such as he had outlined.

He had better luck at Armstrong Siddeley Motors, where the talks were more protracted. During his periods of leave, he visited the firm in Coventry and had many talks with Messrs Viale and Pryor who were supercharger specialists. This line of approach broke down when he received a letter from Major F. M. Green, then the Chief Engineer, which read as follows:

"It seems to me that the whole scheme depends upon obtaining materials which will work satisfactorily at a very high temperature. Personally I doubt very much whether such material is available and this, I think, prevents the development of the internal-combustion turbine engine. I fear therefore that I cannot hold out any hope that this firm will take any serious interest in your proposal".

Whittle had realised that he was in a chicken and egg situation regarding his proposed engine and the materials available, but was determined to break the deadlock: "I was fully aware of the great importance of achieving higher efficiencies for the major components of the engine than had been attained with similar components used in other branches of engineering at that time. In particular, I had made proposals for an improved form of centrifugal compressor and had filed an application for it at about the same time as for the complete engine. In my talks with the Armstrong Siddeley engineers, in addition to trying to interest them in the jet engine scheme as a whole, I also tried to convince them that the form of compressor I proposed was an improvement on the type they were then using for supercharging their engines".

One outcome of his meetings at Armstrong Siddeley was that they advised him to send his proposals to Mr W. S. Farren, whose name was very well known in the aeronautical world and who acted as a technical advisor to the firm. Although Farren agreed that Whittle's compressor proposal was sound in principle, he doubted its novelty, and also said that he preferred the arrangement then in use by Armstrong Siddeley. Thus, Whittle had outlined his proposition to two senior experts in his field, Dr A. A. Griffith and W. S. Farren, and neither had given him any encouragement.

Representatives of aircraft and other firms often visited Felixstowe in connection with the experimental work carried on there. Whittle lost no opportunity in trying to convince some of them of the merits of his jet engine, but without success. The engine was frequently a topic of conversation with the technical and scientific officers at Felixstowe, and was something of a joke amongst his brother officers.

F/O Snaith christened it Whittle's Flaming Touch-hole; he would often greet him with "Well, how's the old flaming touch-hole getting on?" Just one officer, however, took it much more seriously. F/O Rolf Dudley Williams, who was a member of a flying boat squadron then temporarily based at Felixstowe, had shared a hut with Whittle during their first two terms at Cranwell. Little did Whittle realise then how intimately the fates were to weave the threads of their two lives.

Williams' interest was very real, and when he heard that Whittle had applied for only a British patent he made some attempts to raise money from his relatives to obtain American and other foreign patents. He was not successful in this, but retained his belief in the project, and this proved to be a key factor in the subsequent history of the development. He became a lifelong friend of Whittle. In later life he served as a Member of Parliament for many years and was created a baronet.

He had a great sense of humour, as Whittle found out when Williams was his passenger on one occasion in an Avro Tutor with floats. After various aerobatics, Whittle flew inverted for several seconds: "I promptly righted the aircraft when I heard a loud yell. I then looked round to the rear cockpit — there was no sign of Williams! I was horrified. I concluded that he had fallen out! Had he done so, in fact, that would have been the end of him, because we did not wear parachutes in floatplanes.

"I circled round miserably expecting to see a splash when he hit the water. Fortunately, it was purely a leg-pull on his part! He afterwards said he did it because he got tired of several weeks' dirt falling in his face from the floor of the cockpit. Many years later he came across my log book and entered in the remarks column for this particular flight, 'Felt very nasty, RDW' ".

After the episode with Farren, Whittle was forced to realise to an increasing extent that he would need to convince people of the value of his compressor proposals before he could hope to get them to accept the much more comprehensive scheme for a complete jet engine. To stimulate interest, he wrote a paper on superchargers which was accepted for publication in the Journal of the Royal Aeronautical Society.

Whittle's turbojet engine proposal required a compressor

having a pressure ratio of the order of 4:1 and an efficiency of at least 75 per cent. The best aero-engine supercharger of that time was incorporated in the Rolls-Royce 'R' engine powering the Supermarine S.6B which won the Schneider Trophy in 1931. This had a pressure ratio of 1.92 and an efficiency of 62 per cent so, unless a very great improvement on these figures could be obtained, there was little hope for the success of the turbojet engine.

Some time after writing his paper on supercharging, Whittle wrote another paper entitled *The Case for the Gas Turbine* but made no attempt to get it published. This was a significant document in which for the first time he openly discussed the theory of the jet engine. Its contents foreshadowed his later work to a remarkable degree, in view of the fact that he had not then received any advanced engineering training. The paper contained example calculations which showed the big increase in efficiency which could be obtained with the gas turbine at great height due to the beneficial effects of low air temperature. It also contained calculations to demonstrate the degree to which range would depend on height with turbojet aircraft.

Another objective of Whittle's published paper on superchargers was to make a case for using an independent engine for driving the supercharger of the main powerplant. This was a scheme for which F/Lt J. H. McC. Reynolds and he filed a joint patent application and tried to induce firms to take up the proposal, but again without success. Mac, who later became a Group Captain, was Officer i/c Engine Repair Section at the time and said that, as Whittle and he were 'plumbers', they talked the same language but he never heard anything further regarding their joint patent (but the idea was put to use in other countries).

One of Whittle's problems at Felixstowe was the very limited amount of flying he was able to put in, sometimes less than six hours a month. Flying was mostly restricted to about ten or fifteen minutes for each sortie. He did his best to get round this by nominally flying for the purpose of doing handling trials, but he still had time on his hands which he used to maximum advantage.

For six months of his time at Felixstowe, Whittle combined the duties of Station Armament Officer with those of test pilot. This post was normally filled by an officer of the rank of Flight Lieutenant who was an armament specialist. At Felixstowe, however, the duties were more specialised than at most other stations because of the experimental work involved. This suited him: "It was thus rather an unusual task and one which added further variety to an already varied life. My most important duty in this capacity was to carry out the armament trials of a new flying boat which was undergoing tests".

His flying boat experience inspired him to produce a method of representing the field of fire from the various gun positions, and also to devise an enclosed gun turret. He had a wooden mock-up made of the hood and special gun mounting, and spent a considerable time in the drawing office preparing drawings: "I believe, but cannot prove it, that the scheme included a proposal for rotating the turret by hydraulic motor, in which case it may well have been one of the earliest proposals for a power-operated turret".

Whittle's inventive mind couldn't stop producing speculative ideas, which he sent to the Air Ministry for examination. In conjunction with F/Lt F. Kirk, he produced a scheme for an improved method of loading bombs on to aircraft mounted on catapults, and also a proposal for an entirely new type of catapult. Other miscellaneous ideas included a single-fluke anchor and a scheme for simplifying the handling gear of floatplanes. None of these proposals was ever officially adopted except the field of fire scheme, for which he received an expression of the Air Council's appreciation for 'his initiative and ability'.

During his eighteen months at Felixstowe, he only added 132 hours' flying time in his log book, but this had been crammed with valuable experience. He had flown over 18 types of floatplanes, flying boats and amphibians and had qualified as first pilot on flying boats. There were many anxious moments during his catapult testing. One of the most exciting experiences in his flying career occurred during tests to find what was the least safe windspeed along the 'cat'.

It happened during July 1932, when he was carrying out a long series of trials and had to remain aboard HMS *Ark Royal* for practically the whole month. On the sixth and last launch of the series, with no wind relative to the catapult, F/Lt Kirk was his passenger. As the Fairey IIIF left the catapult its nose rose sharply. Instinctively Whittle pushed the control column forward, and after staggering a few hundred yards in a practically stalled condition realised, with relief, that at least the aeroplane was not going to stall and plunge into the sea.

At first he thought that the tailplane had been damaged during the launch, possibly by striking one of the steam cranes, but on glancing back over his left shoulder he saw a body lying face down on the tailplane. It crossed his mind that in some mysterious way he must have removed an airman working on the catapult; but, looking round again, he could see that the body on the tailplane belonged to Kirk, his passenger.

By this time Kirk had struggled round into a sitting position with his back against the fin bracing wire, his legs dangling over the leading edge of the tailplane and his right hand holding on to the fin. Kirk had lost his grip on the rim of the cockpit because his gloves were slippery with catapult glycerine, and then shot to the rear of the long cockpit and bounced into the air, turning as he went. The film record showed that he retained his presence of mind to such an extent that one hand had gripped the fin wire before any of the rest of him touched the tailplane.

When Kirk saw Whittle look round he gave him a 'thumbs up' signal with his left hand. He was really rather a funny sight, because he was wearing a borrowed flying helmet which was much too large for him, and when he opened his mouth the wind distended his cheeks in a most grotesque manner: "He seemed far less alarmed than I felt. My right arm was quivering with the strain of holding the stick forward. I quickly found that it wasn't going to be easy to descend from my height of about 60 feet because when I tried to throttle back the tail dropped due to his weight and the reduced slipstream, so I had to keep the throttle open. I could not turn into wind because Kirk's body was blanking off the rudder completely. Fortunately, there was only a light wind blowing and I found that I had just enough control to force the nose down very slightly, and so I slowly lost height.

"Meantime, a German liner was crossing my path ahead, and the question was whether I could get down on to the water before I flew into her side. I succeeded with about 200 yards to spare, and alighted with the stick fully forward by easing the throttle back. I still had half engine when my floats touched the water".

When Kirk clambered back into the rear cockpit, he nearly put his foot through the after decking of the fuselage, which was the only damage sustained by the aeroplane during the whole incident. Kirk appeared to be calm and collected, but Whittle was almost in a state of nervous collapse and just said, "My God!", to which Kirk calmly responded "What are you worrying about?". Whittle then taxied back to the ship and after being hoisted aboard, they both enjoyed a pink gin reception pressed upon them by a number of very relieved Naval Officers.

A ditching trial of a Fairey Seal landplane on 26 July 1932 was another highlight of Whittle's career as a marine test pilot. The object was to test an emergency air bag for carrier-borne aircraft by deliberately ditching in the sea. No pilot relishes the thought of deliberately pancaking a landplane with a fixed undercarriage on to the sea, despite the fact that a ship was alongside with personnel ready to fish him out and haul him aboard. Only a few days previously a Fleet Air Arm Fairey IIIF, without flotation gear, had ditched and had sunk within 45 seconds, so Whittle was apprehensive about his experiment — especially as he couldn't swim!

There was a strong gusty wind blowing and a considerable sea running when *Ark Royal* steamed to her pre-arranged position off Sandown, Isle of Wight. Whittle was glad of the strong wind, because he knew that it would reduce his speed relative to the water: "I brought the aircraft down into the required position, and pancaked it into the sea from a height of about five feet. As soon as the wheels met the water, the aeroplane buried its nose into the sea and a great sheet of water entered the cockpit. For an instant I thought I had turned right over but though the fuselage reached a vertical position, it fell back. I had no difficulty in inflating and launching the collapsible dinghy which was carried in the rear cockpit. I stepped into the dinghy with an immense feeling of relief and floated away from the aircraft. As I did so I heard a shout of laughter go up from the ship's company. I was told afterwards that this was because I looked like a monkey sitting in the dinghy, but I suspect that it was also their way of expressing a sense of relief".

This ditching episode towards the end of July was Whittle's last flight as a marine test pilot. It ended a month during which he had completed 46 catapult launches, bringing his total to 71. A few weeks later, he received a copy of an extract from a letter, written by the Commanding Officer of *Ark Royal,* addressed to the Vice-Admiral Commanding Reserve Fleet, which read as follows:

". . . I wish to bring to the notice of Their Lordships the very satisfactory work carried out by Flying Officer F. Whittle, RAF, attached to HMS *Ark Royal* from Marine Aircraft Experimental Establishment, Felixstowe, for the present trials. This Officer made a total of 46 catapult launches under varying conditions during the series, and in addition carried out a forced landing flotation test in most realistic conditions and in a praiseworthy manner. His services have been invaluable and his airmanship inspired confidence in all concerned in the trials. His skill as a pilot and in floatplane handling, by making up to nine successive catapult launches in one day, enabled conclusive results to be obtained in the minimum time".

Whittle had, indeed, distinguished himself and needless to say: "I was very pleased indeed with these praises and was encouraged to hope that an Air Force Cross might come my way. I had received broad hints to this effect from senior officers aboard the ship, but if I was recommended — and I have good reason to believe I was — the recommendation did not go through. I was very disappointed and felt, with good reason, that somebody had been very stuffy about it".

Having completed four years of general duties, as every other officer with a permanent commission, he was expected to specialize. The choice lay between engineering, signals, armament and navigation. Engineering was his natural choice, and he was backed up in his annual confidential report for 1932 which strongly recommended him for engineering duties: "A very keen young officer and a useful test pilot. He shows considerable ability in aircraft engineering . . ." As a result, he was posted to Henlow, to attend the Officers Engineering Course beginning in August 1932.

*   *   *

After all the excitement of marine test flying, Whittle found himself back yet again as a student at the Officers School of Engineering at RAF Henlow, situated on the Bedford road about four miles north of Hitchin in Hertfordshire. He had managed to get pleasant furnished rooms in Clifton Rectory, only two miles from the camp. Shortly after arrival he sat for the entrance examination, which all students of a new course had to take.

Whittle was exceptionally well qualified for such a course and this became apparent from the outset when he obtained an amazing aggregate of 98 per cent in all subjects: "I surprised myself and my examiners, and I think that this was the first time that I really realised the extent to which my continuous interest in engineering subjects had improved my knowledge". This result led to his being allowed to take a shortened course. Thus, he was attached to the senior course for lectures and took his final examinations in written subjects at the end of the first year: "The work came so naturally to me that I was soon well ahead of my companions in the next senior year".

His confidence and ability was confirmed in the final examinations when he obtained a Distinction in every subject except Mechanical Drawing. The remarks on his certificate were prophetic: "A very able student. He works hard and has originality. He is suitable for experimental duties".

The course at Henlow marked a change of emphasis in Whittle's career during which his engineering and inventive abilities became paramount, and superseded his obvious potential as an outstanding pilot. He always loved flying, but in the following years it was forced to become more of a sport than a profession.

All members of the course had to keep in flying practice, and the aircraft available for this purpose were de Havilland Tiger Moths which enabled him to keep up his crazy-flying practice. This was frowned upon by the Establishment and Whittle got into trouble for doing it, but his skill came in handy on Empire Day 1934. Henlow, in common with many other RAF Stations, was At Home to the public. The official programme comprised parachute dropping displays with Virginia bombers, alternating with formation flying by Tiger Moths piloted by students of the engineering course.

Whittle was not a member of either of the units taking part and was not supposed to be flying that day, but his luck was in! The Station Commander, Group Captain V. O. Rees, who had previously put a damper on Whittle's crazy-flying activities, felt that the official programme lacked something as it was proving to be too slow. So, he called on Whittle to fill in the gaps with exhibitions of crazy-flying and aerobatics.

Thus, Whittle found himself in a rather curious position by having to give four 20-minute displays whilst doing something he had been censored for doing! At the end of the day he was absolutely exhausted, but totally exhilarated. He had obviously stolen the show — as he was doing on the engineering course! His flying at Henlow included a few hours on the Vickers Virginia, one of which he piloted in the parachute event in the 1932 RAF Display at Hendon.

During his time at Henlow, he continued to do paper work at intervals on his turbojet engine but, though it was often the subject of interesting discussions with instructors and fellow students, there was no progress towards turning it into a reality. All his work to date consisted of calculations and, as yet, there was no sign of anybody willing to back his project. Consequently, he was beginning to feel that it was long before its time.

Despite the demands of an intensive course of study at Henlow, his inventive mind continued to look into other schemes and the most important of these was a new type of aircraft weapon: "In this I was inspired by the bolas used by the South American Indians, which consists of three weights attached to the ends of lengths of rope joined together at their other ends. When the weapon was hurled at an enemy it would, if skilfully directed, wind itself around his body.

"My aircraft proposal was very similar so I christened it The Flying Bolas. It comprised a length of wire with a small bomb or grenade at each end. The idea was that fighters would attack an enemy bomber formation from a head-on direction with one bomb trailing at the end of the wire about 150-200 feet below the aircraft, the bomb at the upper end of the wire being attached to the underside of the aircraft in such a manner that it would be released by a sharp jerk.

"Thus, when the fighter passed a few feet above a bomber from a head-on approach, the wire would engage the wings of the bomber and the momentum of the two bombs would cause the apparatus to wind itself round the wings, whereupon the bombs would explode".

This device was duly submitted to the Air Ministry. A short time later he received a copy of a letter dated 25 March 1933 which said, 'with a view to deciding whether this method of attack is practicable the Council will endeavour to arrange for a practical trial to be made in about a year's time, when a suitable target aircraft will probably be available for this purpose. A further communication on this subject will be addressed to you in due course'.

In the event, Whittle heard no more about it and never knew whether the promised test was ever carried out, but the same idea was exhaustively tried in World War 2. But, at least, he was scoring points with the Air Ministry because their letter went on to say, 'I am to request that an expression of the Air Council's appreciation of the zeal and initiative displayed in connection with this invention may be communicated to Flying Officer Whittle'.

Having had no success with his inventions, he was becoming

rather despondent about the fate of any invention by serving officers relating to Service equipment. He felt there was insufficient incentive for private firms to develop major inventions for Service use, and that when an invention was submitted to the Air Ministry, the inventor was not sufficiently informed as to its fate. Also, that inventions did not receive sufficient consideration before being turned down.

He had therefore come to the conclusion that when an invention had little or no application outside the Service, it was a waste of money to take out a patent. So, he decided that where an invention would find its chief application in the Service he would submit the idea for official consideration but would not take out a patent unless instructed to do so at Air Ministry expense.

There was not a shadow of a doubt that Whittle's main objective in submitting inventive ideas to the Air Ministry was to have the satisfaction of seeing them carried out in practice. But being married and having to live without a marriage allowance meant that he was always short of money: "I would, of course, have welcomed any purely Service rewards which might have resulted".

The Air Ministry had, a short time previously, discontinued the practice of sending one or two officers selected from the Engineering Course to Cambridge University to take the Mechanical Sciences Tripos. Therefore, Whittle sent in a formal application, backed by the Officer Commanding his Course, for his case to be specially considered. His excellent work at Henlow was, naturally, the basis for such a request. However, his inventive potential and enthusiasm had come to the attention of the Air Ministry on several occasions in the past, and this must have been a contributory factor to their decision to allow this officer, as an exceptional case, to proceed to Cambridge University for the two years Engineering Course.

He had completed his course at Henlow at the end of 1933, and was not due for posting to Cambridge until July 1934. To bridge the six-month gap, he was posted to the Engine Repair Section of the Home Aircraft Depot, also at Henlow. His appointment was as Officer i/c Aero-engine Test Benches, and during this period his promotion to Flight Lieutenant was gazetted. He only managed a total of 23 hours' flying in the rest of 1934 and his total flying time, during the two years he was at Henlow, was just over 107 hours.

*   *   *

At the age of twenty seven and with the rank of Flight Lieutenant, Whittle entered Cambridge University as a member of Peterhouse, the oldest of the Cambridge Colleges. He and his wife had the good fortune to rent a pleasant little furnished house in the village of Trumpington. The same house had been occupied by a succession of RAF officers attending Cambridge and, though it was geographically outside the precincts of the University, the Senate had agreed to regard it as being within the precincts for official purposes. For administration purposes he was attached to the Cambridge University Air Squadron commanded by S/Ldr C. E. W. Lockyer.

Apart from his scholastic activities, Whittle was expected to do a certain amount of flying to keep his hand in, and for this purpose would occasionally fly the Avro Tutors with which the CUAS was equipped at RAF Duxford. As at Henlow, the pressure of work made it difficult for Whittle to put in more than a very limited amount of flying.

Being a serving officer, married, living out and several years older than average, set Whittle apart from his fellow undergraduates: "I was never resident in my College and was not expected to dine in Hall more than once a week. However, in all other respects I had to conform to the rules of one 'in statu pupillari' and in theory at least was as much subject to university discipline as any of the undergraduates. It was, for example, an offence to walk about Cambridge without academic dress (cap and gown). If one broke this rule one was liable to be intercepted by the Proctor, assisted by his pair of 'Bulldogs',[1] and subsequently fined.

"However, my comparatively aged appearance enabled me to pass the Proctor without academic dress on a number of occasions without ever being stopped and asked to give my name and college. In a sense I am rather sorry now that I missed this little formality, which is conducted in the politest manner possible. In this and other ways I was largely outside normal undergraduate life and so missed many of the facets of university life, but to a large extent this was compensated by the fact that, because I was older and more serious than most of my contemporaries, I was more diligent in my studies".

Conscious of the fact that the RAF had made an exception in his case in order to send him to Cambridge, Whittle was even more determined to achieve the highest distinction and live up to expectations. The normal period for the Mechanical Sciences

[1]Bulldogs — university policemen.

Tripos was three years, but by virtue of his previous course at Henlow he was expected to take it in two years and so omitted the first year of studies.

He found that it was, in many ways, a big advantage to have gone to university after several years of practical experience: "because I had acquired a strong desire to know the explanations of many of the phenomena I had encountered during this experience. This, of course, was most marked in those subjects which were closely associated with aeronautical engineering. Many items of knowledge which had great practical significance for me must have seemed relatively academic to those who had gone to university direct from school".

Whittle obtained a First in the Mays (the examinations held at the end of the second year of the three-year course, i.e. after his own first year) and he was made a Senior Scholar of Peterhouse. He also received two College prizes, one of which consisted of the two volumes of Stodola's 'Steam and Gas Turbines' which brought back earlier memories. He had dipped into these works as a schoolboy and, although unable to comprehend the theory at that time, he had found them exciting and inspiring. This time he understood them.

In January 1935 his jet engine patent of 1930 became due for renewal. For this a fee of five pounds was required. Shortly before the renewal date he had received an official letter from the Contracts Directorate of the Air Ministry reminding him of the fact, and adding that there was no intention of paying this fee out of official funds.

By then, Whittle had virtually given up hope of ever seeing his invention becoming a reality. He was convinced that it was long before its time, and was not a practical proposition because of the cost and effort required for its development. Also, having acquired a great deal of engineering knowledge as a result of the training he had received since he first had the idea, he had a much fuller appreciation of the problems involved before a paper scheme such as his could be turned into a practical engine. This somewhat 'laissez faire' attitude on Whittle's part at this juncture was foreign to his nature, but there were reasons for his depression. During the past five years since he had taken out his patent it seemed that, despite his efforts to interest people, nobody wanted his invention. Moreover, he could ill afford the five pounds for the renewal of the patent, in view of recent medical expenses arising out of the illness of his elder son and the birth of his younger one.

In the circumstances, Whittle decided against renewal and allowed his patent to lapse: "Though I had lost hope of the successful development of the turbojet engine by January 1935 I had by no means given up invention entirely. On the contrary, I was then very interested in an electro-mechanical device for variable-speed transmission of power for road vehicles and other things". Later, he was able to take out a patent for this invention jointly with the late Dr McCurdy of Corpus Christi College, who furnished the patent fees.

Some three months later, in early May 1935, Whittle received a letter out of the blue which was to re-energise the turbojet project and make it his prime function in life. As he walked into the offices of the University Air Squadron the CO's secretary handed him an envelope: "It did not look at all exciting; in fact, it looked a very ordinary letter. I did not recognise the writing, because it was the first letter I had ever received from the writer".

It was from Rolf Dudley Williams, who had shared the same hut with him at Cranwell and who had taken an interest in his turbojet proposal when they were both at Felixstowe in 1931. Since those days he had heard little of Dudley Williams except that he had retired from the RAF owing to ill health. The letter was handwritten and read as follows:

'This is just a hurried note to tell you that I have just met a man who is quite a big noise in an engineering concern and to whom I mentioned your invention of an aeroplane, sans propeller as it were, and who is very interested. You told me some time ago that Armstrong's had or were taking it up, and if they have broken down or you don't like them, he would I think like to handle it. I wonder if you will write and let me know. My address is:

    c/o General Enterprises Ltd, Callard House,
        Regent Street, W.I.

Do give this your earnest consideration and even if you can't do anything about the above you might have something else that is good.

Please give my regards to your wife. If you like to ring me up at the above address my number is Regent 2934, and I shall be there on Tuesday at 12 o'clock.

            Ever yours, R. D. Williams.'

Whittle didn't react at all when he first read the letter, and stuffed it into his pocket forgetting all about it for several hours. On re-reading it, he decided to follow it up, but mainly in case Williams's contact should prove useful in connection with other inventions.

He replied to Williams on 7 May, telling him that: "I have allowed the patent to lapse. Nobody would touch it on account of the enormous cost of the experimental work, and I don't think they were far wrong, though I still have every faith in the invention. However, if anybody were keen on taking it up I should think it would pay them. There is no doubt in my mind that, as things stand at present, it is the only way to high altitude flying".

A few days later, Williams and a man named Tinling turned up at Whittle's house in Trumpington to talk it over. They were partners in General Enterprises Limited whose chief activity was the manufacture of automatic cigarette machinery. J. C. B. Tinling was another ex-RAF pilot who had been invalided out after being severely injured in a crash resulting from an aerial collision. He was left with a permanent limp.

The net result of the afternoon's talk was that Williams and Tinling agreed to cover the expenses of taking out further patents, and any other expenses which might arise in their efforts to raise money, and would act as Whittle's agents. In return, they would each receive a quarter share of the joint commercial rights. Williams and Tinling were not in a position to provide much money themselves, so the plan was for them to find financial backing in exchange for a share in the rights of the invention.

Although the talks in Trumpington on that Sunday afternoon were optimistic, Whittle did not feel the confidence he was showing. He did not really believe that the time was ripe for an attempt on the turbojet engine, but he encouraged his partners to try and raise money in what he considered the forlorn hope that something would come out of their joint activities. He had had to convince his associates that, although the master patent had lapsed, the patent position could be recovered to some extent by patenting a series of improvements to the original scheme: "As a result of the thinking I had done since 1930 there were sufficient to provide a bargaining basis".

Their objective was to raise £50,000, which they thought would be ample for the development of a complete jet-propelled aeroplane. Whittle was not optimistic in other ways. On 26 May he wrote to Williams saying that he thought it was "not a particularly efficient type of engine, but there is plenty of scope for development. Its virtue lies entirely in its extremely low weight, and that it will work at heights where atmospheric density is very low".

During the next few weeks three provisional patent specifications were filed covering improvements to the original scheme, but this in itself created a problem which was to cause great trouble later on. There was a standard form of agreement for all inventions which the Air Ministry did not intend to sponsor themselves. It gave the inventor commercial rights in the invention, but retained the right of Free Crown User. Such an agreement was obviously a handicap as the government was likely to be the chief and maybe the only customer. Recognising that it was likely to prove an obstacle to raising private money, Whittle attempted to get the agreements modified, but the Director of Contracts refused to consider any alteration.

When discussing the question of financial backing, Whittle was emphatic that in no circumstances should anybody connected with the aircraft industry be approached. He pointed out that if one of the big aircraft firms became involved, then the only thing which could stop them from proceeding independently was whatever patent protection he and the others happened to have at the time. Establishing the validity of patents in court, he said, could be a very expensive business and they were in no position to risk such an action.

Inevitably, things did not go according to plan. Hopes rose and fell as Williams and Tinling did their best to stir up interest. Financiers and industrialists blew hot and cold. At one moment Williams and Tinling would report that they were sure of finding the money almost immediately, only to learn that the financier concerned had cooled off or — in one case — had suddenly gone to sea in his yacht and was inaccessible.

Much later, Whittle heard that a Mr M. L. Bramson was interested in the scheme. He was horrified when he learned that Bramson was well known in aeronautical circles, both as a pilot and as an engineer, and had links with several firms with aeronautical interests. The contact had come through Tinling's father, because Bramson was the nephew of one of Tinling senior's associates. They had no option but to discuss the proposal with Bramson and hope for the best. In the event, Whittle's pessimism about Bramson's aeronautical contacts proved to be groundless: ". . . though it nevertheless remains the fact that our fear of independent action compelled us to a course of events which was not of our choosing".

The meeting with Bramson went well. Both men were pilots and engineers, and spoke the same language. Bramson's initial response to the idea was one of enthusiasm, and he managed to convey the respect he felt for Whittle as an engineer.

Fortunately, Bramson made no suggestion of an approach to any of the aircraft firms, but began by capturing the interest of a firm of investment bankers, O. T. Falk & Partners. As a result, negotiations were opened in the autumn of 1935, between Williams, Tinling and Whittle on the one hand, and Falk & Partners on the other.

Mr L. L. Whyte, MC, represented the investment bankers, though quite frequently Sir Maurice Bonham Carter, one of the Directors, also took part in the discussions. Whyte was a remarkable man, being a scientist, philosopher and banker, which is a most unusual combination. Also, he had a fine war record but he was primarily a physicist, having taken a Cambridge degree in Natural Sciences.

Most of the meetings, over a period of several weeks, took place in Falk's offices at 10 Old Jewry in the City of London. In this traditional financial atmosphere, a novel experience for Whittle, he began to realise for the first time that his dream of a turbojet aeroplane might actually become a reality. His great project was once again in the forefront of his mind, superseding all his other inventive work. So, in addition to his normal studies for the final year of his Mechanical Sciences Tripos, he began working on the preliminary design of an experimental engine, and also doing aerodynamic research under the great Professor B. Melvill Jones (later Sir Bennett Melvill Jones).

In the meantime, Bramson had become a key figure in that Falk & Partners had asked him to act as their consultant, and to write a formal report on the project. Much depended on Bramson's report, which would obviously greatly influence any final agreement. When it appeared that the parties were nearing agreement, Whittle and his associates considered plans for starting practical work. They decided to investigate placing a contract for an experimental engine with a suitable engineering firm — preferably a turbine manufacturer.

At the beginning of November 1935 Bramson delivered his report. This historic document was entirely favourable, and cleared the way for the parties concerned to formulate the details of a final agreement.

In those days Whittle frequently took the family to Coventry to stay with his wife's parents, and so he hoped that the firm selected for the experimental engine contract would be in that general area. During one of these visits he went over to Rugby and had a talk with the senior turbine engineers of the British Thomson-Houston Company, Messrs, Samuelson and Collingham: the same men to whom he had tried to sell his idea five years earlier.

Having been given a general indication of his aims and requirements, they said that BTH might be willing to accept a contract if it was on a cost plus basis. In their opinion, it was too big a shot in the dark for a firm tender, and they would want to ensure that they did not lose money on the contract.

Whittle might have reasonably expected a more enthusiastic reception, bearing in mind that Bramson was behind him and an investment banker of repute was willing to invest money in the project. Such confidence in Whittle's project should have alerted BTH, who had started experimenting with gas turbines on their own account some three years previously, and spurred them to reappraise his turbojet scheme.

For a time there was some doubt whether they would accept the contract, because the work apparently conflicted with a Rolls-Royce proposition. Rolls had asked them to tackle the problem of the exhaust-driven supercharger, and there was a sufficient similarity between the two types of work which might embarrass their relations with Rolls-Royce. However, at this stage, they had at least agreed that the drawings and information which Whittle had prepared for them were sufficient for them to make a start.

The draft agreement between Falk & Partners and Whittle and his associates had been sent to the Air Ministry for approval, but it was some time before this was granted subject to a number of amendments. Eventually, the President of the Air Council (The Secretary of State for Air) became one of the parties to the agreement, which thereafter became known as the Four-Party Agreement, comprising the President of the Air Council, O. T. Falk & Partners, Williams and Tinling jointly, and Whittle.

The Four-Party Agreement was eventually duly signed by all the parties and was dated 27 January 1936. Under the terms of this agreement a company was to be formed with an authorised capital of not less than £2,000 for the purpose of exploiting the turbojet engine. Whittle was to assign all his patent rights to this company, and Falk & Partners were to provide the first £2,000 of capital and had the option to put in a further £18,000 at par within 18 months. In return for the patent rights, Whittle, Williams and Tinling were to have a 49 per cent holding in the company, and this holding was not to be watered down before the capital subscribed for in cash had reached £50,000.

The Air Ministry allowed Whittle to act as Honorary Chief Engineer and Technical Consultant for a period of five years,

'provided always that the work to be done by the inventor under this clause . . . shall not conflict with his official duties, and the time which the company shall be entitled to require the inventor to develop such work and supervision shall not, without the consent of the President of the Air Council, in any one week exceed a total of six hours . . .'

The Air Ministry had insisted on this condition and made it very clear at the time that Whittle's work in connection with the engine was to be very much a 'spare time job'.

This clause, with hindsight, might appear to be rather petty, and Whittle must have smiled when he read that he could only work a maximum of six hours a week for his new company without the consent of the President of the Air Council. But the Air Ministry had to safeguard itself, because Whittle was a serving officer and taxpayers' money was involved. Details of his company formation would be recorded officially, and journalists have a habit of delving into new companies in which serving officers are concerned.

His RAF superiors had looked after Whittle in recognising his undoubted talent, and making an exception, in his case, by sending him to Cambridge because of his performance record at Henlow. The Mays examinations at Cambridge further confirmed their faith in him.

The turbojet project and other inventions which he had submitted from time to time had been products of original thought and, as such, had made an impact on some of those in high places. But now that Whittle had the confidence of an investment bank and a leading consulting engineer in the aeronautical field, who had technically endorsed his project, the Air Ministry was forced to make a major decision.

It is to their eternal credit that they went along with him and agreed to the formation of his new company. Had they realised at the time that they owned an inventive genius who would revolutionise aeronautical technology throughout the world, they might have given him much greater scope, flexibility and backing!

At the time they had other things on their minds. In 1936 the Air Council, under the direction of Marshal of the Royal Air Force Sir Edward Ellington, was busily engaged in building a modern Air Force. The low-performance, fabric covered and partly wooden biplanes of 1934, having fixed undercarriages and fixed-pitch propellers, were to be replaced by high-performance all-metal monoplanes having retractable undercarriages, variable-pitch propellers and enclosed cockpits. The Hawker Hurricane had made its debut in 1935, and Mitchell's Supermarine Spitfire, a distant relative of the Schneider Trophy S.6B, was to make its maiden flight in March 1936. These developments were going on behind the scenes because of the decline in national morale leading up to the Disarmament Conference. It was in this climate that Whittle's company was born.

They called it Power Jets Limited, and it was duly incorporated in March 1936, with an authorised capital of £10,000. The name was chosen as being descriptive of their aims, yet at the same time, unlikely to disclose them. The directors were L. L. Whyte and Sir Maurice Bonham Carter representing the B shareholders (with Bramson acting as alternate director for Sir Maurice) and Williams and Tinling for the A shareholders. Whyte was appointed Chairman, and Bramson acted as official consultant. Whittle, in his capacity as Honorary Chief Engineer was, of course, the mainspring of the new company.

During this time, Whittle had been making frequent visits to the BTH works at Rugby for technical conferences to discuss the design of the experimental engine. It was to be purely an experimental engine for bench test and was not intended for flight, but the design work was based on a flight target: "We had in mind a small 500 mph mailplane, and the engine was intended to provide the power we estimated would be required for this purpose". The engine was known as the WU, for Whittle Unit. Whittle visualised carrying 500 lb of mail across the Atlantic in six hours.

One of the conditions under which BTH accepted the contract was that in the event of success they were to receive contracts for the first 100 engines if and when the engine went into production, provided that their price was not more than 7½ per cent more than their nearest competitor. This condition was to prove a serious stumbling block a few years later.

Thus, the stage was set and the wheels put in motion for the design and manufacture of Whittle's first experimental jet engine. He and Bramson held frequent meetings in London, and many of the engineering decisions which Whittle took at this time were mutually agreed between them.

His tutor at Peterhouse, Roy Lubbock, had become very interested in the engine, and it was through him that the Director of Education of the Air Ministry, W. M. Page, heard of it and also took a benevolent interest. There were now three sections of the Air Ministry concerned, namely, the Contracts Directorate, in connection with the agreements; the Directorate of Education; and the Directorate of Scientific Research, though there were no signs of anything more than a very lukewarm interest from the latter. Dr D. R. Pye, the Deputy Director of Scientific Research and an expert on internal-combustion engines, did, however, reply to a letter saying: "I wish you every success in your bold venture outside the limits of design which have hitherto been built, and shall be very interested to hear how matters progress". But he made it clear in reply to a letter from Bramson that his view was that what Power Jets were doing constituted long-range research.

While he was at Cambridge, it never crossed Whittle's mind that he had taken a tremendous gamble with his RAF career when he committed himself to his turbojet project, and simultaneously graduating with first-class honours in the Mechanical Sciences Tripos. He was totally confident that his jet engine would work, and also that his mental ability would enable him to achieve the highest academic distinction. There was never any question of his being motivated by personal financial gain. The things that mattered most to him were his career in the RAF and an overwhelming desire to bring about a revolution in aircraft propulsion.

The climate at Cambridge was ideal for stimulating his inventive genius, and provided a unique background for him to increase his knowledge of engineering sciences. He was able to discuss his project and learn from leading professors in their various fields, and in this atmosphere he acquired the fullest appreciation of the problems facing him with regard to his experimental engine. He was encouraged by the favourable views of his tutor and of the Professor of Aeronautical Sciences B. Melvill Jones. The latter, however, warned Whittle not to expect too much, and advised him to assume that it would be at least ten years before the sky would be black with jet aeroplanes.

Whittle had occasion to see Melvill Jones quite frequently, because he was assisting him in the Engineering Department's wind tunnel to establish the lost-momentum method of measuring drag. Moreover Melvill Jones, who was a very eminent figure in the sphere of aerodynamics, was a strong advocate of the streamlined aeroplane, and he recognised that his view in this sphere tied in very well with Whittle's engine proposals. His deputy, W. S. Farren, however, was very cynical on the subject. Unfortunately for Whittle, Farren was soon to become Deputy Director of Scientific Research at the Air Ministry.

Chapter 6
The Birth of the Turbojet

From the beginning of Power Jets, lack of finance was a major consideration. Initially, Whittle and Bramson thought that it would be necessary to make the individual components of the engine and test them separately. There were strong reasons for this approach because in many ways they were going beyond all previous engineering experience, and it thus seemed an appalling gamble to aim for the complete engine in one go. However, they soon calculated that their plan for separate component testing would be far too costly. To test the compressor alone, for example, would have required a 3,000 hp electric motor, and a figure of £27,000 was quoted by BTH for a compressor test plant! Therefore, they decided they had no option but to go for the complete engine and hope for the best.

The compressor problem was to become one of their major headaches. In a conventional internal-combustion engine the processes of compression, combustion, and expansion take place in one organ — the cylinder. In contrast, the turbojet engine consists basically of three linked components: a compressor, one or more combustion chambers and a turbine followed by a jetpipe. The compressor draws in large quantities of air and forces it into the combustion chamber under pressure. In the combustion chamber the air is heated by the steady burning of fuel. From the combustion chamber the compressed and heated gases expand through the turbine, thus providing the power to drive the compressor, to which the turbine is connected by a shaft. After the products of combustion have passed through the turbine, there is sufficient remaining energy to provide the high-velocity propulsive jet. When stationary, the thrust is proportional to the speed of the jet; in flight it is proportional to the difference between the jet speed and the speed of flight.

Whittle proposed to use a centrifugal type of compressor, generally similar to the small fan unit of a vacuum cleaner but much larger and, of course, it had to run at very much higher speeds. The supercharger of the then conventional aero engine had a similar type of compressor, usually about 10 inches in diameter, running at a tip speed of about 1,200 feet per second (about the speed of sound). A compressor of this size and speed, in those days, was capable of compressing about 120 pounds of air per minute to a pressure rather more than twice that of the atmosphere.

Up to this time most of the development work on high-speed centrifugal compressors had been in connection with aero-engine superchargers. The compressor that Whittle required for his turbojet was much, much more ambitious, and far beyond anything previously attained with similar components. Though of only 19 inches diameter, it was to be capable of breathing 1,500 pounds of air per minute. When running at full speed it had to produce a pressure of over four atmospheres in the combustion chamber.

To deal with so tremendous a volume of air at such a pressure ratio required over 3,000 hp, and this had to be provided by the small single-stage turbine mounted on the same shaft as the compressor rotor. This turbine was only about 16.5 inches in diameter (a turbine may be thought of as an extremely powerful windmill). Thus, the main moving part of the engine — the rotor — was made up of the compressor impeller, the turbine wheel, and the shaft connecting the two. It was designed to rotate at 17,750 revolutions per minute, which meant a tip speed of nearly 1,500 feet per second for the compressor impeller and 1,250 feet per second for the turbine.

Power of this order from such a small single-stage turbine was well beyond all previous experience. But Whittle felt fully confident that he could achieve his targets for the compressor and turbine, because he was convinced that the way to get high efficiency with these components was to make them do as much work as possible in proportion to their size. He had a formidable task, apart from the problem of the turbine. In the combustion chamber he was aiming to burn nearly 200 gallons of fuel (240 US gallons) per hour in a space of six cubic feet (about the size of a suitcase), which would require a combustion intensity many times greater than any boiler furnace.

Whittle was concerned about the combustion chamber. "I saw no reason why we should not get the combustion intensity, but felt much less sure of my ground, and so decided to seek outside help. On 19 February 1936 I went to the British Industries Fair at Castle Bromwich and visited the stands of several well-known firms who specialized in burners and combustion equipment for boiler firing and other purposes. Without disclosing the nature of the project, I outlined our combustion-chamber problems. For the most part I met with blank astonishment, and was told that I was asking for a combustion intensity at least twenty times greater than had ever before been achieved".

Eventually, he called at the stand of a small Scottish firm, Laidlaw, Drew & Company, and talked to Mr A. B. S. Laidlaw. His attitude was more encouraging. Laidlaw could see no reason why the combustion intensities Whittle required could not be achieved, but agreed with Whittle that they would need to experiment before a combustion chamber could be designed. So the contract for making test equipment for preliminary experiments was offered to Laidlaw, subject to reasonable terms.

All this time, while at Cambridge, Whittle was having to do a lot of travelling in order to get his jet project off the ground. There were frequent visits to London for consultation with Bramson, and others connected with Power Jets; to Rugby for engineering conferences with the BTH turbine engineers; and to Edinburgh to discuss combustion problems with Laidlaw. He usually flew to Edinburgh to combine business with the requirement that he should put in a certain number of flying hours per year. In addition, he was visiting sundry firms in connection with special problems. Among others, he went to the Hoffman Company in Chelmsford to discuss bearings, and to Alfred Herbert in Coventry to discuss the special machining problems of the main rotating assembly.

The pressure on him began to build up as he was forced to concentrate on the engineering problems to be solved. When he visited BTH on 23 March 1936, for example, he was shown a tentative assembly drawing, which was a long way from his conception of the engine, and he had to reject it. This compelled him to specify his requirements more closely, and control the situation. To this end he prepared an assembly drawing and required the BTH engineers to adhere to it. Thereafter things went more in accordance with his wishes, and work on detail drawings started in April.

On the occasion of the Cambridge University Air Squadron annual dinner, in March 1936, he had a stroke of luck. He had invited his Power Jets associates Sir Maurice Bonham Carter, Whyte, Bramson, Williams and Tinling as his guests. Fortunately, H. E. Wimperis, who was then Director of Scientific Research at the Air Ministry, and Sir Henry Tizard, Chairman of the Aeronautical Research Committee, were also present: "There was an opportunity for some informal discussion of the project. We all met and talked to Tizard and this was, I believe, the first occasion on which he heard about it. As a result of this discussion, Whyte sent Tizard a copy of Bramson's report". Such are the wheels of fate, and later Tizard was to be extremely helpful and a good friend. Wimperis had gone on record as saying that it would never be possible to fly faster than the speed of sound. When Williams raised the subject of the Power Jets project Wimperis sarcastically commented that many had burnt their fingers on gas-turbine projects and he didn't "suppose that you, Mr Williams, will be the last". Fortunately, Wimperis retired shortly after this!

Early in April, with Mr W. A. Randles of BTH in charge of the design, the general arrangement was taking shape, and on the 20th Whittle was told that work on detailed drawings had started. There were only about three weeks to go before the Tripos examinations, and Whittle had to cease all work on the engine and hand over to Bramson because he had set his heart on obtaining a First, and he had to make the most of all this short time to have any hope of doing so.

His work on the turbojet had interfered very considerably with his studies, and he had a lot of ground to make up, especially as rather unwisely he had elected to take five A subjects instead of the normal two. Working all hours — he stuck formulae and diagrams around the walls of the bedroom at Trumpington — he made a tremendous effort to regain lost time, but not without some damage to his health. This was undoubtedly due to the excitement and strain of the preceding few months, aggravated by the tremendous spurt that he had had to make. During the examinations in the early part of June he felt unwell throughout, and did not sit one of the papers, but "Fortunately, and rather to my own surprise, I obtained my First".

To have got a First in the circumstances was a remarkable achievement. But Whittle was an exceptional person, who had a very advanced concept of engineering sciences. His studies for his Mechanical Sciences Tripos and his work on the turbojet were to some extent related.

He enlisted the aid of two fellow undergraduates in the design of the compressor rotor. One of these was A. A. Hall from Clare College: "The design of the compressor impeller presented special stress problems, and between us we produced a more satisfactory method of dealing with these problems than any previously known. One of the lecturers, who had specialised in stress work, confirmed that the method was both novel and sound". Hall, later Sir Arnold Hall, was to have a most distinguished career, becoming a leading 'boffin' during the war and eventually Chairman of the Hawker Siddeley Group. Whittle was anxious to retain his assistance, and also that of the other student named Edkins who had become involved, after they had graduated, but unfortunately Power Jets were not in a position to make a satisfactory offer.

In the normal course of events, on the completion of his Tripos course, Whittle would have been posted to engineering duties in the RAF. This would have made it very difficult for him to develop the turbojet project, particularly if he had been posted overseas. Fortunately for him and the aviation industry, his tutor, Roy Lubbock, suggested to Air Ministry that Whittle be allowed a post-graduate year at Cambridge on research work. Lubbock must have made out a very good case, because Air Marshal Sir Frederick Bowhill, Air Member for Personnel, agreed to his request. Whittle was lucky that Bowhill had the post of AMP, because it was he who had been so impressed by Whittle's achievement at Henlow that he had approved Whittle's posting to Cambridge.

This meant, in effect, that Whittle would be free to devote the greater part of his time to the turbojet project. Thus, the RAF and Cambridge University between them were making an invaluable contribution to the very early phases. Apart from that, however, the official attitude of the Air Ministry civil servants regarding Whittle's project remained cynical and uncompromising, as witnessed by DDSR's reply to a letter from Bramson, asking the Air Ministry to do something to get Power Jets special priority on materials for the engine. Pye wrote: "While I fully sympathise with your desire to avoid any such delay, and in normal circumstances it might have been possible to ensure this, the difficulty is that however important the possibilities of the engine may be, it can hardly be regarded as other than a piece of long range research. As such it can scarcely claim priority over deliveries needed for work of immediate urgency".

Ironically, in the same month of July 1936, in Germany the Junkers engine and aircraft companies were merged and the brilliant head of airframes, Herbert Wagner, started a secret cell to build a turbojet — the engine company being too conservative was kept in ignorance of this development. This was to lead to thousands of German turbojets being operational during the latter part of World War 2, but the Air Ministry in Britain knew nothing of this.

Despite Pye's attitude, the initial stages of manufacture started in July 1936. Whittle visited High Duty Alloys at Slough to witness the making of the compressor impeller forging. A few weeks later he was in Sheffield at Firth Vickers, overseeing the forging of the turbine wheel which was not an easy process. Preparations for the combustion tests were also going ahead, and the apparatus was being made by Laidlaw Drew in Edinburgh.

Things were progressing: "We were also collecting together the sundry items required for test purposes — a four-wheel truck on which to mount the engine; a number of test instruments; a small two-cylinder engine for starting purposes, and so on. It was our plan at that time to try and acquire some kind of hut near Cambridge for engine testing, but this plan was abandoned when BTH later agreed to allow testing in their turbine factory".

During this period, Whittle and his Power Jets associates were trying to raise the level of the Air Ministry's interest in the project. Although there were some signs of an increased interest, there had been no indication of any financial help. Whittle had been reporting progress to the Deputy Director of Scientific Research and also had frequent talks with W. S. Farren at Cambridge, who was acting as a consultant to DSR at that time. Whyte was also in regular touch with the Deputy Director and one of his staff — W. L. Tweedie, the first person Whittle had met at Air Ministry in 1929.

Despite the negative attitude, combustion experiments started at the beginning of October 1936. Laidlaw was present at many of these tests, and the various experiments were the result of joint consultation. The apparatus was very crude, but nevertheless seemed to be sufficient to show that the needed intensity of combustion was possible — but they knew that many changes in the apparatus would have to be made before they would have sufficient data to embark on the design of a combustion chamber for the engine.

These combustion tests continued at intervals during the last three months of 1936. The site of the tests was outside the BTH turbine factory and below the overhanging extension of the building housing the turbine factory planning office. This overhead structure gave Whittle and his team some protection from the weather, but its occupants often had a lot to put up with when tests were in progress.

Dense clouds of nauseating fuel vapour and smoke would infiltrate the office above, and at times the noise was deafening, especially when the combustion was unsteady. On one occasion, the staff returned from lunch to find every desk and table swept clear — everything, including pens, papers, inkpots, books and instruments, was scattered all over the floor!

Their immediate reaction was that either a practical joker or a poltergeist had been at work — until another test started up below, and the violent concussions made everything start 'walking' again. One of them averred that even the linoleum on the floor rose and fell in waves when Whittle was at work underneath!

One day when the fumes were particularly dense and obnoxious, the whole of the female staff retired to the ladies cloakroom and refused to return to work until somebody had done something about it. The Chief Engineer of the factory would probably have had a fit if he had seen some of the things that went on outside: "The apparatus was usually anything but leak-proof, and large pools of fuel would collect underneath. Sooner or later flaming drops set them alight and we, conducting the tests, would be stepping between the pools of flame like demons in an inferno".

The turbine drawing office was only a few yards away, so they too got the benefit of the noise and fumes. It was said that Power Jets' drawings could be recognised by their pungent smell of fuel oil, because in the intervals of combustion testing, Whittle would disappear into the drawing office to check them over. (He had to give his approval of all drawings by initialling them, as part of the arrangement between Power Jets and BTH.) Despite the attention which these experiments attracted, surprisingly little information leaked out, and only a few of those actually working on the project knew what it was all about. Some people quite naturally had the theory that Whittle and Laidlaw were trying to produce either a flame thrower or a smoke generator, while others thought they were merely mad! For these tests Whittle had the assistance of one or two of the turbine factory test fitters.

Had the BTH people been told that Whittle was trying to produce a revolutionary engine which would give the country a better Air Force, then nobody would have bothered about the combustion experiments. But they were not told anything, despite the fact that Whittle's project was not then governed by the Official Secrets Act and that his patents had been published for all the world to see.

The Air Ministry had no idea in late 1936 that the Germans were working on similar lines. Apart from Wagner at Junkers, the aircraft firm of Heinkel was also building a test rig to the design of a young engineer named von Ohain. Ohain, who had taken out a patent for a turbojet engine five years after Whittle, in 1935, had been introduced to Heinkel by his Professor, R. W. Pohl, of Göttingen University. He had the advantage over Whittle in that he was backed by Heinkel with their very considerable resources, while Whittle had to depend on the dribbles of finance through a tiny public company.

Von Ohain's engine was basically similar to Whittle's in that he also used a centrifugal compressor, though he used a radial-inflow turbine to drive it. In the long run it proved less successful, and never went into production. It was soon abandoned by the Germans in favour of more promising designs, but, von Ohain's engine did power the small He 178 which first flew in August 1939, but only twice thereafter.

Aero engine manufacturers in Britain, and to a lesser extent in Germany, were conservative in their attitude to potential development. They had enormous vested interests in piston engine power to protect. They did not want to scrap everything that they had worked for, or to start learning a new technology. Hence, they did not see the turbojet as a potential rival to their cherished engines, and followed the prevailing belief that gas turbines don't work! In total contrast to the attitude of the British Air Ministry, the German Reich Luftministerium brought pressure to bear to get aero engine firms to embark on gas turbine work, with increasing success.

After years of calculations Whittle had the shock of suddenly finding himself up against practical problems complicated by severe shortage of money. If Rolls-Royce, for example, had backed him with £100,000 and offered their facilities, he (and they) would have had the test equipment to solve his combustion problems much more quickly and efficiently.

At the end of this first combustion test programme, he and Laidlaw optimistically thought that they had learned enough to go ahead with the combustion-chamber design with confidence. Such optimism was to prove most unjustified.

One of Whittle's major problems was the availability of

materials for the turbine capable of withstanding the combination of stress and temperature which the design required. To some extent there had been a vicious circle operating creating a chicken and egg situation. Until suitable materials existed, a gas turbine was not a practical possibility. On the other hand, until the gas turbine itself existed, there was no demand for the materials.

Yet his turbojet design and the materials problem were inseparable. Looking around to find specialised companies who would be prepared to help him was a daunting and difficult task. His requirements were way beyond existing standards, and his financial resources were totally inadequate to promote the necessary research which manufacturers would have to undertake. Power Jets at this time consisted only of a board of directors with no back-up facilities and little finance. Some manufacturers interested in Whittle's proposals might have been willing to spend money on research and development, provided that the market for an eventual product would support the investment. But Whittle could give no such assurance. Only his drive, brilliance, and ability to sell his revolutionary ideas to hard-headed and conservative engineers got things moving at all.

These visits to various specialised companies up and down the country were to have a greater significance. Whittle was cutting across traditional thinking and waking up British Industry. His challenge to industry to provide materials which would give the necessary strength at the high temperatures involved was to make his turbojet a reality, and within a few years give Britain a significant lead in jet technology.

He was helped, to some extent, in his search for new materials by the increasing demands made on the exhaust valves of existing aero engines. This had resulted in steady progress in developing creep-resisting steels. Creep is the slow stretching which a high stress causes in a material at a high temperature. He was delighted to discover that an austenitic steel known as Stayblade, made by Firth Vickers, would apparently be suitable for the wheel and blades of his turbine: "Materials for the compressor impeller and casing presented a less serious problem, because they were not exposed to very high temperatures. Nevertheless, they had to be of very good quality, particularly in the case of the highly stressed impeller. For this we selected an aluminium alloy known as RR.56 — a product of High Duty Alloys".

*   *   *

During the latter part of 1936 Sir Henry Tizard, the Chairman of the Aeronautical Research Committee which advised the Air Ministry on future research, began to become increasingly interested in the project. Tizard expressed the view that it was about time that someone made a bold experiment of this kind, though he thought that Power Jets would have to be prepared for a long series of costly experiments before a tolerable efficiency would be obtained.

Sir Henry's views and his influence set off a chain of events which began to look promising for Power Jets. The Director of Scientific Research asked Power Jets to submit a write up of the engine, and said that this would be sent to the RAE (Royal Aircraft Establishment) for their opinion. At the same time it was hinted that the Aeronautical Research Committee might take the view that the work of Power Jets might justify some financial assistance from the Air Ministry towards the cost of research.

Dr A. A. Griffith, who was then Head of the Engine Section of the RAE, was asked to study the Power Jets situation and make a report. A favourable report would have meant a great deal to Whittle and Power Jets at this juncture, because official backing from the Air Ministry would have greatly influenced the private sector, and eased the financial situation. Apart from that, Griffith had already established a high reputation in the aeronautical world and his opinion carried a great deal of weight.

As mentioned earlier, Griffith had poured cold water over Whittle's turbojet proposal in 1929 when they first met at the Air Ministry's South Kensington Laboratory. He had for many years been a believer in the gas turbine as a means of driving a propeller, and favoured the axial-flow compressor in preference to Whittle's centrifugal type. As early as 1926 he had been an advocate of the gas turbine as an aircraft power plant, but had hardly been more successful than Whittle in getting official backing. All direct work on gas turbine research at the RAE ceased from 1930 to 1937.

While Griffith was engaged on his report, 1936 ended with most of the detail design work completed, and with manufacture of the engine fairly well advanced. BTH were submitting monthly bills which were paid as the work went along. Total expenditure up to that time was of the order of £2,000.

During the first three months of 1937, while Whittle was still nominally a post-graduate student at Cambridge, steady progress was made in the manufacture of the engine. In the

"IN ITS PRESENT STATE, AND EVEN CONSIDERING THE IMPROVEMENTS POSSIBLE
WHEN ADOPTING THE HIGHER TEMPERATURES PROPOSED FOR THE IMMEDIATE
FUTURE, THE GAS TURBINE ENGINE COULD HARDLY BE CONSIDERED A FEASIBLE
APPLICATION TO AIRPLANES MAINLY BECAUSE OF THE DIFFICULTY IN COMPLYING
WITH THE STRINGENT WEIGHT REQUIREMENTS IMPOSED BY AERONAUTICS.

"THE PRESENT INTERNAL COMBUSTION ENGINE EQUIPMENT USED IN AIRPLANES
WEIGHS ABOUT 1.1 POUNDS PER HORSEPOWER, AND TO APPROACH SUCH A FIGURE
WITH A GAS TURBINE SEEMS BEYOND THE REALM OF POSSIBILITY WITH EXISTING
MATERIALS. "

THE COMMITTEE ON GAS TURBINES

appointed by

THE NATIONAL ACADEMY OF SCIENCES

June 10, 1940

Good thing. I was too stupid to
know this.

Frank Whittle

10 DOWNING STREET

THE PRIME MINISTER

Sir Frank is one of the great engineers of the twentieth century. He has helped to change both the way we live and the world in which we live and his work has made possible the kinds of journey our ancestors never even imagined. His pioneering work on jet engines, his perseverance over the development of the project and his continuing contribution to science and technology are never to be forgotton. His life and work are an object lesson on the creativity and inspiration of British engineering at its best. He has always retained his great. gift of original thought and exposition.

Margaret Thatcher

July 1986

The original WU was Whittle's only engine until its turbine finally gave up the ghost in 1941. By this time the fir-tree root had been invented.

The compressor and turbine of the W.1, the first flight engine. There could hardly be a more simple kind of prime mover than the original form of Whittle turbojet; all you need do is add heat to the working fluid between the compressor (left) and turbine (right).

The original W.1 flight engine outside the Lutterworth works. This was the same engine that today is on view at the Science Museum in London.

George Carter's original drawing for the E.28/39. Other drawings showed the provision for four Browning machine guns.

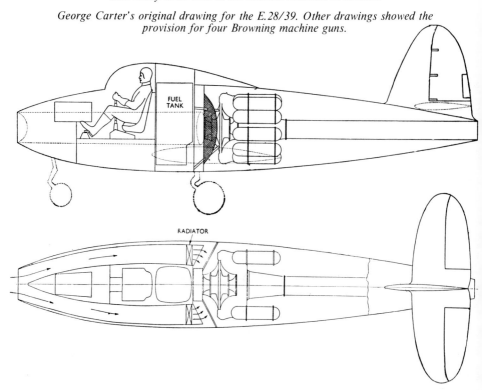

FUEL
TANK

RADIATOR

The E.28/39, after final painting but still with W.1 engine. Later the same aircraft had much greater thrust, and auxiliary tail fins.

The classic moment, caught by an amateur camera; F.W. shakes Gerry Sayer's hand after the first flight on 15 May 1941.

This Wellington bomber was the first turbojet test-bed aircraft. The W.2B is installed for testing, with air inlets at the sides ahead of the original turret mounting.

Conference at Brownsover Hall in 1944: from left, L. J. Cheshire, R. Dudley Williams, Mary Phillips, Frank Whittle, W. E. P. Johnson, J. C. B. Tinling, D. N. Walker and W/Cdr G. Lees.

Brownsover Hall, in 1943 This was the main headquarters office, with a scale compressor, F.9/40 model and (background) W.2B/700 model.

Whetstone, 21 August 1943: Frank Whittle, Sir Stafford Cripps and R. D. Williams.

Whetstone, 21 August 1943: Frank Whittle, Harold Roxbee-Cox (today Lord Kings Norton) and Air Chief Marshal Sir Wilfred Freeman.

Group Captain Whittle and his secretary, Mary Phillips.

meantime, the Department of Scientific Research had hinted that the Air Ministry would want to spend a lot of money on the unit if it came near to success. Whyte, the Chairman of Power Jets, told Whittle that DSR had been subject to winds in high places. The activities of their good friend, Tizard, appeared to be bearing fruit!

During March everything was very nearly ready for the climax of Whittle's life — the first test run of his engine in the BTH turbine factory. During the final stages of preparation, however, there were a few mishaps: "The two-cylinder piston engine for starting proved to be unsatisfactory, and we had to substitute a 20-kilowatt electric motor. We had also slightly damaged the engine during mechanical tests when we had spun the rotor round with compressed air on the turbine. This test was to make sure that the bearings and gears were behaving satisfactorily, but unfortunately the impeller fouled its casing at a speed of 9,300 rpm, and both the impeller and the casing were slightly damaged. The damage would have been more serious if the test mechanic operating the compressed air supply had not been very alert and detected the trouble as soon as it had occurred. Nevertheless, it was an inauspicious start. We could not afford new parts, so had to be satisfied with cleaning up the damaged ones".

During March, Whittle received a copy of Dr Griffith's report upon which much depended. Griffith's final conclusion was: "in its present form the proposed jet propulsion system cannot compete with the conventional power plant in any case where economical flight is demanded (e.g. the transport of the maximum percentage of useful load over a given distance). It is of value only for special purposes such as the attainment of high speed or high altitude for a short time in cases where take-off requirements are not stringent." Griffith made much of the fact that in the absence of propellers the lack of slipstream over the wings would make take-off difficult. He did not recognise, apparently, that the absence of slipstream also meant lower drag.

Whittle himself was more than charitable about the document when he said: "Though this report was somewhat lacking in enthusiasm for the project, it did mark the beginning of official interest in it". Griffith, in fact, had expressed a totally negative view, and ignored all possibilities of future development. He might well have taken into account, for example, that further research and experience would increase the efficiency of components and provide for higher pressure ratios. Although

Griffith's report had to be fair and objective, he might have looked ahead to what would become possible, and given some encouragement to Whittle's project.

This report and a paper by Hayne Constant, once more setting out the case for the gas turbine driving a propeller as a power plant for aircraft, were discussed by the Engine Sub-Committee of the Aeronautical Research Committee. Sir Henry Tizard took a prominent part in the discussions, which led to a strong recommendation that the Air Ministry should take up the development of the internal-combustion turbine as a matter of urgency.

In consequence, the Royal Aircraft Establishment were authorised to go ahead with their proposals for a gas turbine-propeller engine in co-operation with the firm of Metropolitan-Vickers (Metrovick). The arrangement between the RAE and Metrovick was to be similar to that which existed between Power Jets and BTH. Both Griffith and Constant had helped to foster the widespread belief during Whittle's early struggles that not only were axial-flow compressors better than centrifugals but that the latter were a crude idea put forward by Whittle that would never be satisfactory. Nothing could have been further from the truth, as history was to prove in due course.

So Griffith and Constant got the backing they were seeking to develop their gas turbine-propeller project. It does Whittle great credit that he bore no resentment in the circumstances. However, he did receive a letter from Tizard which said: "Please let me know how the tests go. I am anxious that you should not be handicapped by lack of funds in the testing of the unit. Perhaps you will let me know if there is any difficulty in this respect". Unfortunately the implied promise did not lead to any substantial help for some time to come.

Finance had always been a problem and Whittle, during some of his frequent visits to Rugby, had been trying to get BTH interested in becoming shareholders in Power Jets. But their senior executives were still very sceptical about the feasibility of jet propulsion. It puzzled Whittle to reconcile this attitude with the fact that they had been willing to accept Power Jets' contracts, and had driven a hard bargain in the process! He could reconcile this point of view only by the fact that the profits from the cost plus arrangement were negligible by BTH standards, and probably did not compensate the company for some of the disruptions his project was causing.

The time was fast approaching when Whittle would run his engine for the first time, and this was uppermost in his mind during the first days of April 1937. He was confident that it would work — his calculations had proved that — but unsure of what might happen as he opened it up. Nobody, he was sure, had ever started a jet engine before, so he would be making history which was an exciting prospect. The prevailing belief was that it wouldn't even drive itself.

He had had his exciting episodes when he had carried out his crazy flying and floatplane test work, but this was something quite different. His turbojet project was the most important thing in his life, and everything depended on the outcome of the first test run.

Chapter 7
The First Test Run

"A tool is but the extension of a man's hand, and a machine is but a complex tool. And he that invents a machine augments the power of a man and the well-being of mankind".

Henry Ward Beecher.

On 12 April 1937 all was ready for the first test run of the WU (Whittle Unit). There were none of the BTH engineers or any of Whittle's Power Jets colleagues present. Collingham — senior BTH Turbine Engineer — had insisted on this, in spite of their strong desire to watch the proceedings. Whittle was at the controls, assisted by three fitters who had been very much concerned with the building of the engine — Bentley, the chargehand, and his two assistants, Berry and Bailey; Harry Webb, in charge of turbine tests; and Havard and other mechanics of Webb's section.

The engine, mounted on its test truck, was situated on a test site on the gallery of the turbine factory. The jet pipe protruded through a window, a pane having been removed for this purpose. A safety screen had been erected around the engine, consisting of three rectangular sheets of steel plating about one inch thick, two of them standing vertically and the other placed across the top.

This screen was considered to be very necessary because if a turbine overspeeds it is liable to burst, with disastrous results. Pieces may be hurled through the air at speeds of the order of 1,200 feet per second — faster than a pistol bullet. There had been several occasions in the past when steam turbines had burst and killed several people. In one case one of the pieces was said to have been hurled a distance of over two miles.

The truck on which the engine was mounted had had its wheels removed, because of the great weight of the 20 kW starter motor. The instrument panel and controls were mounted at the forward end of the truck. Also mounted on the truck was a hand magneto with leads connected to a high-tension sparking plug in the combustion chamber for ignition purposes. The control panel for the electric starter was several yards away, so Whittle used a system of hand signals to communicate his requirements to the test fitter stationed there. The fuel pump, which originally was to have been mounted on the engine, was driven by a separate electric motor.

When Whittle judged that all was ready: "I had the fuel pump switched on; one of the test hands then engaged the starter coupling (which was designed to disengage as soon as the main rotor of the engine overran the starting motor) and I gave hand signals to the man on the starter control panel.

"The starter motor began to turn over. When the speed reached about 1,000 rpm I opened the control valve which admitted fuel to a pilot burner in the combustion chamber, and rapidly turned the handle of the hand magneto to ignite the finely atomised spray of fuel which this burner emitted. An observer, peering through a quartz observation window in the combustion chamber, gave me the 'thumbs up' sign to show that the pilot flame was alight.

"I signalled for an increase of speed of the starter motor, and as the tachometer indicated 2,000 rpm I opened the main fuel control valve.

"For a second or two the speed of the engine increased slowly and then, with a rising shriek like an air-raid siren, the speed began to rise rapidly, and large patches of red heat became visible on the combustion chamber casing. The engine was obviously out of control. All the BTH personnel, realising what this meant, went down the factory at high speed in varying directions. A few of them took refuge in nearby large steam turbine exhaust casings, which made useful shelters.

"I screwed down the control valve immediately, but this had no effect and the speed continued to rise, but fortunately the acceleration ceased at about 8,000 rpm and slowly the revs dropped again. Needless to say, this incident did not do my nervous system any good at all. I have rarely been so frightened".

They tried again the next evening, after an alteration to the fuel system, but things were even more alarming. The engine accelerated out of control from about 1,500 rpm without the main fuel control being opened at all. The speed rose rapidly, sheets of flame belched from the jet pipe, and clouds of fuel vapour coming from leaking joints were ignited by patches of red heat on the combustion chamber. Flames were dancing in mid-air as BTH personnel, who were at the ready after their last experience, disappeared even more rapidly. Fortunately, once more the uncontrolled acceleration did not take the engine beyond 8,000 rpm.

Later that evening Laidlaw, who was staying in the same hotel — the Grand — in Rugby as Whittle, insisted that the latter drink copious quantities of red wine to calm his nerves after his alarming experience.

They found that there was a simple explanation; owing to an oversight in the arrangement of the fuel system it was possible for the main burner to inject fuel into the combustion chamber every time the fuel pump was switched on. This injection only happened for a few seconds at a time, but fuel pump tests were frequent, and so the amount of the fuel unknowingly injected into the combustion chamber was considerable. The shape of the combustion chamber allowed this fuel to accumulate below the fuel burner, and it was this lake of fuel which was responsible for the runaways.

They then arranged to drain the combustion chamber before each attempt to start, but despite this the engine ran away again on the third attempt. This time because a spring, which formed part of the burner mechanism, was weakened by overheating. (The burner injected upstream and was therefore itself immersed in flame.)

Partly as a result of this experience and partly on Laidlaw's advice, they decided to try downstream injection of the fuel. They then made their fourth attempt and this time ran under control up to 7,600 rpm, but had to shut down when one of the patches of bright red heat on the combustion-chamber walls set fire to the ignition cables.

In further attempts, despite modifications made in efforts to improve the combustion, the engine would not accelerate beyond 8,500 rpm, although it would generally run under control. This was due to the fact that any further opening of the control meant that extra fuel injected was burning not in the combustion chamber but in the jetpipe downstream of the turbine.

This state of affairs led to a dispute between Whittle and Laidlaw: "He wanted to go on with improvements to the downstream system, I wanted to try a system based on the principle of the primus stove, namely, a kerosene vaporizer placed in the combustion chamber with a fuel nozzle injecting upstream. Samuelson and Collingham — Chief Engineer of the turbine factory and his deputy — tended to side with Laidlaw. Nevertheless, I ruled that we should proceed with the kerosene vaporizer, a decision which caused a certain amount of tension".

Upon returning from a visit to London Whittle found that

Laidlaw had more or less convinced Sporborg, BTH's Chief Engineer, Samuelson and Collingham, that he was right about the combustion, and once more there was a heated argument. But Whittle exercised his authority, and the engine was prepared for a test with the kerosene boiler.

Neither Samuelson nor Collingham had been present during a test so far. On the morning of April 17 Whittle gave Collingham a graphic description of the hellish nightmare that had been taking place, and told him how frightened he had been. Collingham was a blunt Yorkshireman and said, "Ee lad, you don't know what it is to be frightened. You should have been standing next to a vertical turbine when it jumped out of its bearings, then you'd know what it's like to be frightened".

He and Samuelson were present when the attempt was made to run with the kerosene boiler: "Starting procedure was normal insofar as anything could be described as normal up to this stage. When I first opened the main control which admitted kerosene to the boiler, the engine accelerated smoothly enough at first, and for a moment or two it appeared to be under perfect control. Then once more it ran away with the usual terrifying crescendo of noise, and a great jet of flame from the propelling nozzle.

"Again there was a rapid exodus. The story goes that Collingham was out of the turbine factory and into the nearby locomotive shed before anybody else got started. As usual, I remained rooted to the spot, not because I was particularly brave, but because I seemed almost to be paralysed with fright. I think that deep down I felt fairly confident that it would not run away to a speed at which it would be likely to burst".

With hindsight, Whittle said that in a sense it would have been too good to be true because, with the available fuel supply, it would have meant an efficiency far beyond their most optimistic expectations. It did not, in fact, exceed half speed on this occasion.

What had happened was that the kerosene boiler had insufficient heating surface, and after a few seconds it primed and liquid kerosene was injected through the nozzle instead of vapour. Thus ended the one attempt to run on vaporized kerosene during this series of tests, though they were to revert to it later.

That evening in the Grand Hotel Whittle couldn't help recalling Collingham's rapid exit in the light of his earlier remarks, and was seized with uncontrollable fits of laughter.

These attacks came on him without warning while he was sitting in the lounge or in the dining room, much to the astonishment of the other occupants. It became so embarrassing that eventually he had to retire to his room to laugh himself out. It was partly a hysterical reaction from severe nervous tension. Later, Collingham said, "I admit I was frightened — in fact, I was badly frightened."

It was hardly surprising that Whittle was beginning to feel the strain again. He had made himself ill with overwork several months previously, when he was striving to get his First in the Tripos Examinations. Since then, the pressure of work on the engine had been steadily building up, and the nervous tension within him had intensified during the terrifying test runs. All this, added to the heated controversy with Laidlaw and the BTH turbine engineers, "had left me completely deflated and I agreed to fall in with Laidlaw's recommendations and to try downstream injection again". Such comment by a tough and uncompromising character like Whittle revealed the emotional impact that the test runs were having on anybody in the immediate area of the engine.

The downstream experiments led to some improvement, and after making various alterations they managed to reach higher speeds under control. But another alarming incident occurred — the compressor impeller seized in its casing at a speed of 12,000 rpm. This brought the engine to rest with a piercing shriek in little more than a second. Bramson was present on this occasion and his instinctive reaction was to turn to run, but before he had taken one step the engine had stopped. Walter Smith, the Shop Superintendent, put his hand on Bramson's shoulder and said, with his strong north-country accent, "It's no use runnin', sir, it'll soon catch yer if it wants!" This remark was most appreciated by those who knew that Walter Smith himself had disappeared down the factory at high speed on at least three occasions.

The damage due to the seizure, and the temporary overheating that had occurred during the uncontrolled acceleration, contributed to a general deterioration of the engine. The blower casing in particular had developed leaks at the joints due to distortion; but as they could not afford new parts, they had to make do with makeshift repairs. By aero engine standards the outfit was becoming little more than a heap of junk, but it had to suffice for another three vital years!

By the end of April it was very clear that they would have to do a lot more work on the combustion problem, and that the compressor was well below its design efficiency. So a number of modifications to improve the engine in both respects were tried.

These efforts to improve the engine by relatively minor modifications continued over the next two months, but with only moderate success. During this period there were a number of arguments between Whittle and Laidlaw, and this resulted in Whyte and Bramson beginning to lose confidence in Whittle. They were naturally impressed by the fact that senior BTH engineers tended to side with Laidlaw, and Whittle sensed that they thought he was being obstinate and temperamental.

This was a particularly difficult and frustrating period for Whittle. He had been trying out all kinds of modifications to improve the performance of the engine without success, and began to realise that he could not hope to reach his target with the engine as it stood. Finally, in late August he came to the conclusion that a major reconstruction would be necessary — which seemed out of reach without money to do it.

Chapter 8
Financial Crisis – The Battle for Survival

Whittle had had to worry about lack of money right from the outset but during the months of May, June and July 1937, the need for further financial assistance reached a crisis point. Falk and Partners, the main source of finance to date, were getting cold feet and seemingly losing faith in the project. In June, Power Jets and the Air Ministry had been negotiating to find ways and means by which the Ministry could contribute to the cost of the work.

Power Jets proposed that the Ministry should buy the engine for £16,000 and leave it in the possession of Power Jets for further development. The Power Jets spokesman had openly admitted that this was more than twice the cost of the engine up to that time (the total expenditure at the end of June 1937 was just under £5,000) but pointed out that if the Ministry was looking for a device by which they could give reasonable help, that was the way to do it. The money would, in any case, be spent on engine development. This proposal, however, was flatly rejected.

The Department of Scientific Research made a counter proposal to the effect that the Ministry might pay Power Jets a sum for a report on tests up to that time and that a research contract might be given to the Company.

While these negotiations were in progress, Falk & Partners, having raised about £5,000 (some of which had come from personal friends of Whittle, Williams and Tinling) were saying that they were having difficulty in raising further money, because of some kind of crisis in the City. Their option to increase their holding to £20,000 was due to expire on July 27, but it became clear during June that they were not going to take it up. Whereupon, Whittle, Williams and Tinling told Whyte that if the money was not forthcoming they would exercise their full rights under the Four-Party Agreement and take over control of the Company.

Whittle, himself, found it very strange that those financing the Company should begin to get cold feet just at the moment when there were clear indications that the Air Ministry was going to help financially — even though such help was likely to be well below that expected.

Whyte had been to see Sir Henry Tizard about this time to have a talk, and a few days later Tizard placed his views on record in a letter (dated 22 June 1937):

> You ask for my opinion about Whittle's scheme.
>
> I think there is nothing inherently unsound in his ideas. He may possibly be somewhat optimistic in some of his predictions, but even allowing for that, I think it is highly probable that if he has the necessary financial support and encouragement, he will succeed in producing a new type of power plant for aircraft. I am particularly interested in this work because I think that if we are to provide the high powers which will be necessary for aircraft of the future, we must develop some type of turbine. Further, the fact that such an engine would use heavy oil is of great importance from the point of view of defence and commerce.
>
> I have a very high opinion of Flight Lieutenant Whittle. He has the ability and the energy and the enthusiasm for work of this nature. He has also an intimate knowledge of practical conditions — this combination of qualities is rare and deserves the utmost encouragement. I sincerely hope he will get the necessary finance because I think you will have to make up your mind that a large expenditure will be necessary before final success is reached. My general opinion of the importance of this work leads me to express the hope that the money will be raised privately so that the knowledge that it is going on will not be widespread.
>
> P.S. — Of course, I do not mean to imply that success is certain. All new schemes of this kind must be regarded as gambles in the initial stages. I do think, however, that this is a better gamble than many I know of on which money has beep spent.

This letter put Whyte and his associates in Falk & Partners in a quandary. But Whittle regarded it as a very valuable letter to have on the record, coming as it did from the Chairman of the Aeronautical Research Committee.

In addition to these encouraging signs the BTH were reacting more favourably to the suggestion that they should take shares. (Though it was six months before they did so.)

Nevertheless, internal tension increased. Falk & Partners wanted time to find the money, and asked for an extension of the option. Whittle, Williams and Tinling agreed to give them time to find the money, but would not agree to extend the option. There was a complete deadlock, which developed into a major crisis on July 8. Whyte told Williams that the method of finance up to then must stop, but in order to carry the Company over the next few days, O. T. Falk & Co would lend a small sum.

The situation was so critical that Whittle reported to the Director of Education that, it was "probable that work would have to stop through lack of money, in which case I would be without official employment".

On the following day, 9 July, Whittle received a copy of a letter containing the Air Ministry's proposal for a research contract. A sum of £10,000 was mentioned, and also a hint that they could hope for a further research contract on the satisfactory conclusion of the one then proposed. But on the same day Falk & Partners formally wrote to Power Jets as follows: "We hereby give notice that we are unable to guarantee any further expenditure by you, but that in order to avoid a stoppage of work we are prepared to finance current expenditure from midnight, Saturday July 10 up to the date of the option, July 22, by way of a loan to you up to sum of £250. This loan will bear interest at the rate of 5 per cent per annum and will be repayable from the first monies received by you thereafter".

Having shut off the financial pipeline, Falk & Partners began to have second thoughts. The Air Ministry's proposal for a research contract, Tizard's letter, and BTH's interest in taking shares were encouraging signs, and the Partners naturally wanted to protect the money they had invested.

A week later, on 15 July, Whyte intimated that Falk & Partners would probably put up between £4,000 and £14,000 within two weeks, whether they retained control or not — on certain conditions. These were confirmed by letter on the following day to the effect that if Falk & Partners did not take up their option, they would be prepared to put in further money to enable work to continue, even though control passed to the 'A' shareholders — providing the latter did not exercise their rights under the Four-Party Agreement. The option expired on 27 July and Falk & Partners continued to finance Power Jets by loan.

The financial crisis was a 'catch 22' situation. The Air Ministry officials concerned wished to make an offer to the Company which would be sufficient to encourage further private finance to back the project, but they distrusted a group of financiers who began to get cold feet, after raising only £5,000.

The Air Ministry's proposed contract worth £10,000 which they submitted early in July was detailed as follows: £1,000 for a report on the first series of test runs — £2,000 for research running up to 14,000 rpm — £2,000 for further research running up to full speed, and then £5,000 for the purchase of the engine.

In August, however, there was a sinister hint that the Contracts Directorate would require assurance of the financial standing of the Company before placing the contract. Matters proceeded very slowly. Towards the end of September Power Jets were told that the Air Ministry would not contemplate an increase in price as a result of major modifications which were then in progress. Then on 1 October, the Ministry said that they would not, after all, buy the engine because of certain contractual difficulties. Thus, the prospective contract was reduced to £5,000 and, even at this figure, it was not signed until the following March!

In the meantime, the BTH had also been blowing hot and cold about subscribing money, pointing out that there was little value in Power Jets' published patents. Whittle assured them that what had been published by no means represented the whole of the patent position, but it was not until January 1938 that they actually put in their £2,500.

The control of Power Jets passed into the hands of Whittle, Williams and Tinling on 1 November, as a result of a supplementary agreement. This modified the Four-Party Agreement and Falk & Partners undertook to find a further £3,000 within fourteen days — the 'A' shareholders agreed not to deprive the 'B' shareholders of their voting rights, or their right to nominate half the Board. But the right to appoint the Chairman passed to the majority of the 'A' shareholders (ie, Whittle).

It was surprising in the circumstances that they retained Whyte as Chairman. Whittle, Williams, and Tinling had a high opinion of his integrity and ability, however, and felt confident that once this particular crisis was behind them that Whyte would further the interest of Power Jets to the best of his ability. Whyte had gone out of his way to convince them of his intense interest in the project, and believed it to be extremely important in the national interest. Finally, the £3,000 which Falk & Partners had undertaken to find, was, in fact, subscribed by J. & G. Weir Ltd, through a nominee.

About July 1937, Whittle's post-graduate year at Cambridge expired, but DSR had been successful in getting the Air Member for Personnel's approval and Treasury sanction for him to be posted to the Special Duty List. Thus, his work on the engine became his official full-time employment. The family therefore moved to Rugby early in October, which made things very much easier for him because of the big reduction in travelling time.

The financial wrangling which had taken place over the past few months had not permitted any acceleration of the development programme. Indeed, there seemed to be some danger that it would be slowed down because BTH were becoming restive. Early in August, Collingham hinted that the BTH might be too busy to continue to do work on Power Jets contracts. However, on 16 August 1937, Sporborg, the Chief Engineer, agreed to go on, though he said the work would have to proceed more slowly than hitherto.

Sporborg also told Whittle that he would have to arrange to do his testing somewhere other than in the BTH turbine factory. With some justification he regarded it as too dangerous in the open factory, and when tests were in progress, other work in the factory was either slowed down or stopped altogether. He was even more emphatic about this on the 23rd when he was present during a test run up to 13,600 rpm. He insisted on a shut down and ruled that in future, tests must not exceed 11,000 rpm during working hours or more than 14,000 rpm in any case. This ruling alone made further testing pointless, so another test site became urgently necessary.

Having considered many possibilities, Whittle came to the conclusion that any other test site would need to be quite near the BTH factory and so he asked Sporborg to rent him a piece of land on the Rugby premises so that a test house could be built on it. Sporborg refused, but eventually offered space in the old, disused and decrepit BTH foundry at Lutterworth, about seven miles from Rugby. It was known as the Ladywood Works.

At this time, Whittle had decided to suspend tests and concentrate on the reconstruction of the engine. Apart from visits to sub-contracting firms and to London for sundry meetings, he spent most of his time in the BTH works. Life was made easier and more efficient at BTH because he had achieved an unusually privileged position. Earlier in 1937, Samuelson had agreed to let him share an office with Randles, who was the senior engineer on the project. Nobody then questioned his frequent excursions into the factory or the drawing office, and to all intents and purposes, he and the BTH engineers and draughtsmen working on the job operated as a single team.

Thus, he was able to oversee the work on the spot and build a personal liaison with the BTH employees concerned. This was to prove invaluable as time went on. Although they did not realise it at the time, BTH were extremely fortunate in having a man of Whittle's calibre on their premises. Events were to prove that they failed completely to take advantage of his genius, and when he made what he believed to be helpful suggestions it was resented.

During the latter part of 1937, Whittle was chiefly preoccupied with the design and manufacture of new parts, and with modifications of the original parts which he still proposed to use for the reconstruction of the engine. He had to use as much of the original engine as possible in order to keep costs down, and much of the design work was governed by this requirement. For example, the same turbine rotor was used, except for new blades; the same compressor casing, though greatly modified, and so on. But none of the original sheet metal components could be used in the reconstructed engine.

Although it had been accepted that there would be no great difficulty in achieving the intensity of combustion required, there were still many problems to be solved: excessive pressure loss, uneven temperature distribution in the combustion-chamber discharge and soot formation had to be avoided; distortion of combustion-chamber parts due to local overheating had to be eliminated, and so on.

In October 1937 Whittle started new combustion tests on the same site as before, and these continued well into December. Once more he collaborated closely with Laidlaw. They tried many experiments, but most of the effort went into the development of a suitable arrangement for the injection of vaporized kerosene, with which they found it was possible to get very short flames.

Whittle always had to keep an eye on costs, and discovered that the monthly bills from BTH were beginning to rise sharply. For the most part they had varied between £100 to £200, but the figure for November 1937 was almost £400, which caused immediate concern to Power Jets. BTH allowed him to check the costs in detail every month which became part of his routine.

He learned a great deal from the process and was also able to achieve savings: "I had, for example, not thought it at all unusual that there should be a few additional test fitters standing around when tests were in progress; I naturally thought they were keen types — until I discovered that they had been booking their time to the job. The Cost Accountant was not, of course, to know who were needed and who were not. Once I was aware of these things I was able to guard against them".

An event of some note in the short history of Power Jets occurred in December when the Company engaged their first employee. He was Mr Victor Crompton, formerly a technical sergeant in the RAF. Immediately prior to joining Power Jets he had been a laboratory technician in the Cambridge University Engineering Department, so Whittle knew him well. He was taken on as Whittle's assistant, and began his duties at the Ladywood Works in the New Year of 1938. Thus, Power Jets began 1938 with one employee and a few odd items of minor equipment (which included one typewriter — Whittle at that time had to do his own typing!) and some rented space in a dilapidated old foundry.

Having an assistant was a breakthrough for Whittle. Up to that time he had to do everything for himself, simply because there was no money to pay anybody other than sub-contractors. Money had always been a problem and would continue to be so for Power Jets but, at least, Whittle was able to start 1938 with somebody to share part of the load.

Apart from money worries, Whittle was uneasy about his prospects for promotion. It seemed probable that these would be affected by his posting to the Special Duties List, because he was still nominally under training. Normally, on completion of a University Course, an officer had to sign an undertaking to remain in the Service for at least five years thereafter. In his case, he had to sign an undertaking to remain in the Service for a period of five years after the termination of his appointment to the Special Duties List. Moreover, for promotion from F/Lt to S/L one was required to pass a promotion examination.

In the event, his anxiety about promotion — and he needed the pay increase and marriage allowance to support his growing family — proved to be groundless. On 6 December 1937 his promotion to S/L was gazetted, and the Air Ministry, recognising that he was too preoccupied, had excused him the examination. This was another farsighted act on the part of the Air Member for Personnel.

Having got his promotion, Whittle had the satisfaction of knowing that his superiors in the RAF (as distinct from Ministry civil servants) were doing all that they could to back him. This was very important to him because the RAF meant everything to him, but his desire to further his career in the Service conflicted somewhat with his equally strong desire to achieve a revolution in aviation. The early part of 1938 was going to be a crucial period, because so much depended on the Air Ministry contract. He was well aware that when such backing materialised, it would undoubtedly have great impact on the progress of his turbojet project.

*　　*　　*

In the meantime, preparations were under way for the move to the new engine testing site. The Ladywood Works had been the BTH foundry, and stood alongside the LNER railway just beyond the northern outskirts of Lutterworth, about seven miles north of Rugby and nine miles east of Coventry. BTH were using a part of it for storage, but otherwise the low buildings were derelict and dilapidated. There was foundry sand everywhere, and its ramshackle appearance and rundown condition were typical of an old and deserted factory.

Whittle and Williams had inspected the premises during the previous month, in December 1937, and decided that it could be adapted to their purposes. They took over a small part of the workshop space, and a section of the building which had been used as offices, at a rental of £200 per year. During the early weeks of 1938 work started on the relatively minor alterations necessary to prepare their section of the Ladywood Works for engine testing. Williams had relieved Whittle of much of the detail, and Whittle himself had the assistance of Victor Crompton.

The mysterious comings and goings at the previously deserted factory intrigued the Lutterworth police. There had been a number of IRA bomb outrages, and the police became suspicious. They suspected that Whittle and Crompton might be

IRA terrorists using the premises to make bombs. Crompton showed one zealous and inquisitive policeman round the parts of the factory which Power Jets proposed to use but, of course, made no mention of what they were up to. The engine was still under reconstruction at BTH in Rugby, and so there was nothing to see — which, if anything, made the police more suspicious than ever. Also, the police may have heard an occasional shot ring out from Whittle's office window when he was shooting at rabbits!

Chapter 9
The Affair of Vortex Blading

While the reconstruction of the engine was in progress at BTH Rugby, Whittle was able to keep a closer eye on the detail design than hitherto. Early in December 1937, something very strange happened in the technical sphere. Whittle made the astonishing discovery that the turbine blades of the engine, as tested between the previous April and August, had been incorrectly designed. Up to this time, there had been various occasions when BTH engineers and Whittle had not seen eye-to-eye on technical matters, but they had usually arrived at a compromise satisfactory to both sides. None of these arguments had been very fierce, neither had they left any permanent scars. But on this occasion, concerning the very principles of turbine blade design, there was a sharp divergence of views. This controversy was to damage beyond repair the relationship between Whittle and some (but not all) of the BTH engineers.

Previously, there had been no argument about turbine blade design, because Whittle had naturally assumed that the BTH engineers were far more competent in such matters than he was, and so he had left it entirely to the experts. He had taken it for granted that the flow of hot gases or steam from a ring of turbine nozzle blades would have the characteristics of a vortex or whirlpool, and had assumed that the steam-turbine engineers had always designed accordingly.

The behaviour of a vortex is a common phenomenon. Everyone will have seen one form when water runs out of a bath, and will have noticed that the water spins more rapidly as it spirals towards the centre. Also, that as the water goes towards the centre it goes downhill: the velocity increases as the pressure decreases. In a perfect vortex of this kind the product of the whirl velocity and radial distance from the centre remains constant. This is the characteristic of a free vortex. The pressure rise from the inside to the outside is caused by the centrifugal force of the whirling fluid.

Whittle discovered that there was a fundamental difference of view on this point between himself and the BTH engineers. He almost could not believe it, but at a meeting on 4 December 1937 his diary recorded: "Am roped into a heated argument which is going on between Collingham, Cheshire, Randles and one of Cheshire's colleagues. The position is that the new nozzle and blade design involves an end thrust on the bearing of 1,500 lb, as against the original 180 lb. Collingham and I say that the bearing could not possibly stand this and the net result is that Cheshire is instructed to return to an impulse section".

Whittle was a very puzzled man when he left the meeting, and spent several days revising his turbine theory and trying to account for so large a difference in end thrust for two designs of turbine blade intended for the same job. He could not reconcile the figures at all, and so set about trying to find out what the engineers in the blade design office had done, without betraying his own ignorance.

When he did find out he was astonished that the BTH engineers had been overlooking a most important phenomenon, namely, the radial pressure gradient which must exist in the whirling flow from a ring of nozzle blades. He discovered this fact on 10 December, whilst talking to Cheshire in the blade design office: "I casually asked him what their figure was for the difference of pressure across the annulus in the clearance between the turbine nozzle ring and the turbine blades. He asked me what difference of pressure I was talking about, so I explained that I meant the radial pressure gradient due to centrifugal force. He said that they did not take it into account.

"I then pointed out that in the case of our turbine wheel, at least, it was very considerable and was accompanied by a correspondingly large velocity variation which would make a very big difference to the calculations of end thrust and of blade angles".

Cheshire explained that it was standard practice in the steam-turbine world to assume that the vapour issuing from turbine nozzles had a uniform velocity and pressure. Whittle was astounded when he heard this, and immediately did some further calculations and showed Cheshire the results. Cheshire was rapidly converted and so was Randles, who said that there was no doubt that the discovery was a matter of fundamental importance, and, as far as he knew, quite a new concept in turbine engineering.

Whittle then did a series of calculations to apply his new thinking to his own turbine blading: "I found that, according to my theory, we needed twice as much twist on the turbine blading as had been provided by BTH in the first design, and that the end thrust was negligibly small".

Although Cheshire and Randles had enthusiastically accepted Whittle's new concept, there was the strongest opposition and obvious resentment within the BTH turbine design department. Whittle sensed that: "No one who has been a specialist in some particular field for years is likely to feel pleased when some young amateur tells him that he has been wrong from the start. In order to drive the point home he had a rather crude sheet-metal nozzle ring constructed, and made a series of experiments using the air supply of the combustion test rig. These largely confirmed his views, and demonstrated that the flow issuing from a complete turbine nozzle ring was a whirling flow rather than a series of more or less independent jets from between each pair of nozzle blades as had been previously assumed. But even these visual demonstrations left Samuelson and one or two others unconvinced, and they remained blindly unconverted for some time.

There was another important piece of evidence to substantiate his theory. A BTH turbine, which had been operated for some time by the purchaser had provided clear evidence that the end thrust was in the opposite direction from that allowed for in the design. This was completely explained by Whittle's vortex theory, but BTH stubbornly preferred to believe that there must be some other explanation!

When the controversy was at its height, a wag in the blade design office composed the following:

> Some steam, as it passed through a nozzle one day,
> Was heard, as it turned round the corner, to say,
> 'Here we go gathering nuts and may,
> Here we go into a vortex'.

> But the poor old steam, it whirled and swirled,
> And left the buckets all twisted and twirled,
> All because someone had plained and not purled,
> And not allowed for the vortex.

> And so at a vortex you must not sneeze
> Or muck about with the vortices,
> Because, if you want high efficiencies
> You must design for a vortex.

Whittle insisted that BTH make the turbine blades of the reconstructed engine in accordance with angles specified by him, and Power Jets took immediate steps to get patent protection for his vortex discovery. News of the patent application did nothing to reduce the resentment within BTH, and the relationship between the two companies was never quite the same again.

When evidence began to accumulate that Whittle might even be right, Samuelson decided to reblade one of their experimental steam turbines in order to test the theory. However, he gave instructions that the tests were to be carried out when Whittle was not in the factory. Although Whittle protested emphatically, Samuelson still refused but, somewhat reluctantly, agreed that Whittle might see the results. These fell short of Whittle's expectations, but nevertheless were a distinct improvement on the best obtained with blading designed by conventional methods.

All this argument had increased Whittle's resentment about the BTH attitude: "In my eyes I had done them a great service, but some of the seniors acted as though I had done them an injury". Before the tests had started, Collingham had wanted him to confirm in writing that the results would be satisfactory: "I said that the most I could do would be to confirm the method of calculation." His response was "You walk in here and tell us we have been all wrong in our turbine blade design. Now we are going to make a test to see if you are right, so we think it's up to you to tell us whether the test will prove the point, or not, otherwise you might come along later and criticise the conditions of the test".

Some time later Whittle saw evidence that turbine manufacturers in other parts of the world were waking up to vortex flow. The Swiss firm of Escher Wyss, for example, had reported measurements of a pressure difference across the nozzle annulus in their company newspaper. Later still he heard that English Electric were designing for vortex flow in the low-pressure stages of one of their turbines. He was told that they had got the idea from their associate company Westinghouse in America. But Whittle had other theories as to how they got the idea. One of the apprentices from BTH, who had been working in the blade design office at the time of the controversy, had left to join English Electric only a mile away in Rugby!

During the same month of January 1938 Dr Griffith told him that the RAE allowed for the vortex effect in a turbine. Griffith also said that they were designing an axial-flow compressor in accordance with the theory.

*   *   *

During the first few months of 1938 the financial position of the Company was still precarious, and every penny had to be watched. Despite the ill-feeling arising from the vortex controversy BTH, after much delay, had invested their promised £2,500. All contributions were gratefully received. Amongst those who put their faith in Whittle by subscribing small sums were Randles, two BTH draughtsmen engaged on Power Jets work — Atkinson and Richardson — and a few of Whittle's personal friends who had only the vaguest notion of what it was all about.

Apart from having to worry about finance, Whittle was seriously concerned about the Air Ministry's attitude during this period, in that they were still very hesitant about risking public money on the venture. Dr D. R. Pye, who was not one of Whittle's staunch supporters, had become the Director of Scientific Research and his deputy was Dr W. S. Farren. After a talk with Farren on the 28 March 1938 Whittle recorded in his diary:

'He says that my general policy has been such that they have not felt that they could give me their confidence. He seems to have several erroneous impressions. He thinks I was connected with the delay in signing the contract. I told him that I had refused to take part in discussions on the subject. I was left still in the dark as to why there should be a misinterpretation of my motives, and feeling rather depressed that this should have happened. I gave him as strong an assurance as I could that I put my duty as a Serving Officer before any commercial interests'.

The delay in signing the Air Ministry contract was due to Whyte, who tried to get more favourable terms. Whittle's view was that they should accept the contract on offer because he was convinced that they would do well enough to induce more favourable contracts later. He thought that the DSR's reservations about going on with Power Jets were due to two factors. The first was the work that the RAE were doing (the RAE had suddenly been authorized to go ahead with the design of their propeller gas turbine project a few days after the beginning of

Whittle's first series of engine tests). The second was that Bramson and Whittle had been impatient to have work started on an experimental aeroplane. In retrospect this is just what should have been done, but DSR felt that they were trying to run before they could walk and should devote all their energies to making the engine work.

That they appeared to lack confidence in Whittle was another matter. Many men would have taken this to heart, but not Whittle — even when the usual series of hold-ups with experimental work were delaying the completion of his reconstructed engine and he was fighting battles on all fronts.

The first test run of his engine had been in April 1937, and it was exactly a year later before he was able to resume test running. The reconstructed engine mounted on its truck was towed the seven miles from the BTH factory to the Ladywood Works. This had been made possible because they had bought a secondhand 10 horsepower BSA car engine to use as a starter motor. This was much lighter than the massive electric motor used previously, and enabled them to mount everything on the truck standing on its wheels.

They did have a small bit of luck when Crompton discovered that a slab in the workshop floor was the cover of a well. This provided a water supply adequate for the engine's cooling system, and thus saved the cost of laying a large-capacity water main. Crompton was still the only Power Jets employee, and Samuelson allowed BTH fitters and test hands to work at Lutterworth as and when required — at Power Jets' cost, of course.

Over the Easter week-end, Bentley, Berry and Bailey — the three BTH fitters who had virtually built the engine — and Crompton and Whittle prepared the reconstructed engine for tests which began on 16 April 1938. Fuel system troubles caused severe speed fluctuations, and during the first few days they could only run at very low speeds: "These troubles — fuel pump failures, swarf in the pipelines and so on — prevented us from running for more than a few minutes at a time until 29 April when we ran for an hour up to the very modest speed of 8,200 rpm. This test was brought to an end when a large cleaning rag, which Crompton was using to mop up oil, was whisked out of his hand and drawn into the engine. I saw it go and shut down immediately, but not in time to save a certain amount of minor damage. I still retain a vivid picture of Crompton (with Whyte in the background) standing frozen with a mingled look of horror and blank surprise".

They did not get very much test running with this edition of the engine because on 6 May, when running at 13,000 rpm, there was a disastrous failure of the turbine. This happened when the engine had been running for 1 hr 45 min — much the longest run to date. The turbine nozzle assembly had fouled the turbine wheel, and the intense rubbing at such a high speed had caused very severe overheating of the blade roots. This caused nine turbine blades to fail. In addition, there was a great deal of secondary damage, partly due to the detached blades and partly due to the severe 'out of balance' caused by the failure.

However, that particular run was significant in that they at last succeeded in getting a few thrust readings. The thrust at 13,000 rpm was 480 lb. It was a rather hazardous business getting a thrust reading, because it was necessary to go to the back of the engine and note the reading of the spring balance which linked the test truck to a post embedded in the test room floor.

The cell used for testing had formerly been the foundry core store, and was rough and primitive. A circular hole in the outside wall had been made for the jet discharge, and a small adjoining room housed the fuel tank. Next to the test cell was the first of what had once been four core ovens; this they had converted into an observation room, though the conversion amounted to nothing more than putting an observation window into the dividing wall. Later, the engine controls were placed in this observation room.

Whittle was very depressed by the breakdown, and reproached himself for the weak feature in the design which was largely responsible for it. Also, at first sight it looked as though very little of the engine could be salvaged.

Power Jets was again in a low financial state which added to his depression: "I had reason to think that Whyte and his colleagues were losing confidence both in the engine and in me, and I supposed that this disaster would destroy their faith entirely. I thought that the effect on the Air Ministry and the BTH would be the same, but in this at least I was wrong".

Only a few days later Collingham remarked that having got so far, if it were their job, they would not stop even if they had to spend a further £60,000. Farren did not seem to be at all depressed by the failure, which revived Whittle's spirits. He had been under a great deal of strain over a long period, and was again suffering from severe headaches and digestive disorders.

After surveying the situation, Whittle decided that another major reconstruction would be necessary. He abandoned the original concept of a single big combustion chamber, and produced a totally new layout incorporating ten small chambers. These conformed with the then-existing ten discharge ducts from the compressor. It soon became evident that this idea would make a much more compact and lighter engine. Though he had proposed multiple combustion chambers in his first patent he had avoided them hitherto, because of the rather elaborate ignition arrangements required to ensure that all the chambers lit up properly. It was obvious that if something went wrong, and one of several combustion chambers failed to light up, or if one or more became extinguished, the effect could be very damaging.

While looking into this problem he hit on the idea of interconnecting tubes, by means of which each combustion chamber would light up from its neighbour, so that it would be necessary to provide initial ignition in one chamber only. He actually provided it in two chambers, as an additional safeguard against a starting failure.

This new arrangement received the general approval of Bramson, BTH engineers, Constant (who was working with Griffith at RAE on their turboprop project), and the DSR. Constant, like Whittle, was a little uneasy about the ten combustion chambers, but thought that Whittle was following a promising line and deserved increased financial support from the Air Ministry.

Constant had been present at an engine test run on 23 August 1937, and had been very impressed. Whittle had maintained fairly good contact with both Constant and Griffith, but had only a slight knowledge of the RAE's own work on gas turbines. This was because it would have been most improper for secret work done by a Government Department to be disclosed to a private company. Whittle had no complaint about this state of affairs, but thought it probable that Power Jets' work was an important factor in stimulating this work at the RAE — and how right he was! He had, however, suspected that the Air Ministry had a natural preference for such work to be done by the RAE rather than by an upstart private company.

While the new combustion arrangement was being discussed, Constant told Whittle that he believed that the Air Ministry intended to request that BTH put Power Jets' work on high priority. He also said that the RAE had already requested Firth Vickers to give Power Jets a high priority on supplies of special steels. It appeared that Constant, at least, was not allowing his RAE work to influence his true judgement as far as Power Jets was concerned.

On 30 May 1938, on the advice of Bramson and Whittle, Whyte agreed that they should proceed with the new reconstruction. Fortunately, inspection had revealed that, with a little ingenuity, much more of the engine was usable than had seemed likely immediately after the breakdown.

Tests on a single combustion chamber verified that the interconnecting tube arrangement would work, and that ignition would spread from one combustion chamber to another as intended: "We did not realise it at the time, but the apparatus we used was very similar to the successful combustion system later developed after many heartbreaking disappointments. This was not the first time that we had been near the design which was ultimately to prove successful without realising it. In the light of subsequent experience it seems that some slight adjustment might have made all the difference, and could possibly have saved at least three years in the development of the turbojet". (This seemingly amazing fact is typical of all really big steps into the unknown.)

*   *   *

The elation over the success of the new combustion chamber arrangement soon evaporated when, at the end of June, the financial problems of Power Jets increased to the point that the Company had only about £1,200 in hand. Whyte hinted that Falk & Partners had several of their companies under review, giving the strong impression that they were losing interest.

Whittle, who had been under very great strain, was getting tired of the continual worry about finance. He wanted to see the Company running on a less 'hand to mouth' basis, and pressed for the raising of more capital.

Whyte argued that it was almost impossible to raise money since the Company had accepted an Air Ministry contract and the work had become subject to the Official Secrets Act. Therefore, he said, it was not possible to tell any potential investor enough about the work to induce them to risk their money. Further, according to Whyte, the strong position of the

'A' shareholders made things difficult. Few people in their senses, he pointed out, would put money into a concern where the inventor himself had virtual control — a comment which naturally upset Whittle!

Whyte, of course, was wearing two hats: one as Chairman of Power Jets and the other as a director of Falk & Partners. He had a moral obligation to both parties, and more particularly to Power Jets. Only a year previously, during the financial crisis which had resulted in control passing to the 'A' shareholders, he had been retained as Chairman because of his integrity, his absolute faith in Whittle's project, and his belief that he was serving the national interest. Now, he seemed to be wavering.

Whittle's immediate reaction was to tell Whyte and the others that: "My time on the Special Duty List is time lost on normal RAF duties, and I do not think it worthwhile risking this damage to my career if the future of the Company is not put on a more certain basis".

Williams and Tinling agreed with Whittle that Power Jets' liabilities must not be allowed to exceed the available cash, and that, unless further capital were forthcoming within the next two weeks or so, work at BTH would have to stop until it was clear that it could be paid for. Williams informed Whyte of their views and, in order to bring pressure to bear, told him they felt they should report this position to the Air Ministry.

This caused considerable tension but, as in the case of the financial crisis of July 1937, Whyte changed his tune. He wrote to Whittle saying, "I appreciate that there are reasons why you personally should feel some anxiety about the position, but I want to give you my express assurance that we will not let the Company get into difficulties. The remarks which I made about the position of the 'A' shareholders were entirely academic, in the sense that it was not in the least in my mind that I might approach them shortly to ask if they would make it easier to place further 'B' shares. This was not in my mind at all. I only meant that circumstances might bring this question up at some later date in the history of the Company".

That letter confirmed their suspicions that Falk & Partners intended to demand the sacrifices of certain of their rights and powers, in return for the finding of further capital. They decided that they would not yield an inch, although Whyte's letter had reassured them in some respects. A few days later Whittle warned Whyte that, if the Company got into debt and this resulted in a modification of the rights of 'A' shareholders, then he and the others would allow the Company to go into liquidation. In this event the patent rights would have reverted to Williams, Tinling and himself, and theoretically, at least, they would have been in a position to negotiate for the formation of a new company. Whyte, stung by this, retorted that, with such power in the hands of 'A' shareholders, anybody who became a 'B' shareholder was a fool!

All this trauma left Whittle worried and despondent. His uneasiness about the position as a whole had reached the ears of Dr Pye and his staff at the DSR. On 18 July 1938 Whittle talked matters over with Pye at the Air Ministry: "Dr Pye said that he was disturbed by suggestions that I was losing confidence in the engine. I told him that my confidence in the ultimate success of the engine was as strong as ever, but I had come to realise that it was going to be a much longer job that I had previously supposed.

"I explained that the mechanical troubles we had been having were disheartening in themselves, but on top of this I had the continuous worry of the financial situation. I also had the feeling that the Chief Engineer of BTH and others were losing confidence in me. In these circumstances my Service career was more important to me, and I was not prepared to go on unless I had a clear indication that the Air Ministry believed that it was in the best interests of the Service that I should do so". This was no bluff. It was a real 'crunch' situation.

Pye could see that Whittle was seeking to get the Ministry to recognise that his work was important to the Service, and that it should be acknowledged as consistent with his duties as a Serving Officer. He told Whittle that it had been virtually decided that he was to remain on the Special Duty List for another year, and asked if that was what he wanted. Whittle replied that he was quite happy to go on if the Ministry considered that that was where his duty lay. Farren, who was present, stated quite bluntly that their whole interest in the job rested upon Whittle. If he gave up, then the work would stop — there would be no question, as far as they were concerned, of appointing a successor.

Thus, Whittle left the meeting with only a verbal assurance that the Air Ministry would allow him to continue his work on the engine for another year. Farren had made it crystal clear that everything depended upon him, and that without him there was nothing.

At Whyte's request, Bramson summarized the technical position as it stood on 19 July 1938, the day after Whittle's meeting with Pye and Farren. Bramson reported that: '(a) The work done to date constitutes a quantitative experimental verification of the principle underlying the Whittle system of jet propulsion. (b) At 73.3 per cent of the design speed, quantitative verification of the jet engine has been obtained, and there is a strong possibility of obtaining it shortly at full speed. (c) Experimental evidence already makes it practically certain that the thermal efficiency of the unit (which has not yet been possible to measure) cannot be so far below estimate as to nullify the positive results. (d) The feasibility of jet propulsion for aircraft has been, for the first time, experimentally established.'

Bramson's last point stated Whittle's greatest single achievement in being the first man to get a jet engine running and, in so doing, prove the basic theory of jet propulsion. The first test run of Whittle's turbojet on 12 April 1937 was to make aviation history, but, because of the British environment, it failed to generate the back-up and financial support he was desperately seeking.

By 30 June 1938 private capital subscribed had reached the sum of just under £13,500, of which about 25 per cent had been found by the 'A' shareholders, Williams, Tinling and Whittle, and their friends. Of the remainder, about half was from BTH and J. & G. Weir Ltd. The direct expenditure on the engine totalled just under £9,000.

In September Whyte received a strong hint from Tizard that there might be a substantial increase in financial assistance from the Air Ministry. Whittle, who had been making further attempts to get the BTH to put in more money, repeated Tizard's comment to Sporborg — the BTH Chief Engineer — that, "a few thousands would be a small insurance for the BTH to pay to be in on the ground floor of what might prove to be a new industry".

It was evident, however, that BTH were sceptical of the value of Power Jets' patents. Whittle felt 'no doubt they (rightly) argued to themselves that they were getting a great deal of valuable experience from the job for nothing'.

*　　*　　*

While the second reconstruction of the engine was in progress, Whittle was able to take the family on holiday to Devon. The year before they had stayed at a farm at Umberleigh, and had very much enjoyed it, and so they went there again. After all the pressures and critical times at Power Jets he needed a break, but this was rather spoilt because he was suffering from very painful ear trouble. Nevertheless it was a welcome relief for him to be away from it all.

Tinling took his holiday at the same time and joined the Whittle family in Devon. In the mornings they usually managed to do a little riding on Brownie, the farmer's pony. The afternoons were taken up by sightseeing along the coast around Croyde Bay. Potting rabbits was then a favourite occupation of Whittle's, and he and Tinling would usually do an evening stint stalking them.

One particular evening they caused a local sensation by going out after dark in Whittle's car with four on board, two armed with 12-bores and one with a .22 rifle: "We went bumping over the fields of the farm with the headlights and guns blazing, trying to make a real hole in the rabbit population. This sounds like a cad's trick, but, in fact, to try and shoot from a car which is bumping over rough fields gives the rabbits every chance. Though bewildered bunnies were dashing all over the place, I believe our total bag was one — and that was one the spaniel caught! All the same, it must have sounded like a minor military expedition, and the combination of the lights and the noise attracted the attention of gamekeepers for miles around. They supposed it was a pheasant poaching trip and made a number of enquiries, but we were not found out".

That holiday was also memorable for their one and only fox hunt: "We were invited to attend a cubbing meet of the South Egerton. The farm had only the one pony, Brownie, and my wife decided to go to the Meet, so up she got at the crack of dawn and off she went. Her experience of riding till then was as limited as my own, and she set off not knowing that she had a five mile hack even to get to the place of the Meet.

A party of us consisting of Tinling, Miss Glen (one of Cochran's young ladies who was also staying at the farm), Harold (one of the farmer's sons), my two small sons and myself, followed in my Lanchester some time later. By the time we caught up with the hunt my wife had had her fill of riding for one day, and so Miss Glen took over Brownie for a time. Then Harold and I each had a turn. In effect, therefore, five of us attended the Meet sharing one horse! Nevertheless, we were in at the kill.

The Hunt Secretary invited my wife to be blooded. She couldn't bear the thought and recoiled in horror. Miss Glen also refused. Though these refusals must have shaken the Hunt Secretary, she came along later and offered the ladies fox pads; again she met with a shuddering refusal and thereafter, no doubt, regarded us as hopeless cases.

* * *

The reconstructed engine was delivered to Lutterworth at the end of September 1938. The three BTH fitters, Bentley, Berry and Bailey, assisted Crompton in its assembly. While the negotiations for a new Air Ministry contract were in progress, the Munich Crisis cast its shadow over Power Jets. The Fighting Services were put into a state of emergency. In view of the state of affairs, Whyte sounded the Air Ministry, and warned Whittle that he might have to leave the work. Whittle urged him to make provision for the work to go on, even if he had to go, but in the event Whittle remained on the Special Duty List.

When the engine in its third form was ready for testing, Whyte ruled that there was to be no running of the engine until the new Air Ministry contract was signed — he didn't want to risk damage while running was not covered by contract. Whittle was impatient, and found this enforced delay intolerable. The relations between the two men once again became strained. Matters came to a head and a few days later, on 10 October 1938, Whyte relaxed a little and agreed that the engine could be run up to moderate speeds. But, on the following day, after one run, Whyte rang up to say that DSR was also concerned about running the engine before the new contract was signed. There was another hold-up for two weeks.

Serious testing of the engine in its third form began on 26 October 1938, after Whyte had phoned the Air Ministry to confirm his acceptance of the terms of the draft contract. The old one had been terminated after a total payment of £1,900 — £1,000 for a report on the first series of tests, and £900 for the proportion of running which had been done in the second series. Under the new contract the Air Ministry agreed to pay for the greater part of the cost of the second reconstruction, and for twenty hours' experimental running at the rate of £200 per hour. The total sum involved was about £6,000.

The delay over test running had, at least, given Whittle a chance to catch up with his flying practice, which was still obligatory. He usually went to Castle Bromwich where 605 (County of Warwick) Squadron of the Auxiliary Air Force was based. Flying gave him an opportunity of blowing the engineering cobwebs out of his system, and the state of international tension provided him with an opportunity for a little authorized low flying — one of his favourite occupations!

About this time, the BTH were staging an ARP (air raid precautions) display so, to make life more realistic, Whittle arranged for a flight of Hawker Hinds from 605 Squadron to dive-bomb the works: "I helped by doing the flying for the rehearsals, during which I simulated the effect of three aircraft diving in rapid sequence so I was able to let myself go!" On the occasion of the actual display (Whittle was not flying), there was a very satisfactory synchronization between the diving aircraft and the explosions arranged on the ground.

For the first few tests of the reconstructed engine a kerosene boiler mounted in the jetpipe supplied fuel vapour to each of the ten combustion chambers. This proved unsatisfactory, because the boiler was too big an obstruction to the flow of the high-speed gases in the jetpipe. Accordingly, it was decided to change to individual vaporizers in each combustion chamber. This meant a temporary suspension of engine tests while combustion tests to evolve a suitable arrangement were carried out. Engine tests resumed in December 1938.

With the Fighting Services in a state of emergency and war clouds looming over the horizon, it became necessary to look into the problems of security at the Ladywood Works. Since obtaining the first Air Ministry contract, Whittle's turbojet project had been subject to the Official Secrets Act. Although the possibility of jet aircraft taking part in the forthcoming war was in the realms of science fiction (except for Whittle and his associates), research projects did require protection. Local police had already been concerned about the goings-on in the old foundry. They thought that Whittle and his associates were up to no good.

Two night-watchmen and, later, a watch-dog, were taken on by Power Jets to look after the premises. Sandy, the watch-dog (price: ten shillings from the Battersea Dogs' Home) had a highly nervous disposition: "Whenever I fired my .22 rifle from my office window in a vain attempt to get a rabbit, Sandy would vanish at high speed and would have to be collected from about five miles away".

At the same time the staff of Power Jets had been augmented by a secretary, Mary Phillips, and an office boy, Hancock, making five employees altogether. Hitherto, Whittle had shared the typing with Crompton, and it was a great relief for him to have secretarial assistance. It meant, amongst other things, that it was possible for him to make much more detailed records of test work. Hancock, apart from doing the cleaning and making the tea, had to collect Sandy whenever Whittle blasted off at a rabbit!

The offices were primitive in the extreme: "Furnishings were few, and mostly purchased by Crompton from secondhand dealers in Lutterworth — piece by piece as the necessity arose. We still had bare floor-boards. The walls were whitewashed unplastered brick. My office was at the head of a flight of stairs at the corner of the building, with the window overlooking the railway. Its situation made telephone conversations somewhat difficult at times. It seemed to me that the engine drivers always chose to stop and blow off steam a few feet from my window. The more obliging drivers would shut off when I waved the telephone receiver at them through the window".

During December 1938 the business of the vortex blading had caused increased tension between Whittle and BTH, and this boiled up to a crisis in mid-month. This revolved around the patent which Power Jets had applied for to protect Whittle's discovery; Whittle had earlier protested to Collingham that though he had rendered what he considered a very great service to the BTH, the only reward he got for doing so was a veiled hostility.

This dissension poisoned the atmosphere between the parties. At a meeting on December 13, Power Jets were accused of thinking more about trying to get money out of the BTH for vortex blading than getting on with the engine. This ludicrous accusation naturally incensed both Whyte and Whittle who were present.

During the ensuing argument, Whittle cited another example of the many ways in which BTH had benefited from his presence in the factory. One had concerned a centrifugal compressor, made by BTH for another firm, which was down on performance until it was considerably improved as a result of a suggestion made by Whittle, but Sporborg's reaction was that it had been an act of interference on Whittle's part in matters which did not concern him!

Two days later the same matter was chiefly responsible for a violent quarrel between Whittle and Samuelson, which ended in Whittle saying that he found it impossible to go on with BTH any more. It seemed to him at the time that that was the end of the Power Jets/BTH association.

However, that evening Whittle and his wife attended the Engineers' Ball in Rugby. Shortly after their arrival Samuelson walked over to their table and remarked that he and Whittle had had a quarrel that morning but, "We are not the sort of people to let it last 24 hours". He then invited the Whittles to join his party, which they did. This olive branch cleared the air somewhat, but the whole incident strengthened Whittle's resolve to aim for the ultimate independence of Power Jets in the matter of design and manufacture. Later, he made it quite clear that, from then on, he would not allow himself to become involved in any discussions on either finance or patent matters with BTH executives.

During January 1939 and the first part of February progress was slow. There were severe speed fluctuations and vibration due to troubles with the fuel system, and it was not until 20 February that they were able to raise the speed above 8,000 rpm. It was depressing for Whittle to learn that the Air Ministry felt that he was not making as much progress as he should, and were getting pessimistic.

On 22 February Farren told him that he, as DDSR, would have some difficulty in making a case to the other Service Departments to secure the retention of his appointment. He went on to say that it was most important from both their points of view that Whittle should produce more results than he had done up to then. Farren pointed out that if Whittle were a civilian there would be no particular problem. But Farren had found himself in difficulty because Whittle, as a serving officer, had made promises which, in effect, were not being kept.

Farren's attitude had put Whittle into a corner. He was faced with the choice between an immediate improvisation to produce fast results, or several months' delay for more extensive modifications. According to Whittle, "This was, perhaps, the most critical moment in the whole history of the development. Had the Air Ministry lost interest in the job, it would almost certainly have meant closing down altogether. Any suggestion of delay at that time would have resulted in the withdrawal of all official support. I was forced into a policy of more haste, less speed".

Lack of money was still a vital factor: "I knew that at least half the engine ought to have been scrapped, because of general deterioration". Such deterioration tended to neutralize any improvement from modifications. The worry of all these things, plus the more direct strain of day-to-day engineering problems, was affecting Whittle's health quite seriously. The ear trouble which had started the year before had become chronic, and he also suffered from frequent severe headaches and indigestion: "I was almost continuously under treatment, and it is probable that these things, too, clouded my judgement".

Immediate improvisations, however, began to produce results. During March, intensity of testing rose, and speed of running increased to 13,500 rpm. Just when things were going well a severe crack near the tip of one of the blades of the compressor impeller was found: "In order to avoid a severe hold-up, pending the manufacture of a new impeller, we cut off the tip of that blade and the tip of the opposite blade in order to preserve the balance. This did not help much because, during another run, in the course of which we reached a speed of 14,000 rpm, another of the tips failed and passed right through the engine — fortunately without doing very much damage".

A spare impeller forging had been ordered some months before, and so the delay, pending the manufacture of the new impeller, was not as great as it might have been. Nevertheless, there was no running for nearly two months.

Farren's straight talking, on 22 February 1939, had reflected DSR's pessimistic outlook regarding Whittle's position. Despite this, Whittle began to receive encouragement from others, although he still had problems and inevitable delays with his engine test programme.

In April, Hayne Constant came clean and said that he was coming to believe that Whittle had, after all, got the basis of a practical aero engine. He said that the effort should be intensified, and that Whittle ought to be developing several engines simultaneously — otherwise, at the rate of work to which he was then limited, he would take about fifteen years, and it would make a nice little hobby for him in his retirement!

Sir Henry Tizard also remained a good friend. Early in May 1939 he told Whyte he was willing to back any further requests for help from the Air Ministry, and that he would use his influence to prevent Whittle being taken away from the work.

Waiting for the new impeller was an anxious time for Whittle. The first impeller had 30 blades, but the new one was to have 29 to avoid resonant coupling with the ten-blade diffuser system. Crucial, in fact, because time was running out, and he had to produce the necessary results to retain the support of the Air Ministry and others involved. The existence of Power Jets was at stake, and success or failure with his turbojet project would naturally influence his career in the RAF.

The pressures upon him were enormous, and it was hardly surprising that they affected his health. He drove himself to the limit, and far beyond. Even Crompton, who had only been working for him for a few months, showed signs of breaking down under the very heavy load, but refused to take a rest. When engine testing was resumed on 17 June 1939, Whittle was keyed up, knowing that he had to have a run of good luck to regenerate confidence in his project.

Fortunately for Whittle and the aviation industry progress was then more rapid than it had been at any time hitherto: "On 23 June we reached a speed of 14,700 rpm; the next day we went to 15,700 and then on the 26th we ran up to 16,000. We did several runs up to this speed on succeeding days and on one of these occasions — 30 June — DSR himself was present".

The visit of DSR to Lutterworth on 30 June marked an important change in the Air Ministry's attitude. Dr Pye saw a test run of the engine of twenty minutes' duration, in the course of which it was run up to 16,000 rpm. He was then shown the results of the tests to date. The chief feature of these was that, though the performance of the engine was fairly well below design at the lower speeds, the discrepancies between actual results and design predictions were decreasing as speed was increased.

By coincidence, Whittle's appointment nominally ended on that particular day. He still had no indication as to what was to happen to him, and Dr Pye couldn't tell him. Pye had requested an extension of the appointment, on the ground that the work could not go on without him. He told Whittle there were two sources of criticism he had to meet: one from the Treasury, who objected to the cost of his appointment, and the other from the Service side, because of the shortage of Squadron Leaders.

Pye then asked Whittle if he was prepared to go on, despite the fact that his work might possibly damage his Service career. Whittle told him that he was prepared to take the risk.

This visit marked a dramatic volte face by DSR. Pye was so impressed with what he had seen that he became a complete convert. He said that he now believed that Whittle had the basis of an engine, as Constant had said a few weeks previously. He agreed that the time had come for an important expansion of the effort, and promised his support for the placing of contracts for an experimental aeroplane and an engine for flight test. He also agreed that the Air Ministry should buy the experimental engine, and leave it in Power Jets' hands for continued development — precisely what the Ministry had refused to do in 1937. One of the big advantages of this last arrangement was that the Ministry would pay for the cost of spares and modifications.

Later that day, when Whittle drove Pye to Rugby Station: "I had the curious experience of having DSR enthusing on all the advantages of the engine; very light weight; no vibration; could run on any fuel; — the lot. His manner of doing so was almost as though he was talking to a sceptic. I was tactful enough not to point out that he was preaching to the first of all the converts. It was a measure of the degree to which Pye was carried away by his enthusiasm".

A week or two later, Power Jets' received the contract for the flight engine. BTH accepted a sub-contract for its manufacture, on a cost-plus basis as before.

One of the future developments, which Pye had discussed with Whyte and Whittle during his visit, was that of making an experimental aeroplane as soon as possible. Whittle had already prepared a layout for such an aeroplane, and showed it to Pye. He told him briefly of the tentative contacts he had had with one or two aircraft firms. These included a visit he had made to the Gloster Aircraft Company's works on 28 April 1939, when he met George Carter, the Chief Designer, Gerry Sayer, the Chief Test Pilot, and Michael Daunt, another of their test pilots. This contact with Gloster had come about through Whittle's old friend, Wing Commander J. H. McC. Reynolds, who was then Air Ministry Overseer at the Gloster works.

Meanwhile test running continued intermittently: fitters and other skilled workmen were still being borrowed from BTH. Combustion continued to be the main problem, so while modifications to the engine at Lutterworth were being carried out, further combustion tests were done at the usual site at BTH Rugby. Whittle and Crompton found themselves shuttling to and fro between Lutterworth and Rugby with combustion chamber components and BTH personnel. Life was hectic, and quite often they would gain a few hours by getting one of the watchmen to do some of the dismantling of the engine during the night. This proved costly when one of them dropped a nut into the compressor intake and didn't report it.

As Whittle began to run his engine more frequently and at higher speeds there were clear indications that the Stayblade steel from which the turbine disc and blades were made was not good enough for the running conditions in the engine: "Had we been clear of combustion troubles, and had the turbine and compressor been as efficient as had been assumed in the design, then theoretically at least, the Stayblade steel from which the turbine blades were made had properties good enough for the purpose. But the component efficiencies were much lower than the design assumptions. Added to this, one of the so far unsolved elements of the combustion problem was bad temperature distribution, which unfortunately usually resulted in the hotter gases impinging on the turbine blades near their roots, where the stress was highest". Saddled with the problems of turbine blades and combustion, Whittle searched for better materials and improved methods. He was working in new dimensions, and only leading specialists in the fields of creep-resisting materials and fuels could help him.

He approached Dr Colin Smithells of Lodge Plugs to discuss the possibility of using ceramics, either alone or in combination with metal. Smithells put him in touch with Dr Pfiel of Henry Wiggin & Co, because he thought there was a good chance of a nickel-chrome alloy (similar to the Inconel used in elements for electric fires) having creep-resisting properties good enough for Whittle's purpose. But Pfiel couldn't help him at that time. This was very unfortunate because, had Pfiel and his colleagues started on the work then, at least a year might have been saved.

*   *   *

All these efforts on Whittle's part, in his quest for new materials and methods, were a great challenge to those in British Industry concerned with high-temperature alloys. His enthusiasm and drive encouraged them to meet the demands of a new technology, which was to revolutionize aero-engine development. It was fortunate for Britain to have a man of Whittle's genius, drive and dedication at this time, because in early 1939 there had been vague references to German work. These came chiefly through Air Commodore Weir of J. & G. Weir Ltd, who were shareholders in Power Jets. A German engineer who had recently joined his staff had said that there were several jet propulsion projects under development in Germany, but he did not know what form they were taking.

We now know that the Heinkel firm made a flight with an experimental aeroplane powered by Von Ohain's engine in August 1939. They were thus undoubtedly the first actually to fly with a turbojet engine, but it was a dead-end effort. Neither the engine nor the aeroplane, however, was considered satisfactory, and German development took a different line. No derivatives of Von Ohain's engine went into production.

The Germans and the British were not the only people working on gas turbines at this time. The Swiss Company of Brown-Boveri had over many years put a considerable effort into the development of industrial gas turbines, and a lecture on the subject was given by their Dr Adolf Meyer to the Institution of Mechanical Engineers in London in February 1939. Whittle, Bramson and Cheshire attended this lecture together. Dr Meyer made no reference to any proposed aircraft application. In the subsequent discussion Whittle pointed out that the gas turbine was specially attractive from the aircraft point of view and that there was a very good reason why it should be more successful in this field than in any other. He was, of course, careful to avoid any reference to its application as a jet propulsion device, or to give any indication of the work he was doing. In his reply Dr Meyer was sceptical about the possibility of an aircraft application.

*   *   *

The outbreak of war was only a matter of weeks away when Whittle started on the design of his W.1 flight engine. Although combustion troubles continued, a speed of 16,650 rpm (ie 94 per cent of full design speed) was attained by the middle of July. There were also signs that things were going to be a little easier financially. BTH had increased their investment by £2,000 and J. & G. Weir had put in another £2,000, thereby increasing their holding to £5,000 — small sums as far as those firms were concerned, but very welcome to Power Jets in the light of their needs!

Towards the end of August 1939 DSR told Whyte that Whittle's appointment was to continue, and that the Air Ministry wanted the work to go on even if war broke out. Thus, the Air

Ministry's attitude to Power Jets had greatly altered. Though test running was temporarily not covered by contract, Power Jets no longer had to feel nervous on this account.

After the outbreak of war on 3 September Whyte, Williams and Tinling gave up their other interests to work exclusively at Power Jets. This was a great relief to Whittle, because it freed him to concentrate on purely engineering problems, and having the companionship of Williams and Tinling, both former RAF officers and pilots, added zest and sparkle to the rather austere and rugged atmosphere of Lutterworth and Rugby.

Dudley Williams' wife, Helen, remembered when they first arrived in Lutterworth: "It was a small place and there was no accommodation to be had. Eventually, after scouring the countryside we found a tiny cottage on an estate. It was terribly primitive with two up and two down, one small sink and water from a well which was some distance away".

By the end of September, when Whyte, Williams and Tinling were devoting their full time to Power Jets, the company began to expand modestly. At the outset, they nearly lost Crompton who received his calling-up papers. Whyte had to take some very urgent steps to retain him. Then an important addition to Power Jets' engineering strength took place in the form of the loan of Mr Cheshire by BTH. Whittle regarded this gesture from BTH as being one of their more important contributions to the work. During September they recruited their first fitter, young Bentley, whose father had already been working on the engine at BTH for over two years. His appointment was followed by that of Leach, who became their first draughtsman.

Whittle had advertised for an engineer to act as deputy to himself. He received 140 applications, of which about 30 were short-listed. None of the applicants had the necessary qualifications, but one of them — D. N. Walker, an able mechanical engineer — was offered a post, and became a very important addition to their design strength. They also began to build up a drawing office and a small workshop, but these were as yet on a very modest scale.

The combustion problem continued to be the main obstacle to the development of the engine, and so the Air Ministry authorized them to install combustion test apparatus at the Ladywood Works to supplement the work they were doing on combustion tests at BTH.

At this time they received further Air Ministry contracts to cover spares for the experimental engine and for the W.1 flight engine, but the most important of the new contracts was for a new and more powerful engine to be designated the W.2. Whittle had for a long time wanted to start the design of a much better and more powerful engine in parallel with the W.1.

Despite the fact that the Air Ministry had issued these new contracts, there seemed to be no sense of urgency on the part of the officials concerned. With the outbreak of war, various sections of the Air Ministry had been dispersed, and the Technical Departments had moved to Harrogate which might have delayed matters. But the Air Ministry's over-caution was making life extremely difficult, because Power Jets had become entirely dependent on Ministry contracts for finance. It was virtually impossible to raise finance from private sources, because the Whittle project was governed by the requirements of the Official Secrets Act — and now Britain was at war! Therefore, the degree of expansion of the effort was strictly limited to what the Air Ministry would sanction.

Early in October, Constant told Whittle that he had been asked by DSR to prepare an advisory report on the whole wartime development of gas turbines. He mentioned that he, personally, was in favour of Power Jets going ahead with eight engines and four aircraft. Also, that he had advised DSR a few days earlier that the Air Ministry ought not to treat the development in a half-hearted way. His opinion was that it should stop it altogether or go ahead at full steam. His attitude led Whyte to record that Constant was the only individual on the Air Ministry side who contemplated applying real wartime methods to the work!

Constant's recommendations, however, failed to help. For the first time Whittle received a hint that some of Power Jets' difficulties were due to the fact that DSR and his staff found Whyte difficult to get on with. Whittle thought that, whatever the rights and wrongs of the case were, there was no doubt that there was some mutual antagonism between the personalities involved, which was a legacy from the protracted negotiations for the early contracts.

Whittle took the view that this state of affairs was largely due to misinterpretation of Whyte's motives by the civil servants concerned. Whyte sincerely believed — and so did Whittle — that the nature of the work was such that it was more appropriate that it should be financed out of public funds than by private capital. On the other hand, DSR and his colleagues had always believed that the bulk of finance should come from private sources, and did not seem to recognise that this had been made virtually impossible by the requirements of the Official Secrets Act. In their eyes, Whyte was fighting to get the State to make payments which would result in large profits going into private pockets. (As though this hadn't been happening for years with the Aircraft Industry!)

So Whyte was in the rather difficult position that, on the one hand, the Air Ministry thought that he was trying to go too fast, and on the other Whittle thought he was not willing to go fast enough. This situation led to strained relations between Whyte and Whittle, and there were indications that these also had been affecting the situation. In retrospect, one feels that Britain has a natural genius for inventing unnecessary problems.

Whittle did not agree with the way that Whyte handled negotiations: "While Whyte was not unconscious of his responsibilities to those who had risked their money in the venture, there is no doubt at all that he was motivated far more strongly than anything else by what he believed to be necessary in the national interest. It was, perhaps, because he allowed himself to be carried away by the intensity of his feelings that he antagonised some of those with whom he had to deal. They were not used to contacts with individuals who could express themselves with his degree of intensity.

"Whyte had right on his side but, like so many others throughout history, had to suffer for it. The feeling spread from one official to another that Whyte was difficult to deal with. As happened with me later, influential individuals who had, as yet, no opportunity to judge for themselves, became prejudiced in advance. Had I not been so intimately concerned with the engineering side of the job, similar antagonism would have led to my separation from it".

Despite the cautious attitude of the Air Ministry just after the outbreak of war, there were useful additions to the staff of Power Jets. By the end of January 1940, the total strength of the Company was about 25, including the three full-time directors. There were now four draughtsmen, headed by R. H. Rout, and four additional engineers. Together with Cheshire and Walker they were to form an important part of Whittle's team.

Wing Commander George Lees, OBE, was the most senior, and he became Whittle's deputy. Whittle knew him well because George Lees had been one of his former instructors, both in the

Apprentices' Wing at Cranwell and on the Engineering Course at Henlow: "He was several years older than I was, but his amiable nature and his very flattering respect for me were such that I felt no embarrassment in having my former instructor as my deputy". Like Whittle, Lees was posted to the Special Duty List for work with Power Jets. As the Education Branch had been put into uniform and given ranks, George joined with the rank of Wing Commander. But when war was declared Whittle, himself, had to wear uniform with the less-senior rank of Squadron Leader!

The other three engineers were all very young and relatively inexperienced, but with high academic qualifications. Whittle put more weight on intelligence and engineering training than on day-to-day experience. He wanted the best brains he could find, and the right temperament for the work required from them. The three men he selected were W. M. Ogston, R. G. Voysey and R. D. Van Millingen.

Ogston had graduated at Oxford with First Class Honours in engineering, and his rather unusual personality was manifest in his interview when Whittle gave him a very intensive oral examination: "I was in the habit of putting many questions which I did not expect them to be able to answer, chiefly to test their intellectual honesty. I rejected many applicants because they attempted to bluff their way through instead of having the honesty to say that they did not know.

"Ogston did his best to convince me that he did not know anything. When he told me in effect that he really was not very much good for our purposes, I said 'Well, you obtained First Class Honours, didn't you?' — he replied, 'Yes, but I had to work far harder than anybody else to do it'. Fortunately, Whyte and I had a very much higher opinion of him than he seemed to have of himself, and he duly became one of the most valuable members of the team".

The other two young engineers were also well qualified: "Voysey had graduated at London's Imperial College of Science and Technology, and was a Whitworth Scholar. In his interview he exhibited a quite remarkable range of engineering knowledge, and an obvious ability to apply it. Van Millingen was a graduate of Edinburgh University, and clearly possessed inventive genius".

Other recruits to the staff, as part of the expansion policy which Whittle regarded as modest, included two sheet-metal workers, Truan, the accountant, and two or three additional office staff.

In modest plans for further extension, they hoped to obtain sanction to spend approximately £10,000 on workshop equipment. This, it was thought, would have enabled them to become largely self-contained in providing experimental components for the engine and auxiliary test apparatus. But Whyte would not contemplate spending such a large sum at that particular time, and this led to a certain amount of internal friction once again. This breach was to widen as time went on.

Meanwhile, the preliminary design of the experimental aeroplane was crystallizing. Whittle had drawn up a broad specification in July 1939. At that time Power Jets were hoping that the Ministry would place the contract for the aeroplane with Power Jets, who could then sub-contract it to an aircraft company — either Gloster or one of the other firms with whom Whittle had had preliminary talks. Later that month Wing Commander Reynolds visited Power Jets, and brought with him a drawing of George Carter's first proposal.

At that time, Gloster were working on a twin-boom fighter project with a Sabre engine driving a pusher propeller. George Carter, having taken out a patent for a gas turbine unit at the age of 22, had become intensely interested in the Whittle project. He was instantly converted when he first saw Whittle's engine running. His first idea was for a tail-first canard fighter which was very different in arrangement from Whittle's own proposals or indeed from any convential aircraft at that time. But Power Jets felt that to combine so radical a departure in aircraft arrangement with such a novel type of powerplant would be taking too big a chance.

In the original specification Gloster were required to design an aeroplane which could ultimately be converted into an interceptor fighter. It was to be quite a small aeroplane of an all-up weight of about 2,800 lb, though it had to carry four Browning guns. Carter's later proposals were more conventional, and Power Jets and Gloster found themselves in good general agreement in a very short time.

During discussions Whyte put forward the idea that, in addition to the special aeroplane, they should aim to convert some existing aeroplane into a flying test-bed. Air Commodore Weir had urged this course on him, and had suggested a Wellington for this purpose. However, nothing was done at the time to follow up this proposal, although very useful work was done with a Wellington Flying Test-Bed at a later stage.

Whittle and his colleagues did not succeed in persuading the Air Ministry to place the experimental aircraft contract with Power Jets. Eventually the Gloster Aircraft Company received a direct contract from the Ministry, under the specification E.28/39. (The idea that it should be a fighter had been abandoned.)

There followed frequent exchanges of visits between Lutterworth and Gloster Aircraft. The most frequent visitor was R. W. Walker, George Carter's chief assistant on the project, and he was often accompanied by Messrs James and Lobley. Whittle recounted an amusing story concerning one of those visits:

"On one occasion when Walker from Gloster entered my office, he found a group of us on our knees studying a blueprint on the floor. This amused him considerably, and he mentioned that their people had come to refer to Power Jets as The Cherry Orchard. I asked why Cherry Orchard? He explained that the atmosphere at Power Jets reminded them of the play by Chekhov in which various characters would appear on the stage, say something quite irrelevant, and then disappear again. (Not having seen the play I didn't know to what extent this was a true misrepresentation of it.)

"I asked him why he thought Power Jets was like that, so he said that, in the first place, Power Jets was quite different from any other engineering concern he had ever seen. He went on somewhat as follows: 'A small boy comes through one door carrying a cup of tea. Then you jump up, pick up a rifle and fire it through the window. Next, one of your directors appears, to ask whether he can afford to have a three-inch gas pipe put in. Then the same small boy comes through another door with another cup of tea —'

"While he was still speaking, one of the two doors of my office was thrown open by Cheshire who appeared, poised, with a blotting-pad held aloft and triumphantly announced 'Rocking Blotters!' This was to apprise us of the fact that a luxury item, for which he and others had been agitating, had at last been supplied. This incident did nothing to diminish our Cherry Orchard reputation. (Somebody else likened the Ladywood Works to the typical wicked professor's hideout!")

Whittle recalled another incident in keeping with this atmosphere which occurred about that time: "Crompton came into my office with a very worried expression and said, in low dramatic tones, 'You would not be sitting there, sir, if you knew what was going on underneath'. 'What's that?' I asked. He replied in an even more sinister tone, 'Voysey's boiling cordite'. Then, feeling he had done his duty, he disappeared rapidly.

"This statement was a slight exaggeration, but not without foundation. Immediately below my office was a small cubicle which we were using as a kind of laboratory. Reg Voysey, who had joined us in January 1940, was making experiments with the object of evolving a starter motor for the engine operated by cordite. When Crompton accused him of boiling cordite he was, in fact, merely melting it in a flask over a Bunsen burner".

These anecdotes reveal the funny side of life in the drab, pinchpenny and sometimes frightening atmosphere of the Ladywood Works. Years later, Voysey remembered those times and his impressions of some of the cast at Power Jets shortly after he joined the team.

"My time with Power Jets", he said, "was the happiest and most exciting period of my life. Intellectual honesty pervaded throughout, and there was a streak of nobility in the characters involved because they didn't need to be mean. People sorted themselves into age groups rather than rank. These comprised the early twenties, thirties and a few forties, who were all on christian-name terms amongst themselves.

"I addressed Whittle as Squadron Leader Whittle, and my seniors as Mr Whyte, Mr. Tinling and so on. Williams was the man who called everybody by their christian name, and instigated the practice. He was a light-hearted, somewhat flippant character, extremely good with people and a sound thinker who, even then, had political ambitions. Tinling, his partner, was much more serious and a man of unfailing integrity. They seemed an odd pair and yet they worked well together and had a lot in common, especially the noble RAF code which, like Whittle, they clung to.

"Whyte had lectured in physics, and had a mystical interest in the subject which was one of the oddities of his character. He was about 5ft 9in tall, with good shoulders and a full chest making him appear biggish. His fleshy face betrayed a vague sandy colour under the skin, and he had brown eyes and golden-brown hair flecked with a few specks of grey. Always dressed in a well-cut suit, he wore gold-rimmed glasses and my impression of him during my first interview was that he was a bit tricky, because he tried to catch me out. There was an intellectual coldness about Whyte and, as time went on, I began to realise that while Whittle wanted cash flow to develop the project, Whyte was primarily concerned with getting the best deal.

"In those days I regarded anybody of thirty or more as being old, and W/Cdr 'Daddy' Lees was in that category. He was a big, genial man with pale blue eyes and a typical RAF moustache. There was a father/son relationship between him and Whittle which had developed ever since Whittle was an apprentice at Cranwell and Daddy Lees was one of his instructors. Lees always spoke good sense and was quite selfless, almost priest-like — in the best sense.

"Leslie Cheshire, on loan from BTH, was one of the older men in the team. He was slightly built and had a wrinkled face and a small head, which I found most disconcerting bearing in mind all the brains he had in it. He was easy to get on with, a gentle man and, in his way, a quiet rebel who served as a chopping block for many of Whittle's ideas.

"The thing that I most remember about Frank Whittle at that time was his total absorption in what he was doing — a total concentration which impinged itself on the atmosphere surrounding him. It was very hard for anybody to evaluate him, because he was a many-sided person who had a charming naiveté. He trusted people, and believed that everybody was motivated by common good. I had the utmost respect for him as a leader and, of course, for his genius".

Chapter 10
The Birth of the Meteor

After the Air Ministry's cautious approach following the outbreak of war, two important visitors saw demonstration runs on the experimental engine towards the end of January 1940. As a result, things started to move. They were Air Vice-Marshal Tedder (later Marshal of the RAF Lord Tedder), Director-General of Research and Development, and Sir Henry Tizard, Chairman of the Aeronautical Research Committee, who came on separate occasions.

Both were impressed by what they saw. Tizard, who came on January 24, commented drily, "A demonstration which does not break down in my presence is a production job". He also said that they had got much further with the combustion problem than he had been led to believe, and added that if he had been responsible for that engine he would have been very proud of himself.

The talks which followed the demonstration run covered a lot of ground. Whittle showed proposals that he had drawn up some time before for a high-altitude bomber (Bramson had written a memorandum on the subject). Also discussed was the possibility of pilotless missiles powered by turbojet engines. In June 1939 Whittle had suggested this to DSR, but had been told to concentrate his energy on the development of his engine.

Tizard's view of these proposals was that they were too advanced for this war — although history was to prove him wrong, because the Germans did develop jet flying bombs and rockets. However, Tizard promised to help in having extra test equipment for the engine authorized, and to support a programme which would enable Power Jets to gain experience in development and manufacture. The latter was particularly encouraging for Whittle, who wanted Power Jets to be in control of that situation.

Tedder's visit on 29 January 1940, in heavy snow and biting cold, was equally encouraging. The engine behaved reasonably well during the demonstration test run, and Tedder was duly impressed. Again Whittle pointed out that his chief need was for more extensive test equipment to enable Power Jets to do individual tests of the compressor, turbine and other items.

However Tedder thought that such test apparatus would take so long to make and install that it would not make any useful contribution to the war. Nevertheless, he wrote to Whittle saying: "How glad I was to have an opportunity of seeing your child in action. It really is a fascinating and impressive job and, having seen it, I shall certainly feel even more than before that it is up to me to do all I can to help it forward".

Though Tizard's views of their progress with the combustion problem were encouraging, they knew that they had a long way to go. It was not for lack of effort, as Whittle recorded: "At the time of Tedder's visit we had experimented with no less than 31 different types of vaporizer, not counting many of the modifications to some of the types tested, but we were still in trouble with coking up of vaporizer tubes, local overheating, distortion, and bad temperature distribution at the outlets from the combustion chambers".

In addition, there were main-bearing failures, almost certainly due to foundry sand which dropped like fine rain from the crevices in the roof when the engine was running. Even so, the design of the W.1 flight engine was well advanced and the preliminary design of the W.2 was in progress. The design target for the W.2 was a maximum thrust of 1,600 lb, as compared with 1,240 lb for the W.1.

The two engines were basically similar, but there were a number of important differences. In the W.2 these included the substitution of air cooling for the turbine wheel (the need to avoid water cooling jackets was underlined by the freezing troubles they had had).

To add to his problems at this time, Whittle was becoming more concerned and irritated by the growing antagonism between Power Jets and BTH. Their association had been a very mixed one, in that BTH were not only contractors charging for work on a cost-plus basis but also, at the same time, shareholders in Power Jets. Bad feeling and resentment on BTH's part seemed to have its origin in two chief sources: one concerned Power Jets' patent policy in connection with vortex-design turbine blading, and the other sprang from the increasing frequency of technical disagreements between certain engineers and Whittle himself.

BTH's rancour over Whittle's discovery of vortex theory has already been mentioned. The tension on the technical side was basically between Whittle and senior BTH engineers. He said "This was, perhaps, aggravated by the fact that Cheshire, Randles and many others in more junior positions were on my side. These and others, including factory personnel working on the job, were enthusiasts and exhibited a strong loyalty to me personally. It may be guessed, therefore, that there were times when my position was distinctly uncomfortable". (Randles and two BTH draughtsmen, Atkinson and Richardson, had previously backed their faith in Whittle, and invested their own money in Power Jets.)

Whittle felt that the technical disagreements had their origin in the very different backgrounds of the BTH engineers and himself: "I was an aeronautical engineer trained to think in terms of very low weight and great precision. My experience had given me a clear picture of the special problems peculiar to an aircraft power plant, such as the need for rapid starting, quick response to control, and ability to cope with a range of operating conditions as wide as from take-off conditions in the tropics to high-speed manoeuvring at very great heights where the air temperature would be 50 degrees C below freezing point. I saw these things through the eyes of a pilot, as well as through the eyes of an engineer.

"The BTH engineers were steeped in an entirely different tradition. Their outlook was appropriate to the manufacture of large stationary electric generators for power stations and the like, largely constructed from massive castings and forgings weighing many tons and installed on heavy, rigid foundations. To save on manufacturing costs was far more important than to save on weight. Many of them had been 20 to 30 years or more in their profession, and had little or no connection with modern aerodynamic theory. I had the advantage of coming, more or less, fresh from university, with the added qualification of having worked under Professor B. Melvill Jones on aerodynamic research".

Though Whittle's project primarily involved a turbine, it was a field of engineering very far removed from the BTH engineers' previous experience. Apart from that, there were other difficulties: the machine tools in the factory were old and correspondingly unsuited to the work, and the factory was not temperature controlled — an important condition where great precision is required. Many of the factory personnel were so accustomed to dealing with far heavier components that they found it difficult to adjust their methods to relatively delicate work.

For example, the arc welding of stainless steel presented difficulties in any case, and the combustion chambers of the W.1 needed to be fabricated from Staybrite steel sheet only $\frac{1}{64}$th inch thick. Whittle was told bluntly that this was impossible, so he got hold of one of the most skilful welders and more or less challenged him to do something which hadn't been done before and, after a little experimenting, the man succeeded. (Later, on Voysey's initiative, Power Jets became expert at seam or stitch welding of very thin sheet metal.)

Whittle was fighting an uphill battle all the time and it is quite remarkable, in retrospect, that the work was done as well as it was, in view of the unsuitable circumstances. Sometimes, he said, "It was a bit like expecting the makers of Big Ben to make a good job of a lady's wrist-watch".

His obvious impatience about these things caused irritation amongst certain members of BTH staff, who began to look upon Power Jets work as a nuisance. Some were still sceptical about the real importance of the job, and doubted its success. At least one of the senior BTH engineers had proved to his own satisfaction that the jet engine could not compete with conventional power plant for aircraft, and aired his views!

The deteriorating situation at BTH caused Whittle to conclude that something must be done greatly to reduce the dependence on BTH. His prime aim was that Power Jets should be equipped to do most of the work, which would enable him to control the situation completely as far as the engineering and development of the project was concerned. But however fast the firm expanded, it could not hope to recruit sufficient personnel and equipment to make a material difference within a few months. Therefore, he decided to look around for another sub-contractor.

There were other reasons which influenced him in that respect. Certain Ministry officials thought the time had arrived to hand the whole job over to one of the established aero-engine manufacturers. In this connection, W. L. Tweedie of DSR had specifically mentioned Armstrong Siddeley. The Gloster Aircraft Company, who had a direct contract from the Air Ministry to manufacture the experimental aeroplane, were part of the giant Hawker Siddeley Group. This Group also included Armstrong

Siddeley Motors, who made radial aero engines such as the Lynx and Jaguar. Hugh Burroughes, a Gloster director, was keen to enter into an agreement whereby the Group would make both the airframe and Power Jets' engines, thus marrying up a composite deal.

Burroughes' enthusiasm, however, was not shared by his own Board who were not keen to take on such a revolutionary project. Also, Whittle himself made it quite clear that he was very strongly opposed to any such course. He did not want to be committed to a manufacturer of orthodox powerplants. Apart from the fact that his turbojet project was an entirely new concept, demanding different engineering skills and unbiased thinking, he was sensitive to the danger of aero-engine manufacturers muscling in on his project and taking it out of his hands.

In looking around for a suitable sub-contractor, it happened that Tinling's wife Nancy was a close friend of Barbara Wilks, the wife of Maurice Wilks, Chief Engineer of the Rover Car Company. This link led to a meeting between Maurice Wilks and Whittle towards the end of January 1940, at which Whittle suggested that Power Jets should place contracts with Rover. Wilks promised to discuss the matter with his brother, S. B. Wilks, the Managing Director. He indicated that his brother would probably be willing to do work for Power Jets, and that they might also be interested in a financial share in the venture.

As a sequel to this meeting, Whittle, Williams, Tinling and W/Cdr Lees visited the Rover works outside Coventry for a conference with the Wilks brothers. They explained the nature of the required development work, the need for full-scale compressor test apparatus, additional engine test houses, and so on. Whittle said that the figure needed to carry out this intensive development programme was about £150,000.

The authorized capital of Power Jets at this time was £50,000, of which only £23,000 had been issued. The unissued £27,000 'B' shares thus represented a little more than a 25 per cent holding to anybody who took them up. Whittle put it to the Wilks brothers that, 'a holding of this magnitude in Power Jets, in view of the state of development reached, was worth £270,000'.

S. B. Wilks was a little surprised at the amount of money that the Rover Company would have to put up, and said that they would expect to feature largely on the manufacturing side. He also said that it would be difficult to find so large a sum, but Whittle gained the impression that Wilks intended to explore ways and means. It was agreed that Wilks should talk to Major G. P. Bulman, Director of Engine Development at the Air Ministry, and Whittle suggested that he should also talk to Tizard and Tedder.

Bulman's reaction to Wilks' approach was to trigger off a series of events which caused Whittle great anxiety about the future of Power Jets. In a letter to the Rover Company, Bulman implied that those firms who already had an interest in Power Jets Limited should have no difficulty in providing any necessary further finance. The same letter virtually refused permission for Maurice Wilks to see the engine, and advised the Rover Company 'to tread warily'.

Thus it was that the Ministry, which had hitherto been charging Power Jets with not doing enough in the way of private money, started to undermine their most important steps in this direction.

Whittle found himself in a complex situation, in which it was impossible to obtain any clear official policy from those whose attitudes varied like straws in the wind. In referring to a Government Department he said that, "It is, of course, misleading to say that the Air Ministry thought this or thought that, especially in a case like ours, where the officials differed widely in their views. In conversation, it was difficult to tell whether an official was giving his personal views or expressing the official policy with which, privately, he may have disagreed".

There was a formidable array of officials each having a finger in the pie. As Director-General of Research and Development, Tedder was responsible to Air Marshal Sir Wilfred Freeman, Air Member for Development and Production, who took a keen personal interest in Power Jets' work. Below Tedder and responsible to him were Bulman and Pye, Directors of Engine Development and Scientific Research respectively. Others who had a large say in Power Jets' affairs were W. S. Farren, W. L. Tweedie (Scientific Research) and certain officials of the Contracts Department. Tweedie, in particular, seemed to have a very large influence, and was the one who authorized or refused permission for many of Whittle's proposals.

A typical example of official indiscretion and ineptitude occurred during an informal discussion between Whittle and Farren on 16 February 1940. Following a conference at the RAE, Farren made a series of comments about the position of Power Jets which disturbed and depressed Whittle profoundly. In an effort to scotch what seemed the probable course of events, he wrote to Farren, as follows:

"During our conversation at lunch yesterday you made various remarks, some of which were to the following effect:

1. People who had put their money in Power Jets were an unselfish crowd of people who had done a very good job of work, and that there was no hope of them ever getting any return on their money, and that in fact they would be very lucky indeed if they ever made good their loss.

2. The Air Ministry would not allow Power Jets to become a manufacturing organisation and intended to keep it as a small organisation, and that for manufacture some existing firm would be used.

3. That nobody would make anything out of this engine, because it belonged wholly to the Air Ministry and the Department would see that nobody made anything out of it. There would only be the normal legitimate manufacturing profit (from which Power Jets was excluded).

4. That the Air Ministry did not like Mr Whyte's suggestion of an organisation to handle manufacture in which Power Jets would be part owners.

5. That it was not healthy for an organisation such as ours to depend so much on Air Ministry money; that it should get private money as well, but that it was of little use anybody putting money into Power Jets because if they did so they would lose it, there being no way by which they would get a normal return, Power Jets having no patent position by virtue of the fact that the Air Ministry controlled the situation in this respect, and no manufacturing rights.

6. That the Air Ministry would not place orders with Power Jets for other than experimental engines, and definitely would not place orders for other engines through Power Jets."

Whittle went on to tell Farren that: "It is fortunate that I regard the above as expressions of your own opinion, and not as those of the Department, as otherwise I would be most upset, since it would seem to me grossly unfair that the Air Ministry should allow Power Jets to ripen the fruit and others to pluck it.

"I am not after big dividends myself, but at the same time it would weigh heavily on me if I thought that many individuals who had put their money in largely because of their faith in me were not to see a just return on that money in the future.

"In any case I regard Power Jets' organisation as almost as much my creation as the engine itself, and for that reason I want to see it expand. It is in a sense my only command and I believe that Power Jets as such could handle this job in its future stages better than some existing aero-engine firm, who would probably rather kill it than get on with it.

"We have plenty of evidence that the wolves are gathering round the door, and I have a very depressing feeling that your sympathies lie with the wolves".

Whittle sent a copy of this letter to Tedder who replied saying, ". . . Don't worry about what Farren might have said on financial matters which are not his concern. Neither he nor I are in a position to discuss the financial aspects of the Company, either in the past or in the future.

"On the other hand, I dislike wolves as much as you do, and you can be assured that my sympathies do not lie with them . . ."

Farren realised that he had spoken out of turn when he saw a copy of Tedder's letter, and phoned Whittle on February 23 trying to put matters right: "He said I had misunderstood him; that his own feelings towards Power Jets were all that they should be. What he had tried to do was to point out what undesirable things might happen. He went on to say that he agreed with everybody else that Power Jets had done a marvellous job of work and that he felt as others did, that it would be unjust if they did not reap some benefit from it."

Nevertheless, it will be seen that Whittle's recorded impression of Farren's remarks proved to be a fairly accurate forecast of official policy which was put into effect in March and April 1940.

Things were going badly for Whittle at this time. On the day before Farren's conciliatory telephone call of February 23 there had been a very unfriendly meeting with BTH, resulting in another crisis in their relationship. BTH knew that Power Jets were looking around for alternative sources of manufacture, and resented it. Sporborg said that BTH would do no further work on the W.2 pending a decision as to where further orders were to be placed. There was an angry exchange between Sporborg and Whyte because they disagreed completely about what had been said at a meeting a few days earlier. Though, as a result of some pressure from the Ministry, BTH agreed to resume work on the W.2, the atmosphere was far from cordial.

Negotiations between Power Jets and the Rover Company had

continued, despite Major Bulman's interference, with both sides making proposals which the other side found unacceptable. Each time Power Jets gave ground the Wilks brothers 'upped the ante', and Whittle began to distrust their motives. Nevertheless, Whyte, Williams and Tinling believed that a worthwhile deal could be made, until the Air Ministry threw another large spanner in the works.

On 26 March 1940 Tedder presided over a conference at Harrogate during which the main lines of official policy were defined. Whittle understood that an important part of the background of this meeting was that Freeman and Tedder had decided that the jet engine was to be included in a list of potential war winners, and that the work was to be given a corresponding priority.

The Wilks brothers of Rover were present, and Power Jets was represented by Whyte and Whittle. The other Ministry representatives were Pye, Tweedie and an official of the Contracts Directorate. Sporborg of BTH had excused himself, and was to meet Tedder in London the next day.

The purpose of this vital meeting was to reach conclusions which would enable development work to proceed as fast as possible. Tedder said that he was not expecting production plant to be laid down yet, but development and design work was to be done with production in view. The Ministry had decided that the work must proceed with the greatest possible speed, as it was believed that there was a good chance that engines could be in production in time to be of use in the war. The Ministry, he said, proposed to give direct contracts for development engines to the Rover Company. He decreed that there was to be a very intimate basis of co-operation between Rover and Power Jets.

In the course of the discussions regarding the form such co-operation should take, Tweedie stressed the fact "that the Crown had free use of Power Jets' patents and therefore he did not see that they had anything to offer in return for finance". S. B. Wilks pointed out that the Air Ministry appeared to hold all the cards. Tedder agreed with a grin and, waving his hand in Whittle's direction, added "including the Joker".

Tweedie even expressed himself against the Air Ministry giving any further contracts for development engines to Power Jets — he thought they should go direct to Rover. It was also made clear that Power Jets were not to be allowed to manufacture engine parts themselves. Thus, Whyte and Whittle were put in a position of having to fight for the very existence of Power Jets. They argued that much quicker development would be assured if contracts were placed with Power Jets who would then sub-contract them to the Rover Company. But the Air Ministry were totally opposed to this, pointing out that Power Jets would be proceeding without having any experienced production people on the job. Apparently it was not realised that experience of conventional production methods might be more a handicap than a help in such a new sphere of engineering.

In retrospect Whittle was convinced that much of what had been said by certain of the Ministry representatives and S. B. Wilks was based on meetings between them before this particular conference. He had never known what had been going on behind the scenes between the Rover Company and Ministry officials and, if this were true, then he thought that Tedder was unaware of it. Tedder seemed to be the sole protector of Power Jets.

Whittle was not a cynical man by nature, but thought at the time that: "It must have seemed a wonderful opportunity to the Rover Company. They were to be given a free pass into a new industry, and to be subsidised by Government contracts into the bargain. They knew that most of the officials concerned wanted to see the job in the hands of an established engineering concern. They could see that a good deal of personal antagonism existed between certain civil servants on the one hand and Whyte and myself on the other.

"The engine itself appeared a nice simple piece of engineering — so simple that even a young RAF Squadron Leader had been able to design it! Seemingly, if they played their cards right, there was little to prevent them taking over the whole job completely. The Ministry would be the main customer, and so any Power Jets patents, valid or otherwise, would be no obstacle. They had to be careful with Tedder of course; he at least intended to protect Power Jets, but he was a Serving Officer and couldn't afford to ignore the advice of his technical advisers. Anyway, there was a war on and in all probability he would fairly soon be moved to an Operational Command, whereas the civil servants would remain".

Had Whittle believed the Rover Company were capable of making a better job of the project than Power Jets, and that they really had the national interest at heart, his attitude would have been very different. As it was, he was convinced that nobody was more qualified to manage the engineering side than himself, and that Rover's main object was to make the most of a favourable opportunity to get in on the ground floor of a new industry absolutely free of charge.

At a meeting at S. B. Wilks' house on 31 March 1940 the negotiations between Power Jets and Rover for a financial link finally collapsed in a thoroughly poisoned atmosphere. This breakdown was inevitable after the Harrogate meeting when Power Jets' bargaining position had been completely undermined, partly by the promise of direct contracts to Rover, and partly by the remarks that Tweedie and others had made to the effect that, since the Crown had free use of Power Jets' patents, the Company had nothing to offer in return for finance.

Whittle pointed out with great emphasis that the £50,000 Rover were being asked to subscribe, in return for a considerable shareholding, was required for development work and that every penny of it would be spent on such work. Rover as shareholders would be getting much of the benefit and, furthermore, a good deal of the money would be spent on sub-contract work with the Rover Company — but it was all in vain!

Their reaction was a studied list of negative criticisms: Power Jets' assets were worthless; they did not like the structure of Power Jets; the balance sheet did not show a good position; the work was still a gamble, and Power Jets had not achieved so very much after all; they doubted Power Jets' ability to carry on with the work; and there was always the possibility that the Air Ministry might decide to post Whittle elsewhere.

Meanwhile, there had been at least one meeting between the Ministry and BTH, at which Power Jets was not present, when it had been agreed that BTH were also to receive direct contracts. Power Jets heard about this only when they went to Harrogate on 12 April for a further meeting with the Ministry, and were told that BTH and Rover would share the production of jet engines. Direct contracts were to be placed with both firms, and Power Jets were to hand over all drawings and information, and to give them every assistance in their power and to co-operate on the closest possible basis.

Power Jets was to be maintained as a research organisation only.

Contracts for further development engines beyond the W.2 would be placed direct with the two firms (thus revoking a decision on 26 March at the previous Harrogate meeting to give Power Jets a contract for three further experimental engines).

As a result of this meeting it became obvious that Power Jets were being pushed further and further into the background. Whittle was extremely depressed: "Everything possible was going wrong. The moves which the Ministry hoped would speed up the work would, in my view, have exactly the opposite effect. For example, any work BTH did on their direct contracts would obviously receive priority in their factory over their work for us, so that far from any speed-up on our work, the very opposite would happen.

"The Rover Company were also to get direct contracts and to do the development work which I regarded as properly the function of Power Jets. I was absolutely convinced that neither BTH nor Rover were competent to do the development work".

Although it had been agreed that Power Jets was to be maintained as a research organisation, Tweedie had been opposed to any important further extension of Power Jets' test facilities, but Tedder had ruled that they should be equipped to carry out research work efficiently. Any further equipment authorized, he said, would remain the property of the Ministry.

Whittle still hoped that Power Jets would continue to dominate the design and development of the engines which the two firms were to make, but this hope faded later in the month when it was ruled that the firms concerned would be responsible for their own drawings and development.

By the end of April 1940, Power Jets' position had been gravely weakened. They were compelled to hand over every scrap of information which they had accumulated to two large firms without any safeguards whatsoever. Perhaps the one thing that was saving them from complete extinction at that time was the fact that Tedder recognized that Power Jets still had an important part to play. In a Minute dated 28 March he described the Power Jets' design team as "the key to the whole project . . . (whose) continued existence was vital".

Whyte made determined attempts to obtain safeguards regarding patents, and also to get the position about design responsibility cleared up. On 18 April he spoke to Tedder on the telephone, and apparently there was a heated conversation in which Tedder accused Whyte of obstruction and hinted that the AM might have to use the big stick on Power Jets.

In Whittle's eyes, Whyte had been making perfectly reasonable attempts to secure safeguards, but his efforts came to nothing because neither BTH nor Rover would agree to various schemes put forward, including one from the Contracts Directorate. The problem was never solved, and several months later it was ruled that the matter should be left to arbitration after the war.

Although frustrated by events and worried about the future of Power Jets and himself, Whittle's prime concern was always for the job itself. He expressed himself forcibly on that subject to Wilks and Tweedie: ". . . if it is the aim of the AM to put this job into production in the shortest possible time this is not the right way to do it. The responsibility for design is far from clear. If I am to remain responsible I must be closely adjacent to the design drawing office concerned. In my opinion the design cannot be dissociated from the drawings".

Whittle knew what was likely to happen: "If the work were successful, the firms concerned would get the credit, but if things went wrong then Power Jets would get the blame". Events were to prove how correctly he had foreseen the consequences of the AM's policy of this time.

The situation came to a head on 9 May when Whittle received a letter from Tedder saying, in effect, that because of the ill-feeling which existed, the desired co-operation between Power Jets and Rover was not possible, and that from then on the two firms would act independently. On the following day he went to Harrogate to see Tedder to attempt to have the decision reversed, because he regarded independent action by the Rover Company as being even worse than the earlier policy.

The moment was ripe for such a meeting from all points of view. In parallel with official policy, decisions which had been made earlier in the year, and associated with them, the Gloster Aircraft Company were authorized to proceed with the design of a twin-engined interceptor jet fighter, to specification F.9/40, and to prepare for its production. The authorization to go ahead with the design of an actual fighter, without waiting for the experimental E.28/39 aeroplane and its engine to be flight-tested, was striking evidence of the change in attitude towards the potential of the Whittle engine. The resulting fighter ultimately became known as the Meteor, which took part in the latter stages of World War 2 and in the Korean War.

Tedder opened this talk by telling Whittle that he had been very worried about the way things were going. Whittle replied that he was also very worried and had given up trying to understand recent events. The AVM[1] suggested that a good deal of this worry was unnecessary, and that the root of the trouble

[1]AVM — Air Vice-Marshal.

was Whyte's unreasonable attempts to obtain water-tight safeguards on all points, because he did not trust the Ministry's undertaking (the moral obligation): "I told Tedder that he was misunderstanding Whyte completely, and though I did not get on with Whyte too well myself, I felt bound to say that if he really understood Whyte's motives, he would find they were all he wished them to be. Whyte was acting in what he undoubtedly believed to be the best interests of the nation".

Tedder considered that he had put Power Jets in a very strong position, but they did not seem able to see that this was so. He said that he had made his mind up very definitely some time before that in no circumstances would he allow a small company to be swallowed up by two large ones. He added that this was still his attitude, in spite of severe provocation.

During the ensuing discussion Whittle repeated his arguments against the Ministry's policy. They then had a talk with Sir Wilfred Freeman. This was Whittle's first meeting with the Air Marshal whose first words were, "What shall we do about this bloody man Whyte?" Whittle again defended Whyte adding that, "Whyte has very good reason to be uneasy about patents".

They then discussed whether or not Power Jets could co-operate with Rover. Whittle thought that they could in spite of past difficulties, saying that he did not see how the policy of non-co-operation could possibly work. At this juncture, Freeman said that his view of Whittle's functions was that they ought to be broader than they had been hitherto: "He suggested that I was attending too much to detail. I replied that there were still many design points which I felt I could not entrust to others as yet, though I was doing my best to train other engineers. I put it to them that the broader functions that Sir Wilfred seemed to have in mind would be best fulfilled if I were formally made the Chief Engineer of the whole project, but both Tedder and Freeman were non-committal on this point.

"I hinted at my dissatisfaction that most of the Ministry's decisions had been taken without giving me a hearing beforehand, and commented that I did not think the Ministry officials concerned had any comprehension of the enormous amount of work Power Jets had to do.

"Sir Wilfred turned to Tedder and asked him if I was a difficult fellow to get on with, adding: 'he seems to be a reasonable enough being in this office'. Tedder smiled and said I was a little difficult at times. In our earlier talk, Tedder had remarked that I had to be regarded somewhat as a prima donna — very important, but needing to be handled gently. I said to Freeman that I hoped that time would show that I was not as difficult as Tedder implied.

"In a short further talk with Tedder alone, after assuring me that he would reverse his decision that Rover and Power Jets should act independently, he remarked that he had been glad to have had a personal talk, and said he wished that talks with other people had been of the same kind, adding "you and I speak the same language".

That remark of Tedder's meant a great deal to Whittle, and had a wealth of meaning for him: "It implied that as members of the same Service, we shared a tradition and a concept of duty and integrity which set us apart from many of those — Civil Servants and others — with whom we had to deal — and a long way apart from some".

Whittle left the meeting determined to do all he could to clear up difficulties. Nevertheless, although quite sincere in his intentions where the Rover Company was concerned, he had no real belief that the Ministry's policy could be made to work. In retrospect it seems incredible that he should have been left in that exposed position. Those in high places, having recognised his genius, might well have backed him up in the national interest, and allowed him to get on with the job. Instead, he was forced to fight on all fronts.

On 10 May, the very day that Whittle met the Air Marshals to clear the air, Hitler suddenly unleashed his Blitzkrieg machine, and the Panzer Divisions were grinding across the plains of Europe. Within weeks the Germans had occupied almost the whole of Europe, and Britain was isolated. Chamberlain was replaced by Churchill as Prime Minister. The Battle of France had been lost and the battle for Britain was about to begin.

Meanwhile, Whittle and George Lees had visited the Rover works with the specific intention of sorting things out with the Wilks brothers. The talks went very well indeed, and Whittle took the initiative in inviting them to attach one of their engineers to Power Jets on loan to help Power Jets and acquire experience useful to the Rover Company. He also suggested that a similar arrangement might be extended to cover test hands both from Rover and from Joseph Lucas Ltd (who were to co-operate with Rover on combustion development and other special problems). Later, on 18 May, he wrote to Tedder to the effect that present relations with the Rover Company were going well, and he would do his best to maintain them.

One of the consequences of the change of Government with Winston Churchill as Prime Minister was the formation of the Ministry of Aircraft Production, with Lord Beaverbrook as Minister. As a result, the Technical Departments of the Air Ministry were transferred to the MAP. Britain's plight was desperate, and major policy changes within the industry were to be expected.

On 20 May, Power Jets received a telegram removing all priority from their work because it had been decided to concentrate the maximum possible effort on urgent short-term requirements, particularly fighters — over 450 Hurricanes and Spitfires were lost in the Battle for France. Aircraft in production were given absolute priority, to the detriment of new projects. These panic measures proved to be shortsighted due to muddled thinking, and had a damaging effect in the case of Power Jets.

From the wording of the telegram it seemed as though Power Jets' work would stop entirely, but the next day Tweedie said that it did not necessarily mean that all work stopped. That work which did not conflict with urgent aircraft work, he said, could go on, but Rover would shut down entirely because of their commitments on aero-engine manufacture.

BTH took the instruction to mean that all work would stop. Quite soon afterwards Tedder told them that work could continue if it did not interfere with priority work, but it was some time before they resumed. This period of uncertainty came to an end after three weeks, when priority was officially restored on 11 June 1940. This vacillation must have been depressing for all concerned. It was Whittle's view that the momentum lost was equivalent to several months' delay.

But there were signs that things might change for the better. In the same month, Dr Harold Roxbee Cox (later Lord Kings Norton) was appointed a Deputy Director of Scientific Research and was given authority over all aspects of gas turbine development — he had previously been Superintendent of Scientific Research in the RAE and as such had been present at conferences relating to the E.28 and other aspects of Power Jets' work. However, the official attitude towards gas turbines at this time was that they weren't exactly paramount. Turbines were not to be Roxbee Cox's only concern; he was to have the responsibility for a number of other special projects for the next

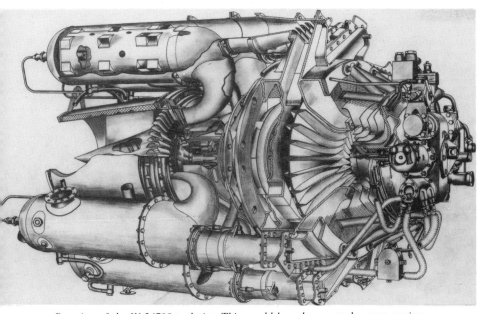

Drawing of the W.2/700 turbojet. This would have been a truly great engine, had it been allowed to be used.

Posed group beside the first F.9/40: from left, John Crosby-Warren (test pilot); Michael Daunt (test pilot); Frank McKenna (general manager, Gloster Aircraft); Frank Whittle and George Carter (chief designer).

Mike Daunt getting ready to fly the F.9/40 Meteor. He survived being sucked into the engine inlet!

At Brownsover Hall; Dudley Williams, Frank Whittle and J. C. B. 'Col' Tinling.

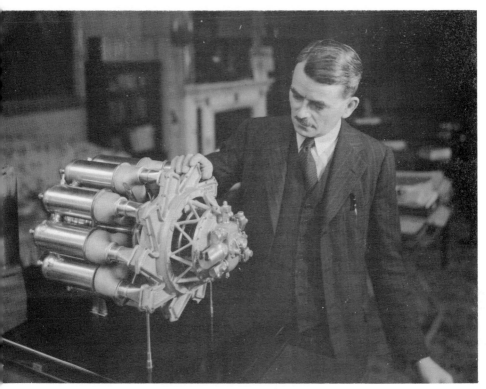

Frank Whittle and a model of the W.2/700 to about one-third scale (Brownsover Hall, 1944).

The three musketeers: Williams, Tinling and Whittle, who bore the main burden for so long.

A Gloster Meteor III, powered by Derwent I engines and with sliding (instead of hinged) cockpit canopy.

Rare moment of relaxation at Brownsover Hall in 1944: Cheshire, Williams, Whittle, Tinling, Walker, Lees, Johnson.

The Boss shakes hands with his Power Jets team in 1945: from left, J. Hodge, unidentified, W. Cooper, A. Simmons, Whittle, R. Feilden, D. Walker, D. Shepherd, R. Voysey and H. Cowan.

Later in the war the E.28/39 was powered by much later Power Jets engines. Here test pilot S/L Moloney and engineer S/L Cracknell pose by the original aircraft with new W.2/700 engine (No 15) in March 1945.

Installation of the powerful W.2/700 in the E.28/39 in March 1945.

General Ira C. Eaker, of the US Army Air Force, invests Frank Whittle with
the American Legion of Honor at the Pentagon, on 15 November 1946.

Arranged by General Electric, Sir Frank became a good friend of his unknown
rival, Pabst (Hans) von Ohain. They are still good friends.

At the great Patchway Works in 1959: Sir Stanley Hooker (Bristol Aero-Engines, formerly of Rolls-Royce) and Sir Frank compare technicalities.

two years. He was to be assisted by D. G. Tobin, who had become the channel for most of Power Jets' dealings with the Ministry — Tobin had been appointed as a contact man during April, to keep an eye on liaison between PJ, Rover and BTH.

Whittle hoped that the moment had arrived for a drastic revision of policy, but Roxbee Cox intimated that there would be no important changes. He did, however, imply that Power Jets could expect more lenient treatment in the provision of equipment for research functions. A few days later Power Jets were told that new test houses would be sanctioned, and that they would receive contracts for certain items of test equipment.

On 9 July Whittle was summoned for an interview with Lord Beaverbrook. "I missed what might have been an excellent opportunity to get the policy changed", he said, "I saw him for about three minutes. He fired a series of questions at me, the first of which was, 'What have you got tucked away'? I replied, 'A very good engine, sir'. I did my best to answer the rapid bombardment of questions to which I was subjected, without knowing what lay behind them.

"The Beaver asked me what I thought of Ministry policy. I felt that this was too complex a subject for a very short interview, so I replied that the decisions had been too recent for it to be possible to judge how they were going to work.

"After the interview I was still ignorant of the reason for the summons. It was not until a long time afterwards that I heard that knowledge of our work had been withheld from him because it was feared that he might consider it to be an interference with immediately urgent requirements, and that, having heard of it indirectly, he sent for me to find out what was going on. However, the axe did not fall, and indeed Lord Beaverbrook's parting words to me were to the effect that as soon as we were ready for a prototype fighter to take the engine we should have it".

*   *   *

Whittle had been promoted to temporary Wing Commander on 1 June 1940 — his thirty third birthday — against a background of national disaster. On 22 June France surrendered and everybody suddenly woke up to the fact that an invasion of Britain could be imminent.

During the battles along the Western Front, aircraft losses had been heavy. Later, the Germans admitted a total of 1,065, and the RAF 959, of which about half were fighters — at every stage of these battles the high-speed monoplane fighter had been the key. The battle for France had left Fighter Command's defences at their lowest ebb, with the RAF desperately needing more Hurricanes and Spitfires to defend Britain against the powerful Luftwaffe.

It was in this climate of national crisis that Whittle had been summoned to meet Beaverbrook whose influence, business acumen and enormous vitality was already beginning to make an impact on the problems facing the aircraft industry. The Beaver had to take a short-term view and concentrate on those aircraft already in production to the exclusion of prototype projects. It is quite remarkable, in the circumstances, that the Whittle project was allowed to continue. Work was never suspended on the construction of the Gloster/Whittle E.28 — Britain's first jet aircraft — and priority was restored to Whittle's engine work two days after his meeting with Beaverbrook. In the light of history great credit is due to Beaverbrook and his advisors that they did not wield the axe at this critical time, because the turbojet project was not then of immediate wartime significance and the E.28 was a totally new kind of aircraft — though one of unique potential.

Whittle had missed an excellent opportunity of getting official policy changed when he met Beaverbrook. He was anxious to speed up the development of his project because he believed that sooner or later Britain would be attacked by very high-altitude bombers and that the only effective defence would be jet fighters. This belief strongly governed his actions and those of his associates. But he never again had the chance of a full-blooded confrontation with The Beaver, who was just the sort of man to appreciate his problems and eradicate his difficulties.

During the five years which had elapsed since he received Dudley Williams' letter in early May 1935, Whittle had been obsessed with his turbojet project weathering one crisis after another. This obsession, which went far beyond the bounds of normal dedication, had completely dominated his life. All his time and energies had gone into the task, with the result that he had neglected his family: "I don't think Dorothy could really accept the fact that her little man was working on something of great importance. And, of course, I couldn't put her in the picture, and she wouldn't have been interested if I had tried. She was, and is, very artistic and her mind moved in a world far removed from science and engineering".

As the pressures on him built-up during the late thirties, his cigarette smoking had increased dramatically to as much as three packets a day: "My heaviest consumption was while doing theoretical work, especially when drinking numerous cups of tea, but I never inhaled". He also began drinking on social occasions and found it very helpful in overcoming acute shyness (from which he has never been free). This introversion undoubtedly helped to convey the impression that he was reserved and a bit stand-offish.

The fact was that Whittle had very little time for conversation except for shop talk. Arnold Hall (later Sir Arnold, Chairman and Managing Director of the Hawker Siddeley Group) remembered him at Cambridge University: "There was a knock on my door and Whittle stood there with a roll of papers under his arm — a small figure bubbling with enthusiasm and exuding vitality. Within a minute or so his papers were spread over the floor and we were discussing how I, and a chap named Edkins, could help him with stress calculations. He could talk of nothing else but his engine. Even when driving his car he would glance over his shoulder at me in the back seat, spouting statistics and formulae. I think it is a very important thing in understanding this man to realise that he did the almost impossible in getting a First, despite the fact that he was devoting so much of his time to his invention".

Whittle continued to do the almost impossible in keeping Power Jets and his turbojet project alive. It cost him dearly as far as his health was concerned. From the summer of 1936 he had increasing problems, experiencing frequent and severe headaches and indigestion. During 1939/40 he was plagued with staphylococcus infections. Boils, some of which were very large and inconveniently placed, necessitating the use of an inflated rubber ring, and painful furuncles in the ears, all combined to pull him down.

It was not until 1940 that he started on the downward path with sleeping pills, tranquillisers and stimulants, and becoming something of an addict: "I now realise that I started down this slippery slope more or less by mischance. In 1940 I suffered a lot from nasal congestion for which an over-the-counter remedy in those days was a benzedrine inhaler. I rapidly became an addict without realising it, and would be sniffing away every 15 minutes or so. When I suffered rapid heartbeat, feelings of tension, anxiety and insomnia I did not make the connection: I assumed these things were due to overwork, frustration and the race with time. So, when I appealed to the doctor to help me with insomnia, it never occurred to me to mention the benzedrine which, with hindsight, was a major cause of many of my problems".

* * *

During the months of June, July and August 1940, preceding the Battle of Britain, the close collaboration desired by Tedder between Power Jets, BTH and Rover failed to materialise. Having obtained direct contracts from the Ministry, BTH and Rover became more secretive about their work: "We heard that BTH were working on the design of the engine and that they were putting up test houses, but we did not hear about these things officially. Rover were photostating copies of Power Jets' drawings, with all references to Power Jets removed and no acknowledgement of the origin of the drawing". This, of course, was a gross breach of copyright — tantamount to forgery.

Whenever things went wrong either BTH or Rover would go behind Whittle's back to the Ministry and blame Power Jets, their argument being that they were the practical engineers and Power Jets were not more than gifted amateurs. Their main contact was Roxbee Cox, who had only been in the job for a short time. Whittle knew what was going on and his view was that: "Roxbee Cox could scarcely be blamed at this stage for believing much of what he was told by BTH and Rover. Technical points were the chief source of dispute and so he probably tended to weigh the background of engineering experience of these two firms against the seemingly limited experience of a relatively junior RAF officer".

Whittle was in a very precarious position. He had previously floated the idea to Tedder and Freeman that he should be made Chief Engineer of the entire project which would have given him control, but Tedder thought that such an appointment would be distasteful to BTH and Rover.

Not to have been given his 'Command' was a great blow to Whittle and it hurt him deeply. He had not merely been concerned about his own reputation. His basic reason for broaching the subject was that he was convinced that he and his team were the only people competent to control the design. But they were wholly financed by the Ministry at this stage, and, in the light of events, their survival as a team hung on a very delicate thread.

With hindsight, it seems incredible that Whittle didn't get the backing for which he had asked. The turbojet was his baby, which he had created, nursed and developed from the cradle. He and he alone had given it life, and in so doing had opened up new horizons in aviation technology. The very least that Tedder and Freeman could have done was to have given him his Command and given him all necessary support to bring his turbojet project to fruition.

That the RAF Air Marshals should have let him down was the unkindest cut of all. Sir Arnold Hall described Whittle as a child of the RAF, the perfect officer with a sense of duty bred into him. He was invariably right, he said, because he worked everything out in meticulous detail. He was right about choosing a centrifugal compressor in the first instance, which simplified everything and saved a lot of time. Looking back, he remembered that Whittle was talking about ducted fan engines in the early days and even before the War he knew the way Civil Aviation would go — and it did, first with the Comet. He had remarkable genius and foresight.

In Hall's opinion, Whittle should have been made Chief Engineer of the entire project which, he said, would have saved a lot of time and tangles. Whittle was a great engineer, very highly qualified and pioneering a new concept of aviation engineering involving light weight, great precision and revolutionary creep-resisting materials. BTH and Rover, by comparison, were engaged in heavy industry and traditional in outlook.

The late Sir Stanley Hooker said of him: "Whittle had an unrivalled grasp of the fundamentals of thermodynamics and aerodynamics, and he never did anything until he had given it the deepest and most logical consideration. As I came to understand his work, I realised that he had laid down the performance of jet engines with the precision of Newton, a feat whose magnitude he never appeared to appreciate. For the preceding 30 years the performance of piston engines in flight was known only to a very rough approximation based on inaccurate empirical formulae, yet Whittle predicted what a jet engine would do before he had ever made one. Today, 40 years later, his formulae are used unchanged. They are of such precision that it is more accurate to calculate the performance of jet engines, including the most modern fan engines, than it is to attempt to measure it either in flight or in the astronomically costly test plants which attempt to simulate flight conditions on the ground. And this is true from take-off to the speed of Concorde, and beyond. Indeed, the pen really is mightier than the spanner!".

Although Whittle was still not put in control of the engineering work, his anxieties regarding the future of his Power Jets team were soon to be dispelled. Tedder, in this respect, was as good as his word, and during the latter part of 1940 Power Jets received substantial Government backing and expanded more rapidly than at any previous time.

This expansion began during the final phase of the Battle of Britain, when the country's independence hung in the balance. The key to survival had been the production of enough fighters and the training of enough pilots to combat the Luftwaffe. Aircraft production of all types had virtually doubled from 860 per month in March 1940 to 1,601 in August, of which about one-third were fighters. It was during that year that aircraft production really got under way in this country.

Rolls-Royce had been working to capacity manufacturing their Merlin engine which powered both the Hurricane and the Spitfire. Despite this pressure, Rolls also had the development facilities and the manufacturing back-up greatly to accelerate the Whittle project. It is arguable that the nation would have been far better served if a Whittle/Rolls combination had been instituted during 1940.

After the formation of MAP, Power Jets began to expand a little more rapidly, and by 1 September 1940 the total strength was about 70 including the full-time directors and personnel on loan. The additions to the engineering team were in keeping with Whittle's high standards; Hawthorne, Bone and Feilden (like himself) were all First Class Honours men of Cambridge (Hawthorne, later Sir William Hawthorne, had also taken his doctors's degree at the Massachusetts Institute of Technology, so he had quite exceptional qualifications).

The experimental engine was still the only engine in existence. Though progressively deteriorating, it was being used for combustion development. Experiments were made on a combustion system which vaporized the fuel (kerosene) before injection, but it was never really satisfactory. A tantalising thing was that seemingly good results on the test rigs could not be reproduced in the engine. Eventually the MAP arranged for

Power Jets to use a large compressor for high-pressure combustion tests. This compressor formed part of the plant used in the construction of the Dartford tunnel under the Thames on which work had been suspended.

Some useful work was done on this rig but the answers were mostly negative. It was found that the vaporizing system being used in the engine would stand endurance running in the Dartford compressor rig, so it appeared that the pressure conditions did not, after all, account for the differences in behaviour between the rigs and the engine.

The chief reason for these differences was discovered by W. E. P. Johnson, Whittle's old RAF colleague and earliest associate on his jet proposals, who had joined Power Jets in April on loan from the RAF to which he had been recalled at the outbreak of war. Johnson made a full-scale model of a combustion chamber with transparent plastic material (Rhodoid). With the aid of wool tufts and smoke, Whittle and his associates were able to observe the airflow as it entered the phantom combustion chamber: "This simple but valuable piece of apparatus taught us a lot. It became obvious that the differences which had puzzled us were mainly due to the differences in the pattern of the airflow entering the chamber".

However, a much more significant development occurred in July 1940. Isaac Lubbock of the Asiatic Petroleum Company, who had been advising Power Jets for some time past on combustion and fuel problems, invited them to see a combustion chamber of approximately the same size and form as that used in the engine, and with which Shell engineers were experimenting in their Fulham laboratory. The fuel was injected in a fine mist of liquid droplets through a controllable atomising burner. Power Jets combustion engineers started work on it on 19 July, and within a week Whittle was able to report to the Ministry that tests were sufficiently promising to justify the making of a set of similar combustion chambers for the engine. Lubbock also contributed by lending Power Jets a burner expert, J. R. Joyce.

Despite a series of initial troubles when adapted to the engine: "the introduction of the Shell system may be said to mark the point where combustion ceased to be an obstacle to development".

By now the space at Ladywood works was seriously outgrown. People were falling over each other, almost literally, because at one time some engineers were obliged to sit and work on the stairs leading to Whittle's office! A railway coach which stood on a siding outside the works became the office of the combustion engineers, of whom Dr Hawthorne, Darling, Bennet-Powell, and Flight Lieutenant Bone, were all on loan from the RAE.

This by no means met their needs, and so a few rooms were rented in Brownsover Hall, an old country house about three miles from Rugby on the Lutterworth road. The former dining room became an excellent, though rather small, drawing office and the accommodation was used by the design staff. But the pressure on space continued to grow at Ladywood, and temporary wooden huts were erected to satisfy immediate needs.

Extra equipment was badly needed. In August 1940 they had only one machine tool — a lathe! The figure authorized for Power Jets' requirements in equipment and buildings was £27,000 — about the price of three engines. With the exception of the internals of the combustion chamber, they were still entirely dependent on BTH for manufacture. Efforts to get additional sub-contract capacity had largely been frustrated, with the result that they had to take on a fair proportion of the work themselves. The Ministry, as usual, was slow to accept the situation, and only after continuous pressure did Power Jets succeed in getting piecemeal sanction to build up a workshop capable of making engine components.

Despite the difficulties and frustrations, slow but steady progress had been made throughout 1940 on the engine which would power the E.28 on the first jet flight, and the power plant for the twin-engined Gloster F.9/40 fighter, the Meteor.

About the middle of 1940 it was decided to use a spare rotor which was being made for the experimental engine and certain components originally made for the W.1 (which were considered to be below standard for an engine which had to be airworthy), to construct an experimental version of the W.1. This composite engine was designated the W.1X.

The W.1X proved to be a very valuable engine indeed. Before completion it was sent to Gloster and used as a mock-up for the installation of the W.1 in the E.28. Whittle and George Carter, the Gloster Chief Designer got on very well: "If the excellent liaison between Carter and his team and me and my team had been a model for others at least two years — probably three — could have been saved. The W.1X was installed in the aeroplane almost without a hitch".

Both the W.1X and the W.1 embodied modifications dictated by experience with the experimental engine.

Whittle had felt it necessary to test certain of the special features of the F.9/40's W.2 engine in advance if possible, and so, in February 1940, he produced a design which was really a compromise between the W.1 and the W.2. This was designated the W.1A. Its stated purpose was to prove such special features of the W.2 as the air cooling of the turbine disc and the novel compressor intake arrangement. The Ministry eventually gave Power Jets a contract for a W.1A, and this was also sub-contracted to BTH.

Shortly before this, it had been decided that there were to be two E.28 prototypes, the second one having a high-speed wing profile. This second aeroplane was to be powered by the W.1A, for which most of the design work was done by Power Jets, with some of the details being left to BTH.

The W.2 being made by BTH on Power Jets' contract was, after a certain amount of argument, being made to Power Jets' design. In contrast, the W.2 being made by the Rover company, on direct contract from the MAP, differed from Power Jets' design in a number of ways. These were chiefly in such features as bearings and auxiliary drives, but for the main components, namely, the compressor, the turbine, and combustion chambers, they were conforming to Power Jets' design. They did not have the knowledge to do anything else.

Whittle had done the design calculations for the W.2 but, owing to pressure of work, he had limited himself to calculations for the full-speed conditions. The increase in engineering staff now made it possible for him to do performance calculations in greater detail. The results made him very uneasy about the design. They revealed that, if their assumptions proved to be over-optimistic, there would be a severe penalty. Whittle reported this fact to the Ministry, and Power Jets then started on a complete revision of the design, designated the W.2B.

By the end of 1940 practically the whole of Power Jets' design effort was devoted to the W.2B. By then it had been decided that the W.2B was to be the power plant for the Gloster F.9/40.

BTH also called the engine they were making on their direct contract a W.2B. This was rather confusing because it differed in many ways from the Power Jets W.2B, though of the same general arrangement. The only direct contributions Power Jets made to it were the supply of initial design figures and the design of the combustion equipment.

The design target for the Power Jets W.2B was a static thrust of 1,800 lb, though it was agreed with the RAE that, for the purposes of aircraft performance and so on, it would be assumed that at full power it would deliver 1,600 lb.

A feature of both the W.2 and W.2B was the very simple engine mounting: "We intended from the first that engine changing should be a very swift operation, and in this we were undoubtedly successful. It took about thirty minutes to change an engine in the Meteor. This was one of the many ways in which the strong Service associations of many of the Power Jets' personnel was reflected in the design. Williams, Tinling, Lees, Johnson, Crompton, Bone and myself either were, or had been in the RAF. And by the end of the year, we had Flight Sergeant King and other airmen on attachment".

*   *   *

In those critical days of 1940, when Britain stood alone, the nation thought that a German invasion was imminent. Only the good old English Channel separated the island from Nazi-occupied Europe. The British people were expecting Hitler's Blitzkrieg machine to strike at any moment, heralded by an avalanche of bombs and German paratroopers dropping out of the sky.

Road blocks were set-up at major crossroads, and signposts were either removed, painted out, or turned round to confuse an airborne enemy. Local Defence Volunteer (later Home Guard) forces were formed, some armed only with pitchforks and staves, and instructions went out that church bells should ring only as an invasion alarm.

German fifth columnists and saboteurs were known to have infiltrated Western Europe, and the British were told to be on the lookout for spies and report anything seemingly suspicious. The Government promoted a 'careless talk costs lives' campaign with the slogan 'be like Dad — keep Mum'. The atmosphere throughout the country was apprehensive, but the public inspired by the resolute leadership of Winston Churchill were determined to resist to the last.

During the critical period of May 1940, Whittle and his

associates considered the possibility of duplicating their work on the other side of the Atlantic. They felt that if the Germans got to know what they were doing, they might deem it well worth while to make a special effort to wipe them out. So they suggested to the Ministry that the whole job should be moved to Canada. Later, they modified their views and thought it would be sufficient to send a nucleus across to duplicate the work, but nothing came of those suggestions except that sets of blueprints were sent to Canada as some kind of insurance.

The secrecy and national importance of his work made Whittle react in other ways: "I had quite an exaggerated idea of the bomb worthiness of Power Jets; not only did I think the Ladywood Works likely to be bombed, but also thought that there was a distinct probability of something in the nature of a raid by parachute troops. Since our sole defence at night, when the Battle of Britain was at its height, was our two night-watchmen, I decided that some of us ought to sleep on the premises as an additional guard. At first my colleagues were reluctant to accept that this was necessary, but after a short period, during which I supplemented the night-watchmen on my own — sleeping on a camp bed in my office — the idea became more generally accepted and a group of us took it in turns. (Fire-watching had not yet become a national institution.)"

Whittle found an element of fascination in this night-guard business. The nights were mostly fine, and if there were sundry minor discomforts, it was a relief for him not to do the Rugby-Lutterworth drive in the black-out with the heavily hooded headlamps that everyone was compelled to use in those days. He used to get quite a thrill wandering round the almost deserted works on a still night with searchlights eerily sweeping the sky.

There was one daylight raid on Rugby by a single raider. It happened on a Sunday afternoon, when Whittle was at home. A few minutes after the sirens had sounded the alert, complete pandemonium broke out. He rushed to the window in time to see a twin-engined bomber flying low in the direction of BTH let go a stick of bombs. The noise was out of all proportion to the raid, because every gun-crew for miles around had been waiting for something to happen for so long that none of them was losing an opportunity to let fly! The excitement was all over in about thirty seconds, and nobody was seriously hurt. BTH escaped with superficial damage to the office block; nevertheless, he heard the next day that Power Jets' work had suffered because, when the bombs fell, a workman holding one of their badly needed compressor impellers was so startled that he dropped it. It had to be scrapped.

Despite the compact target presented by the BTH works, the large railway goods yards and junction, and the English Electric Company's works, Rugby caught the fringes of the blitzes on Coventry but otherwise suffered little from enemy air raids, and the small town of Lutterworth escaped completely. There were other indirect delays at the Ladywood Works, through bomb damage, but generally speaking, air raids did not cost them more than a few weeks.

Chapter 11
More Trouble and Further Expansion

During the autumn of 1940, Whittle made continued efforts to bring about changes in policy. When Air Chief Marshal Sir Wilfred Freeman and Roxbee Cox visited Power Jets on 18 October, he was told that Rover had accepted the proposal that their first W.2B should be made to Power Jets' design except for the most minor modifications. Also, Roxbee Cox said it was proposed that BTH should do the same.

This policy was confirmed in Tedder's letter of 22 October to all parties concerned and represented some improvement from Power Jets' point of view, because it was a step in the direction of proper engineering control.

At the same time, Whyte again made a strong appeal to Sir Wilfred to put Whittle in control of the whole of the engineering side of the work, but Sir Wilfred would not agree for the reason previously given by Tedder, namely, that it would be distasteful to Rover and BTH.

However, the policy, as laid down in Tedder's letter, was never implemented because neither BTH nor Rover would agree to the conditions. Naturally, Whittle was very depressed: "It is beyond my understanding why it was that the Ministry was almost brutal in the way in which they forced Power Jets to toe the line, but seemed completely weak and powerless where the other two firms were concerned. We dared not say no, but the other firms could and did say no repeatedly. Nearly every time they did so, the Ministry gave way".

Although Whittle never gave up trying, the inescapable fact emerged, during the autumn of 1940, that he was never going to be given control of his brainchild. Lord Kings Norton (Roxbee Cox), when looking back, thought the notion that Whittle was incapable of controlling his own production was very doubtful. In 1987 he said, "Everybody needs help, of course, but with the right help, I think that Whittle could have produced Whittle engines". In this respect, Whittle's workshop experience was so extensive and wide-ranging that his knowledge of manufacturing techniques was unrivalled by any engineer or technician of the other two firms or by anyone in the Ministry itself. There must, therefore, have been reasons, which one can only surmise after so many years, for depriving him of his natural inheritance.

Primarily, Whittle was governed by the Establishment. Policy decisions were usually the outcome of collective thinking involving the AM, MAP, Treasury, senior civil servants, and scientific advisors concerned with the aviation industry. Tedder and Freeman, Whittle's bosses, were part of that machinery and did not act without consultation on major issues.

Tedder was a distinguished officer far removed in character from the commercially minded Sporborg and Wilks; but, like Whittle, he was naive where commercial greed was concerned. Moreover, he was not a professional engineer, and was obliged to rely on civil servants in the Ministry for advice. Although very intelligent and knowledgeable, he was too much of a gentleman to believe that anyone could put their commercial greed before the interests of the nation in time of war.

Tedder, who had backed Whittle throughout, would undoubtedly have given him his Command; but it was not politic for him so to do — the inference being that it would be distasteful to both BTH and Rover! Tedder was in a powerful position and a strong character, so the decision not to give Whittle full authority revealed the strength of the antagonism within the Establishment and the industry.

Such antagonism was to be expected, because Whittle led the world in his thinking, which naturally evoked the full blast of criticism from the cynics, and from those who were incapable of understanding his genius. The aviation industry, which Whittle was about to revolutionize, was traditional in outlook, conservative by nature, and deeply suspicious of young men like Whittle who, in their opinion, were "too clever by half". Sir Stanley Hooker, talking of his own experience with Rolls-Royce remarked that: "I could never hope to become an accepted designer, because it takes 20 years of dedicated application to become that".

The fact that Whittle was a relatively junior serving officer categorized his status in the eyes of some of the disbelievers, who automatically dismissed Power Jets as small fry. But in March 1940, when Whittle's jet engine was included in a list of potential war-winning devices and given corresponding priority, it suddenly dawned on them that he really had something, and those with vested interests became apprehensive.

D. R. Pye, Director of Scientific Research, and his henchman Tweedie were experts in conventional piston engines. Apart from aero-engine superchargers, neither was familiar with turbine theory, and so, perhaps, subconsciously at least, they dreaded the day when their specialist knowledge would go on the scrap heap. They and their fellows in the Directorate of Engine Development might be said to have had an intellectual vested interest opposing anything which might undermine their status as experts.

Tweedie of course, had been the spokesman for the Ministry in the flat rejection of Whittle's invention in 1929 and the continued coolness thereafter. He must have been conscious that he was more responsible than any other individual (except, perhaps, A. A. Griffith) for delaying the turbojet by at least a crucial six years. Unfortunately for Power Jets, Tweedie had been, and continued to be, the Ministry spokesman on the day-to-day development at Ladywood, and no additional expenditure under Ministry contracts was possible without Tweedie's approval. It is very probable for obvious psychological reasons that Tweedie could not help allowing resentment to colour his attitude and actions towards Whittle. He appeared to be personally responsible for the parsimonious treatment of Power Jets, and, in Whittle's eyes, was a drag on progress and an influence on Ministry policy out of proportion to his status.

During the latter part of 1940, some six months before the first flight of his engine in the E.28, Whittle, by virtue of his genius, had been thrust into the aviation power game which was not his style. In the first place, he was not a political animal, had no time for small talk, and lacked commercial experience — all he wanted was sufficient backing to allow him to get on with the job. He wasn't concerned with image building and even begrudged the time, which he could ill afford, that he had to spend with visiting officials. His overriding objective in life was to give Britain jet fighters as quickly as possible and nothing else mattered. In this respect, he had something in common with R. J. Mitchell[1] who had regarded the creation of his Spitfire in much the same way, knowing that it was going to be a race against time.

Such dedication in a man sets him apart from others, and this was one of the reasons why Whittle had continual problems with BTH and Rover. BTH's main concern was in the design and

---

[1]R. J. Mitchell — designer of the Spitfire fighter.

manufacture of industrial steam turbines, and Rover were occupied in manufacturing vehicles (which had been halted in favour of war production) and in sub-contract work, including the production and repair of Bristol aircooled piston aero engines. Both companies' work on the turbojet project disturbed their pattern of profitable business and this naturally resulted in friction and resentment, which has already been described in some detail.

Whittle should, of course, have been given total control of his project from the outset, as part of Ministry policy. The Air Ministry had agreed that he should control the design work but did not implement this in its entirety, leaving him in an invidious position which prompted argument and bickering between the parties concerned. This failure on the Air Ministry's part enabled BTH and Rover to exploit the situation to their advantage. They were both established private commercial companies with a profit motif and in the longer term they hoped, by amending Whittle's designs, to market their own jet engines.

It was a messy situation resulting from a naive policy for which Tedder must, at least, take some of the blame. His attempts to paper over the cracks failed to achieve mutual co-operation between the firms concerned and he allowed the situation to drift. Unlike Power Jets, BTH and Rover were not wholly dependent on Air Ministry contracts and so Tedder had more clout with Power Jets than the other two companies. Thus, Whittle was often made to toe the line while the others, in many respects, were allowed more freedom without recrimination.

*   *   *

In October 1940, after victory in the Battle of Britain, the decision was taken to go ahead with the production of the twin-engined F.9/40 jet fighter project. The rate of production to be planned for was 80 airframes and 160 engines per month, which meant considerable expansion for those involved.

During the months of November and December 1940, Power Jets' staff was increased by 53 personnel, but this growth was only a small proportion of the total expansion. The work of Power Jets, Gloster, BTH, Rover and Vauxhall was supplemented by ancillary work in other places. Lucas were increasing their efforts on combustion development. The firm of Ransome & Marles and the National Physical Laboratory had started work on bearing tests. The Ricardo Engineering Co were assisting Power Jets on certain problems, the Mond Nickel Co and Firth Vickers were working to produce improved materials for turbine blade and combustion chamber parts. The RAE were doing wind-tunnel tests for Gloster and advising and assisting Power Jets in sundry ways.

The Ministry's policy was, at least, not lacking in boldness, and rather surprising in view of the fact that certain high officials believed that the aeroplane would be unstable with this novel form of propulsion. It was also courageous, bearing in mind that, though the W.1X was nearing completion, Whittle's battered experimental engine was still the only engine running under its own power and no flight tests had yet been made.

The general expansion, following the decision to go ahead with the jet fighter project, put increased pressure on Power Jets and a very large proportion of the effort of their design and drawing-office staff was devoted to providing information for other firms. This seriously affected the amount of work they were able to do on direct development themselves. Not only that, but they were inundated with visitors who naturally wanted Whittle's time: "I don't think the Ministry officials concerned had any conception of the load that was imposed on me by these numerous visits. Each one would mean the loss of at least half a day, and each would mean a tedious repetition of things I had said over and over again ad nauseum"!

But there was one visit which Whittle would never forget — that of Air Chief Marshal Sir Hugh (later Lord) Dowding — Commander-in-Chief, Fighter Command, during the Battle of Britain. Whittle felt uneasy before 'Stuffy' arrived because certain previous encounters with him were associated with trouble.

"I felt sure that something was bound to go wrong. It did. While the experimental engine was running, I took him round the outside of the test houses. It was impossible to speak because of the noise. As we stood about three yards away from where the jet nozzle protruded through an aperture in the test-house wall, I pointed to the nozzle, meaning to imply 'That's the business end of the engine'.

"He misunderstood my gesture and, before I could stop him, walked rapidly in the direction indicated. Suddenly a mighty invisible force wrenched open his raincoat and sent him staggering across the concrete — his brass hat rolling away on to the grass. I stood petrified with horror, and when Sir Hugh recovered himself, apparently unhurt, I could scarcely move and certainly could not speak".

Fortunately, someone had seen the incident through an observation window and shut the engine down. Sir Hugh, pardonably terse, asked the horrified Whittle if he wasn't going to show him something, so Whittle dumbly led the way into the test house. Only those in the Service would really understand what a junior Wing Commander felt like when he nearly blew an Air Chief Marshal, of great repute, into the next county.

Until that moment Whittle had not realised how deceptively invisible the jet was to a stranger: "There was no trace of smoke or anything else to show the presence of the powerful blast, though several yards down-wind it was more obvious because of the haze of foundry sand raised from the ground and the waving trees in the hedgerow".

By lunch-time, however, Dowding had recovered his good temper sufficiently to joke about the incident, and Whittle thanked his lucky stars that Stuffy had escaped so lightly!

Chapter 12
The First Flight –
15 May 1941

The honourable career of Whittle's first experimental jet engine, the WU, ended on 22 February 1941 — nearly four years after its first run — when it was damaged beyond repair by a failure of the rim of the turbine wheel.

It ended its career in glorious fashion. During the last seven weeks of its life it did approximately 100 hours of running, making a total of just under 170 hours from the completion of its second reconstruction in October 1938. The two most noteworthy runs were one of a little over 8 hours at 14,500 rpm, and one of just over 10 hours at 14,000 rpm.

Although these speeds corresponded to cruising conditions only, this remarkable performance by the old warhorse had a major psychological effect on many of the people concerned. It came at an opportune time. Power Jets already had the W.1X and were making substantial progress with it, despite two or three bearing failures. The W.1 was received from BTH in February 1941 as a group of sub assemblies, but, not wishing to risk it until they had eliminated all the snags by experience with the W.1X, Whittle refrained from putting it on test for the time being. However, it did not stand idle as it was sent to Gloster as a mock-up to complete the installation arrangements in the E.28 airframe.

The Gloster/Whittle E.28/39 was completed at the beginning of April 1941, and as the W.1 had not yet run it was decided to use the W.1X for the taxiing trials. All the initial construction of the two prototype E.28s had been carried out in the experimental shop at Brockworth, a few miles to the south-east of Gloucester. But, because of the threat of renewed large-scale bombing, the prototype to be ready first was discretely moved to a garage in Cheltenham previously occupied by Regent Motors.

In this garage, protected by an armed policeman, a small band of craftsmen fitted the various pieces together. Secrecy was vital, and it was surprisingly good. Only those directly concerned with the machine had any idea that it was being built. On 7 April 1941, the E.28 Pioneer, powered by Whittle's W.1X. engine — which had been built out of unairworthy parts and was suitable for taxiing trials only — was handed over to the pilot for test.

Gloster's Chief Test Pilot was P. E. G. (Gerry) Sayer, who had visited Lutterworth on a few occasions to familiarise himself with the engine controls and to get some idea of the engine characteristics. The late John Grierson, an outstanding jet test pilot himself, described Gerry as being a particularly fine type of chief test pilot, who combined a high degree of personal charm and leadership with an unequalled skill in handling an aeroplane. He had known Whittle many years.

On that day of 7 April, Whittle and Cheshire went down to Gloster's airfield at Brockworth. Walker and others from Power Jets were already there. Whittle, who was determined to climb into the cockpit and do some taxiing trials himself, recorded events:

"The trials began that evening but there was little done because the light was fading by the time the aeroplane was ready. We had set the throttle stop to limit the engine speed to 13,000 rpm. The grass aerodrome was rather soggy from rain so that it required 12,000 rpm before the aeroplane would start moving and at 13,000 rpm it would only move at about 20 mph.

The look of disappointment on Gerry Sayer's face was obvious. He evidently thought the engine would never develop enough 'urge' to get the aeroplane off the ground. We were not worried, because we knew how rapidly the thrust increased at the upper end of the engine speed range. I assured Gerry that with increased engine speed he would find things very different. He did not look convinced.

The next morning we removed the throttle stop and adjusted the relief valve in the fuel line to give a maximum engine speed of 15,000 rpm. With this limit I made a few taxiing runs in which I reached a maximum speed of about 60 mph. It was a thrilling experience for more reasons than one. It was clear that we should not be short of thrust when we used the permissible maximum of 16,000 rpm. Also the complete absence of vibration, the big reduction in noise as compared with conventional aircraft, the excellent view from the cockpit, and the simplicity of controls, all added up to an impressive combination of characteristics. I felt that the engine instruments left something to be desired, but otherwise, so far as one could judge from a mere taxiing run, everything seemed very satisfactory indeed.

Sayer then did a little taxiing with the same limit on engine speed.

After lunch we increased the engine speed limit to 16,000. With this setting, Sayer taxied off to the downwind edge of the airfield. This action caused us to suspect that he intended to do more than merely trundle over the grass, though we had warned him that the engine was thoroughly unairworthy. It had never been intended for flight in the first place, and it had had a number of misadventures on the test bench which had rendered it even less fit to fly than when first built.

Sayer turned into wind, and increased the engine speed to the maximum permitted while holding the aeroplane back with the brakes. He then released the brakes and rapidly gained speed. We saw his elevators go up in an effort to get the tail down. He was a little too successful in this, because the tail 'blister' struck the ground and the aeroplane pitched forward on to its nosewheel again. Nevertheless, a second or two later it left the ground and, after being airborne for about 200 yards, landed. Sayer taxied back and repeated the performance twice more, the third take-off being very clean and smooth. Each time the airborne distance was 200-300 yards.

These proceedings must have caused very great astonishment to many people who could not help but see the aeroplane but who, up to that moment, had had no knowledge of it. One spectator was an American mechanic, working on the wing of an RAF Stirling bomber. He nearly fell off in surprise". More significant was the fact that the E.28 flew dead straight. Many experts had predicted it would do almost everything except this!

Sayer's pilot notes regarding engine performance were as follows:

"The engine is very smooth indeed, and no vibration was observed in the pilot's cockpit.

"The throttle control, however, is too coarse, a large increase in engine revolutions being obtained with very little forward movement of the throttle lever.

. . . the engine ran very well indeed throughout the taxiing trials".

Whittle never had any doubts about the outcome of the Brockworth trials. He knew that his engine would perform, and that Gloster Aircraft would provide a good machine. The fact that he himself had actually been propelled to the point of becoming airborne by his brain-child never crossed his mind. He was too pre-occupied with more pressing matters, and there was much to be done before the E.28 could prove his turbojet in sustained flight.

After the taxiing trials, the machine was returned to another garage in Cheltenham which Gloster had taken over as a dispersal. A new nosewheel leg giving longer travel was fitted, and work began on the retracting mechanism of the undercarriage, which had not been tested before the taxiing trials. Dowty Equipment made the undercarriage, which had their 'knee-action' levered-suspension units for the main wheels but one of conventional type for the nosewheel. There being no hydraulic pump on Whittle's W.1 engine, retraction was effected by means of an hydraulic accumulator. Before each flight this was charged up to 1,500 lb per square inch by a hand-pump in the cockpit. Then, when the undercarriage was selected up, the retraction was brought about automatically by the accumulator, without the need for any further pumping by the pilot. As an emergency measure, there was a compressed-air system, worked off a bottle, for 'blowing' the undercarriage down should a failure occur in the hydraulics. The flaps were operated hydraulically, direct from a hand pump.

Three days after the taxiing trials the W.1 ran for the first time. The first test had been delayed pending the completion of modifications dictated by the experience with the W.1X. This experience proved invaluable, because the W.1 went through its acceptance test, and its 25 hours' special category test without any hitch whatever. The engine was shipped for installation in the aeroplane at the beginning of May. For the purpose of the flight trials the Ministry had ruled that it was to be limited to a maximum speed of 16,500 rpm, at which the thrust was 860 lb (as compared with the full design thrust of 1,240 lb at 17,750 rpm). However, it had been run up once to 17,000 rpm, at which speed the thrust was 1,000 lb. It was cleared for ten hours' flight testing by the MAP.

It had been decided that the E.28 would make its maiden flight from RAF Cranwell. Gloster's aerodrome at Brockworth was considered to be unsuitable, because it was far too small, with no runways, and surrounded by hills, whereas Cranwell had a long runway with clear approaches amid flat open countryside. Also, it was easier to preserve secrecy out in rural Lincolnshire rather than in the crowded Gloucester-Cheltenham area surrounding Brockworth.

Cranwell was a particularly appropriate choice because it was there, as a cadet, that Whittle had written the thesis which became the starting point of his subsequent work on jet propulsion. It had taken him thirteen years to come full circle, back to Cranwell, with his turbojet dream at last a reality.

He went up to Cranwell with D. G. Tobin, the Resident Technical Officer at Power Jets, on the evening of 13 May 1941. They expected the flight trials to begin on the 14th. The weather on that day was not good enough for a first flight; so Whittle borrowed an Avro Tutor to blow out the cobwebs. He had not flown for nearly two years, and was pleased to find himself completely at home up there as though he had been flying regularly.

On the morning of the next day, 15 May, the weather was still quite unfit for test flying, and so he returned to Lutterworth: "The truth is that my mind was so firmly fixed on the target of getting W.2B-powered Meteors into production that the E.28 had come to seem comparatively unimportant relative to this aim". But, later on, when he saw the weather improving he hurried back to Cranwell, where he could see patches of blue sky and noted that the cloud base had lifted considerably.

At 7.35 pm Gerry Sayer began taxiing out to the eastern end of the long runway. Whittle and some of his Power Jets associates had gone by car to a point about 400 yards along the runway. At about 7.40 pm Sayer was completing his final checks prior to take-off. He made sure that the cockpit hood was fully opened; set the elevator trimmer to give a slightly forward load on the control column, and checked that the flaps were retracted before opening up the engine against the brakes.

The wind from the west was light and bitterly cold, as Gerry Sayer released the brakes and the little E.28 accelerated rapidly as, using the steerable nosewheel, he held her straight along the runway heading towards the open fields in the line of flight towards Leadenham. There was little tendency to swing, and after a run of five to six hundred yards he eased her airborne, purely on the feel of the elevators.

She looked a neat, beautiful little aeroplane climbing slowly up to 1,000 feet. Then Sayer retracted the undercarriage and, trailing a faint wisp of smoke, she disappeared from view behind cloud banks. For several minutes, all that the spectators could hear was the distant smooth roar of the engine. Then she came in sight again as Sayer made a wide circuit preparatory to landing. As he came in, it was obvious that he had complete confidence in the aeroplane. He approached the runway in a series of quite steep gliding turns as though he had flown the machine for hundreds of hours. Those watching who were pilots sensed that Sayer felt completely at home as he made a perfect landing, slightly on the main wheels first, before dropping gently forward on to the nosewheel. The first flight had lasted 17 minutes.

Whittle found it difficult to describe his emotions during the flight: "I was very tense, not so much because of any fears about the engine, but because this was a machine making its first flight. I think I would have felt the same if it had been an aeroplane with a conventional power plant making its first flight. I do not remember, but I am told that shortly after take-off, someone [thought to have been Johnson] slapped me on the back and said, 'Frank, it flies!' and that my curt response in the tension of the moment was: 'Well, that was what it was bloody-well designed to do, wasn't it?' ".

Before Gerry Sayer had time to get out of his cockpit, Frank Whittle and George Carter (Gloster's Chief Designer) rushed up to shake his hand and offer their congratulations. It was a historic moment for British aviation. Yet, despite frantic efforts by Johnson, they had failed to persuade the Ministry to send a professional crew to Cranwell to film the event and indeed, Tobin was the only MAP representative present. The only film taken was an unauthorized unofficial one made with a hand camera which turned out to be a very disjointed and amateurish effort. So, the first flight of the E.28 Pioneer, which was to change the face of the aviation industry and sign the death warrant of conventional power plants, was never properly recorded, either photographically or as a detailed document.

Up to that moment nobody had thought of a celebration and it was too late in the evening to make special arrangements. But somehow or another, the staff of the Officers' Mess managed to produce the necessaries for a very pleasant impromptu party. RAF Cranwell was then commanded by Air Commodore (Daddy) Probyn, who had previously known Whittle well. Probyn took a keen interest in the E.28 and did everything possible to help Power Jets, including the provision of accommodation on the station.

With various interruptions due to weather, but no delays for any other reason, the flight trials continued for the next twelve days, and the ten hours' flying for which the engine had been cleared were duly completed in 17 flights. There was no trouble whatever with either the aeroplane or the radical engine. The tests were, in fact, so successful that jet propelled flying appeared to be almost too easy. It was not even necessary to inspect the engine. This last caused particular astonishment to the Gloster crew. In their experience it was usual for the engine mechanics to take off the cowlings immediately after a test flight for a thorough engine inspection. They were therefore dumbfounded when, as soon as the E.28 had taxied into the hangar after its first flight, the Power Jets' crew, in effect, dusted their hands and disappeared — they knew that all was well from the smooth note of the engine! This first E.28, in fact, continued as a flying test bed for a series of engines throughout the war, until it ended up honourably in the Science Museum.

The top speed reached with the W.1 was 370 mph in level flight at 25,000 feet — above the then top speed of the Spitfire. It was achieved by a temporary increase of rating of the engine up to 17,000 rpm, corresponding to the test bench thrust of 1,000 lb. After test results had been more carefully analysed by Gloster and the RAE, it was concluded that the performance of the E.28 was better than had been predicted. Possibly because the high-velocity propelling jet had a beneficial effect on the airflow over the rear end of the fuselage, thus slightly reducing drag — a factor which had not been taken into account in performance estimates.

The fact that the E.28 Pioneer had exceeded expectations reflected the very highest credit on all those involved in the project. At this time it was a very rare thing indeed for the performance of a new type of aeroplane to exceed design estimates. But this was only part of the outcome of the E.28's success. Whittle — who had been the first man to get a turbojet running — had thrust Britain forward into the Jet Age and stood the aviation industry on its head, though it was to be some time before this was generally accepted.

It was natural that such performance from a completely novel type of engine should make a radical change in the attitudes and thinking of nearly everyone concerned in aviation engineering. The electric news from Cranwell galvanised the Establishment, and on 21 May 1941 a large number of officials, headed by Sir Archibald Sinclair the Secretary of State for Air, arrived by road and air to watch a demonstration flight. Gerry Sayer brought gasps from the uninitiated onlookers with a high-speed run downwind, when the strange whistling roar of the propellerless engine rivetted their attention as they watched the E.28 pulling up into a steep climbing turn and shoot skywards. The absence of a propeller was a source of amazement, and few of those privileged to see Sayer could have had any doubts that they had witnessed the beginning of a new chapter in aviation history. Fortunately, the weather held off just long enough for the flight. Almost at the instant that Sayer landed, it began to pour with rain.

There were, of course, the most stringent security precautions. The aeroplane was housed in a hangar at the extreme western end of the south aerodrome, and was guarded day and night by Gloster's security police. Nobody, except those holding special passes, was allowed within several hundred yards of the hangar. All the RAF personnel at Cranwell were naturally taking a lively interest in the proceedings, and it was impossible to conceal entirely what was going on.

One of two officers watching the E.28 take off was heard to ask, "How the hell does that thing work?" His companion replied, "Oh, it's easy, old boy, it just sucks itself along like a Hoover". Dan Walker of Power Jets was amused to hear one officer — not knowing that Walker was one of the engineers intimately concerned — assure everybody in his immediate vicinity that the power plant was a Rolls-Royce Merlin engine driving a small four-bladed propeller inside the fuselage. He stated positively that he had seen it!

One of the more amusing stories about the impact made by the E.28 on the uninitiated came from the Officers' Mess. One officer at least was greatly disturbed at what he had seen and sat with a puzzled frown. When asked what was troubling him, he replied that he had seen a strange aeroplane going like a bat out of hell and there was something odd about it, but he could not think what it was. After a pause, he said, "My God! chaps, I must be going round the bend — it hadn't got a propeller!"

*   *   *

In Britain, the success of the E.28's flight tests induced the Government to lay plans for quantity production of the W.2B as the power plant for the Meteor fighter. At a meeting at the MAP presided over by Tizard, it was decided that the production target was to be a total of 1,200 engines and 500 aircraft — these to begin to appear in June and July of 1942. It was estimated that there was a chance of completing the 500 aircraft by the spring of 1943.

About this time in late May/June 1941, Power Jets were experiencing surging problems with the W.1A and W.2 engines — the forerunners to the W.2B, which was scheduled for quantity production. Surging is an intermittent reverse flow in the compressor which occurs if the mass of air flowing into it is below a certain critical value. When it occurs in a jet engine there are a series of fearsome bangs. The W.2B was still on the drawing board, and Whittle was highly conscious that a great deal of development work would be necessary before it was fit for such production.

In a letter to Tizard on 27 May 1941 he expressed his uneasiness:

"I want to say with the greatest possible emphasis that what is now needed is the maximum possible concentration of effort on the development work at Lutterworth for the next two or three months, and that anything which detracts from this concentration should be cut out until our primary object is attained, i.e. the development of the W.2B up to the point when it can safely be launched into production.

"The responsibility that rests on my shoulders is very heavy indeed. We are faced with two alternatives — either we place a powerful weapon in the hands of the Royal Air Force or, if we fail to get our results in time, we have falsely raised hopes and caused action to be taken which may deprive the Royal Air Force of hundreds of aeroplanes that it badly needs. Therefore I say that we must be given every help in the task and be kept from all unnecessary strain or else I must ask to be relieved of the responsibility.

"Everything now turns on getting the test bench results and we have not got them yet, and we shall not succeed in getting them in time unless the effort is as intense as I have indicated above.

"I feel confident that the job can be done in the end, but that is not enough, it has to be within the next two or three months, and nothing that Rover's or the BTH or anybody else tries to do, starting virtually from scratch, can really affect the development within that time.

"What is required is concentration of effort on those features of the W.2B which are in doubt, rather than the frittering away of energy on the design and making of alternative structure, gearboxes, fuel systems etc, etc, such as is going on in the BTH and the Rover Co, all of which will be a costly waste if nobody succeeds in making a turbine which will do its job.

"We know the gearbox works, we know the fuel system works, we can feel fairly confident of the combustion chambers and blower, but there is grave doubt about the turbine end at present, and by far the greater part of the total effort should be directed to solving that problem. The BTH can help immensely, by making a series of alternative wheels for several W.2Bs (to Power Jets' drawings), otherwise made by the Rover Co, with the assistance of the Coventry Gauge and Tool Co.

"Failing this, it is my duty to say that I cannot guarantee success before the end of the year".

This powerful letter had little effect, and nothing was done to take the pressure off Whittle and help him overcome his problems. On the contrary, there were many signs that the Ministry intended to place even greater reliance on the Rover Company — despite the successful flight trials which could scarcely have been a more forceful demonstration of Power Jets' capabilities.

Following a visit to Rover's factory at Barnoldswick, near Clitheroe, Dr Hawthorne of Power Jets reported that Maurice Wilks had shown him a tentative layout of a unit comprising a two-stage single-sided compressor arrangement followed by a 30-inch straight-through combustion chamber and turbine wheel. Hawthorne also said that the establishment seemed to be primarily devoted to development and testing, with the main engine building work being sub-contracted. It appeared to him that Waterloo Mill was a Rover version of the Power Jets' set-up, with probably more facilities for production in the offing.

Hawthorne's report thus confirmed that Rover were putting a very elastic interpretation indeed on their function of 'development for production', and that they intended to embark on all aspects of development.

This revelation naturally incensed Whittle, but he was too preoccupied at the time to do much about it. On 4 July 1941 Whyte resigned as Chairman and Managing Director of Power Jets. Whittle appointed Tinling as Chairman, and he and Williams became joint managing directors. Whyte's resignation was really the culmination of a long period of differences of opinion with Whittle, but Whyte did not sever his ties and remained as a member of the Board.

Shortly after the success of the E.28 flight trials it was hardly surprising that some of those whose noses had been put out of joint began a campaign of harmful propaganda. Some of this was directed at Whittle himself, and it was soon being bandied about that he was an awkward and difficult man to get on with. So much so that, when Whittle was about to meet certain people for the first time, he found that they had all kinds of preconceived ideas about him.

The late Sir Stanley Hooker of Rolls-Royce refuted any such suggestion saying that: "In the more than 40 years that I have known him, we have never had a disagreement. Although Rolls-Royce were destined to take his engine away from him, I personally have never had anything but encouragement and generous help from him. Naturally, after the great struggle and frustrations he had in getting his ideas and engine accepted, he resented the criticisms of those who were now climbing on to his bandwagon. There were plenty of such people, and plenty of criticism when his W.2 ran into such difficulties".

Criticism, however, was not confined to Whittle himself, and stories began circulating that the fuel consumption during the flight trials had been far too high. This propaganda to discredit the jet engine began to have an effect at the Ministry. Both Bulman, the Director of Engine Development, and Roxbee Cox expressed their concern, particularly as sub-contractors, including Rover, were talking about it.

Fortunately, Whittle was able to cite some test results recently achieved with the W.1A, which proved that the fuel consumption was not more than 8 per cent higher than the predicted value, and was probably less.

When Constant of the RAE saw the test results he was very impressed, and urged Whittle to report on them as soon as possible, so that they could be used as a counterblast to some of the nonsense being peddled around. It was an uplift for Whittle, at that particular time, to have someone of Constant's intellectual stature support him against the conniving activities of those who were spreading false rumour and gossip.

Constant, whose association with Dr A. A. Griffith in the RAE team, actually put him in the rival camp, had a strange personality. Whittle described him as being tall and slim, taciturn and unemotional: "In meetings he would calmly smoke his pipe and remain silent, but when he did speak it was always very much to the point — often asking a very incisive question. When I first knew him he was a Communist, but, I think, a very academic one. I never heard him parade his views, and I am sure they never affected his loyalty. He had quite a good presence yet he was a bachelor and, as far as I could tell, had little or no interest in women. But he was one of the very few of the more influential individuals concerned who supported me during the severe technical and other controversies. He was that rare thing — an intellectually honest man".

While Whittle was positive about Constant's fairness and his support, others at Power Jets thought the opposite, although they did not have Whittle's opportunities for judging the man. They felt that Constant sat on the fence and pursued his own interests whenever it suited him. However, there were no such doubts in the Power Jets camp about such people as Bulman and his deputy Ross.

The period from June 1941 and for some months thereafter was a critical time for Whittle, who was grappling with major development problems. Bulman, who had never been disposed towards Whittle's revolutionary engine project, was involved at the very heart of the arguments and controversies. He had been Director of Engine Production since 1939 and as such wielded a very powerful influence over Whittle's affairs.

Before becoming a civil servant, Bulman had been a Major in the Royal Flying Corps and was a smallish, sturdy, clean-shaven and tough character with a military air. Wedded to piston engines and allied to conventional manufacturers, he had adopted a cynical and uncompromising attitude towards Power Jets from the outset. Whittle's meticulous diary of events shows quite clearly that Bulman and his deputy Major Ross sided with Rover and BTH on almost every occasion.

With hindsight, it was a tragedy that MAP allowed relations between Power Jets and the Rover Company to ferment and deteriorate, particularly at this time in mid-1941 when plans were being formulated for the production of the Meteor — Britain's first jet fighter. Good relations between Power Jets, Rover and BTH were vital to ensure that no time was lost in giving the RAF jet aircraft. But such a relationship depended upon Ministry policy being fairly and firmly implemented, allowing Whittle to control design and development and the other two companies to amend his designs only for production reasons. In the event, Bulman allowed Rover to meddle with Whittle's designs without prior consultation or consent, and failed to give Whittle back-up when he most needed it.

There were two factors which should have dominated Ministry thinking and action during 1941. The first was the race against time to provide operational jet aircraft to counter German developments in that direction. Intelligence sources had revealed that it was likely to be a very close and highly significant race. Germany had six teams working on jet engines, had flown test-beds, had one jet-powered aircraft, were about to fly the He 280 and Me 262, and had half-a-dozen other projects in hand. Britain knew nothing of this.

The other factor was Whittle himself, who — alone in Britain — was the key figure in winning this race. That the MAP should have taken the pressure off him, given him full support and allowed him to get on with the job has previously been discussed. The fact that they did not do this is part of history, and resulted in severe confusion and delays which were seriously to jeopardise the Meteor production programme and place an intolerable and ceaseless burden upon Whittle.

Chapter 13
The Bandwagon

The principal aero-engine firms were Rolls-Royce, Armstrong Siddeley (a member of the Hawker Siddeley group), Napier, the Bristol Aeroplane Company, and the de Havilland Engine Co. With the exception of Napier, all these firms became interested in aircraft gas turbines during 1941.

The late Lord Hives, Chairman and Managing Director of Rolls-Royce, first met Whittle in 1940 when the Battle of Britain was carving up the skies over southern England. At Stanley Hooker's instigation, he visited Lutterworth with Hooker to see Whittle's new engine. This proved to be a historic meeting, which ultimately put Rolls-Royce into a commanding position in the field of aviation gas turbines.

The visit by Hives and Hooker followed a visit by Hooker and Constant. When Hooker reported back to Hives the latter asked, "What power does it produce?" Hooker replied, "About 1,000 pounds of thrust". Hooker went away and did some slide rule pushing and then returned to Hives, "Do you know what the thrust of a Merlin in a Spitfire is at 350 mph?" he asked, "No", said Hives, "How much?" "1,000 pounds" said Hooker. Hives at once arranged for an early visit to Lutterworth!

Before this, Rolls-Royce had been working on a turbojet scheme to the design of Dr A. A. Griffith. This was a very ingenious but much more complex arrangement than anything Whittle was doing, and still in an embryo stage.

Whittle personally conducted Hives around his meagre facilities and showed Power Jets' one and only engine, and talked at length about his progress and ambitions. Hooker records that at the end of the tour Hives turned to Whittle and said: "I don't see many engines. What is holding you up?"

Whittle then explained his difficulties in getting certain components made, whereupon Hives said in his typical broadminded way, "Send us the drawings to Derby, and we will make them for you". He said nothing about payment. Whittle vividly remembers that, during this visit, he stressed the great simplicity of his engine. Hives drily commented, "We'll soon design the bloody simplicity out of it!"

Thus, the Derby Experimental Shop began making turbine blades, gearcases and other components for Whittle's programme which opened up a fruitful technical co-operation between the two companies. Whittle had a great deal more to fear from Rolls-Royce, from a commercial point of view, than he did from Rover who were beginners, but there was no reserve whatever on the part of Power Jets in such technical collaboration. Whittle explained that: "this was based on our respect for their outstanding engineering ability, particularly in the field in which we were engaged. I believe that this respect was mutual".

When Whittle was having surging problems with his engine there was no test rig in Britain with sufficient power to test his compressor. Later, Rolls-Royce built one at Derby using a 2,000 hp Vulture piston engine and a step-up gear made by putting two Merlin propeller reduction gears in series and driving them backwards, to achieve the 16,500 rpm required by Whittle's W.2 compressor. The late Sir Stanley Hooker, a leading expert in supercharger design, remembered noting, with envy and admiration, that Whittle's compressor had an efficiency of 79 per cent, within 1 per cent of Whittle's theoretical figure!

The de Havilland Engine Co had also been drawn into jet engine development by Sir Henry Tizard after the trial flights of the E.28. Major F. B. Halford, their Chief Engineer, had already had some association with the project as an adviser to Vauxhall Motors before that firm dropped out. The de Havilland proposals were beginning to take definite form at the end of June 1941. They were embarking on the design of a jet engine and of an aeroplane to be powered by it — this was the birth of the Goblin-engined Vampire. The engine, originally known as the H.1, was to be much larger and more powerful than Whittle's W.2B and was to be designed for a thrust of upwards of 2,700 lb. It differed from Whittle's design in that it had a single-sided centrifugal compresser and straight through combustion chambers. Oddly enough it was more like Whittle's 1930 concept as depicted in his first patent than were Whittle's own designs.

Once more Power Jets was expected to co-operate fully and supply all the necessary information, which placed a heavy burden on Whittle and his team who had their own problems and were grossly overloaded. Whittle had asked the MAP on several occasions for additional help, but to no effect. However, most of the information required by de Havilland reached them via the RAE, who were closely in touch with both Power Jets and Halford. In addition, Power Jets gave more positive direct assistance, particularly on combustion-chamber design and testing.

Whittle had strong reservations about what he regarded as another diversion of effort: "This was based on our view that nothing should distract us from the task of getting the Meteor powered by W.2Bs into production at the earliest possible moment. I did not believe that any major departures in engine design could lead to an engine which would be in production in time for the war. On the contrary, the additional competition for sub-contract capacity and material supplies was likely to put back the date at which the Meteor would become operational".

In the event, Whittle proved to be right in that Halford's Goblin-engined Vampire never quite became operational during the war, nevertheless it became a very fine aeroplane. But, ironically, because Rover's devious conduct delayed Whittle's W.2B, it was Halford's H.1 engine which powered the first flight of the Meteor on 5 March 1943.

The other two firms who became involved in aero gas turbines were Armstrong Siddeley and Bristol. Armstrong Siddeley initially did project work on a rather complex scheme proposed by an engineer named Heppner. However, this did not proceed beyond the paper stage, and was subsequently dropped.

Certain contacts between Power Jets and the late Sir Roy Fedden and F. M. Owner of the Bristol Aeroplane Company led to proposals for combining jet engines and piston engines, but these were subsequently dropped and Bristol concentrated on the development of propeller turbines.

Metropolitan-Vickers were also involved in the business, working on the RAE-Metrovick F.2 jet with an axial-flow compresser. This was the final outcome of the years of effort by Griffith and Constant.

Now that many firms, all of whom were potentially dangerous competitors, were entering the aircraft gas turbine field, Power Jets' chances of survival were becoming increasingly slim. What, in more normal times, would have been vital trade secrets had been freely supplied to possible future rivals. The whole of the equipment operated by Power Jets was the property of the State. The company's only tangible assets were its patent rights, and such protection that these afforded applied only to non-Government contracts of which there were none!

From time to time there had been suggestions that Power Jets should become partly or wholly Government owned, which would have provided the protection they needed. At the time of the flight trials and thereafter, Tizard repeatedly argued that the sums of public money spent on Power Jets could not be justified unless the Government holding was substantially increased. He and others seemed blind to the fact that even larger sums were being allocated to Rover and BTH.

The Treasury, however, turned down Tizard's proposal on broad grounds of public policy, although Ministry officials, including Roxbee Cox, favoured the plan. Finally, on 10 September 1941, in a further attempt to clear up the matter, Tinling wrote a long and very carefully considered letter to the Minister of Aircraft Production setting out in detail the difficulties of the Company's position as a consequence of Ministry policy, and some broad principles for consideration.

In effect, Tinling was seeking something more specific than Tedder's assurance of a moral obligation to protect the Company.

After a lapse of over two months, the Ministry replied in a long letter (dated 24 November 1941) in which not one of the points of principle which Tinling had sought to have recognised was conceded. Indeed, if anything, it seemed to represent a retreat from Tedder's undertaking, because of the following:

"The Company is being financed from public funds and this will continue so long as it is deemed necessary. It is impossible for the Minister to give any undertaking in this respect beyond what may be contained in current contracts".

The letter contained an important admission that while the Ministry had forced Power Jets to disclose all its technology, they had been too weak to make other firms toe the line. The relevant section read:

"In so far as information or knowledge has been divulged which is not the subject of a patent the position is more difficult. The Company is aware of the attempts made by the Department to secure certain undertakings from third parties and the lack of success attending these efforts. The Minister is not unsympathetic to the Company's representations although the

Company was bound to make disclosure. It is not possible at this stage for the Minister to define the Department's attitude to this question more closely than to say that the Department would not be an assenting party to the exploitation for commercial purposes by third parties of information obtained from the Company for military purposes and not otherwise procurable. The Minister considers that this problem must be left for consideration in the light of the circumstances prevailing if and when it arises".

The above quote tells the whole story, and demonstrates the frustrating position in which Power Jets found themselves, fighting a Ministry policy which Whittle knew from the outset would never work. Apart from this, he knew in his heart that this lack of control on the part of the Ministry would, in the longer term, enable others to step in and squeeze out Power Jets and perhaps attach him to one of the other firms.

In March 1941, General Henry H. 'Hap' Arnold, Chief of Staff of the US Army Air Corps, was on a fact-finding mission in Britain and was astonished when, by chance, he learned that Whittle's engine was about to fly. He was aware of British jet patents and after checking out the Whittle project he was convinced that the British invention could become the springboard for America's entry into the Jet Age. He quickly made arrangements for Whittle's W.1X engine to be shipped to the USA, and picked General Electric to build it under licence. In April he asked GE to send a good engineer to Britain to work with Colonel A. J. Lyon of the US Army Air Force in London. Within a few months contracts were signed between the British and US governments for rights to build the Whittle engine in the United States. On 1 October 1941 the W.1X disassembled to packing-case size, accompanied by a Power Jets team comprising Dan Walker, Flight Sergeant King and G. B. Buzzoni, was flown to Bolling Field, Washington, in the bomb bay of a Liberator. They arrived at GE's works at Lynn, Massachusetts, on the 4th.

The PJ team, huddled in the bomb bay, had been worried that the pilot might pull the wrong toggle and deposit them in the drink. Towards the end of the flight they were so cold they almost wished he would. Buzzoni, a very capable fitter, commented on landing that, "The first time I fly I have to fly the bloody Atlantic!"

This was a little over 9 weeks before Pearl Harbor, so the US was not yet in the war. The US Government gave an undertaking that they would use the information for war purposes only. At the end of the war the UK Government released them from this undertaking for the magnificent sum of $800,000!

Thus America received a virtually free passport into the field of aero gas turbines, entirely brought about by Whittle's guts and determination to bring his project to fruition. The deal with America was indicative, and could not have come at a better time. There was some hard bargaining taking place between the two countries over lend-lease deals during this period, when America was neutral and Britain, fighting alone, desperately needed American arms. This reciprocal arrangement regarding the Whittle project was proof that Britain was in the forefront of a new aviation technology, which gave the country added status in American eyes just when she needed political and economic support in the USA.

The Americans, by nature, wasted no time in tackling the jet project, which Arnold and the National Advisory Committee for Aeronautics considered to be of vital national importance. It was naturally a top secret project, and only a handful of people concerned knew what was going on. Arnold quickly decided that GE were the best company, because of their experience in steam turbine technology and in superchargers. Like Whittle, Arnold did not approach traditional piston-engine manufacturers, being convinced that they would be sceptical of such a radical and unorthodox development. In August 1941, about three months after the first flight of the E.28, GE received a contract to build 15 Whittle engines designated as Type I-A. Bell Aircraft, of Buffalo, New York, were selected to build three aeroplanes, to be powered by the I-A. The Americans were off to a good start, helped by Whittle and his associates. Only thirteen months after General Arnold's historic Washington meeting, on 2 October 1942, the XP-59A Airacomet made its maiden flight — some six months before the British Meteor became airborne!

During the latter part of 1941 it was at last conceded that Power Jets should be equipped to make experimental engines. The capacity authorized was defined as that necessary to make engines and spares up to an equivalent of twelve complete engines per year.

The Ministry belatedly recognized that it was impossible to accommodate the necessary expansion at Lutterworth, and at the end of October 1941 authorized the building of a new factory on a site just outside the village of Whetstone about four miles south of Leicester and about nine miles from Lutterworth.

The growth of the industry had led to the formation of the Gas Turbine Collaboration Committee, whose purpose it was to encourage and guide collaboration amongst all firms engaged on gas turbine projects. The first meeting was held on 1 November 1941. At first, Whittle had his reservations: "Frankly, we at Power Jets did not receive the proposal with any enthusiasm, because it seemed likely to complicate matters and add yet further to the burden on us in supplying information. Later, we became enthusiastic supporters, and I am firmly convinced that Britain owes much of its technical superiority in this field to the GTCC. There were many intrinsic difficulties in the proposal, but somehow or another, under the skilful chairmanship of Roxbee Cox, a good deal of thin ice was skated over very successfully".

Whittle was a very tired man towards the end of 1941, exhausted by a four-and-a-half-year struggle with formidable engineering problems, overwork and frustration. He was also very depressed about the outcome of MAP policy and was suffering from insomnia, irritability, lack of appetite and other severe anxiety problems. These symptoms had gradually grown worse until he was forced to stop work on 10 December 1941.

On that day — three days after the Japanese attack on Pearl Harbor had brought America into the war — the dreadful news of the sinking of the *Prince of Wales* and the *Repulse* was announced: "I heard the news from Cheshire, who burst excitedly into my office to tell me. I was so shocked that I temporarily lost all self-control. I sprang to my feet and pointing to the door, shouting 'Get out — get out'. I find it hard to explain why I acted so violently in those particular circumstances, especially as Cheshire and I were close friends and there was nothing he personally had done to annoy me.

"Somehow the sinking of those two mighty ships affected me profoundly, partly, perhaps, because I had spent sufficient time at sea with the Navy in the past to know to what extent one's ship becomes one's home; partly also, I suppose, because, to my mind, the Navy still symbolised the might of Britain. In my depressed state the news sounded like the knell of doom".

Knowing that there was something seriously wrong, Whittle stopped work then and there, and went home. This was the first of three nervous breakdowns which Whittle was to suffer and he was in the Military Hospital at Oxford for about ten days, in the care of Group Captain Symonds (later Sir Charles Symonds), the RAF's senior specialist in neurology.

It was to be expected that a man like Whittle would find inactivity intolerable, and he returned to work after an absence of one month: "long before I was fit to do so, but I regarded myself as being on light duty for a time".

He came back to learn that Air Marshal Linnell (who had taken over from Tedder about a year earlier) had virtually changed the position overnight, in that he had ruled that Power Jets' work was to come under the Director of Engine Research and Development instead of under the Director of Scientific Research. This meant that Major A. A. Ross (Bulman's deputy) could give rulings affecting Power Jets.

During Whittle's absence a meeting chaired by Ross on 23 December 1941 was used to redefine the relative functions of Power Jets and Rover. Ostensibly, the purpose of the meeting was to make decisions on certain technical matters relating to the W.2B, especially the fuel system. In practice, all the former restrictions on the latitude of design permitted to Rover were removed. To add to Whittle's irritation, somebody reported that at one meeting during his absence, his views on a certain matter were quoted, and a certain senior MAP official had said, "It's no use taking any notice of Whittle — he's gone round the bend".

By the end of January 1942, Power Jets had three engines of the W.2B type, namely, two Rover-built engines and a third which they had built with the aid of sub-contractors. These were not complete engines, because in practice a good deal of 'cannibalising' was going on through shortage of parts. More often than not, they could only run one particular engine by borrowing parts from another. Additionally, the W.1A, destined for flight in the E/28, had been successfully cleared for flight during the previous month.

In their progress report covering the period up to 4 February 1942, Rover also claimed a substantial advance with the surging problems. Whittle learned that: "They had delayed surging to above the full speed of the engine, and had obtained a thrust of 1,644 lb at the surge speed, namely, 16,750 rpm with an exhaust pipe temperature of 628 degrees Centigrade. This was with their own design of compressor casing; thus they were closely in parallel with us even to the extent that they found that several of the turbine blades cracked and they had exhaust assembly failures. They had also had a thrust-bearing failure".

These comments by Whittle clearly indicate that the Rover engineering team were learning fast. Therefore, he might be accused of having been a little unfair in his judgement of their capabilities. This, however, was not the prime cause of his discontent. He had never liked the details of the MAP arrangement for Rover to manufacture his engine but, more important, he mistrusted Rover's motives — particularly those of the Wilks brothers.

BTH had also succeeded in raising the surge speed to a little above the earlier limit, and claimed a thrust of 1,667 lb. So, the bogey of surging was appreciably receding, and being replaced by the problem of turbine blade failures. Unfortunately, the apparently encouraging results at the beginning of 1942 were not maintained during the rest of the year, which proved to be a critical one for all those concerned in the business.

*   *   *

In a letter dated 12 January 1942, Hives of Rolls-Royce invited Whittle to Derby to discuss a proposal that they should build their version of a Whittle engine. Hives recognised the need for Rolls to take immediate steps to get more actively into the business, and a link with Power Jets was a logical step. Hives and Whittle had previously got on well together, and the simplicity of the Whittle-type engine had strong appeal to Rolls, whose aim was to develop such an engine on a short-term basis.

Negotiations went well, and it was agreed in general principle that Power Jets would be the main contractors and would place a sub-contract for the work with Rolls-Royce. On 30 January 1942, Hives visited Power Jets and made it clear that he intended to be in the forefront of post-war jet engine manufacture, and for that reason he wanted to go further than establishing technical collaboration between the two companies. He went on to say, in effect, that a commercially negotiated link-up was essential.

Hives left no doubt in Whittle's mind that Rolls-Royce had realised that at the end of the war there would be an absolute glut of Merlin engines, which threatened stagnation in the aero-engine business unless Rolls had something on the go which rendered the Merlin obsolete. In effect, Hives admitted that Whittle had revolutionized the aero-engine business, but he gave the impression that he was in no hurry to conclude a deal. Whittle, for his part, gave an assurance that Power Jets would give Rolls-Royce the option of a first refusal in respect of any scheme put forward.

In the event both sides waited for the other to make a first move which never came, and a golden opportunity was lost. Whittle was hampered by not knowing what was the bargaining position of Power Jets, and also felt it inappropriate, as a serving officer in uniform, to concern himself with commercial negotiation. Hives, who had inspired, directed and led the great contribution to the war effort that Rolls-Royce were making was, in all respects, a 'colossus' in the field of aero-engine design and manufacture. In his position he would naturally expect the junior partner to make the first move — he could afford to play a waiting game, confident in the knowledge that he had a first refusal on any competitive deal involving Power Jets. Whittle, for his part, just did not realise that Hives looked upon him as a spokesman for Power Jets in commercial matters.

This would have been the right moment for Power Jets, and for the country, to form an alliance with, and work under the umbrella of, the giant Rolls-Royce company. The climate was right for it. Things were looking good following the enormous success of the E.28, and in the progress then being made in ironing out the snags of the W.2B which was to power the Meteor.

However, technical collaboration between the two companies did go ahead, and the MAP eventually approved their proposals (though after some months' delay), whereby Power Jets received a contract for the design and development of six engines, and they immediately placed subcontracts with Rolls-Royce. The Rolls-Royce engine was known as the WR.1, and was a scaled-up version of the W.2B designed for a thrust of 2,000 pounds. However, the project was overtaken by events and was abandoned at a relatively early stage of development. Its size was too great for the Meteor, and there was no other aeroplane in sight. Meanwhile, RR also continued to struggle with the complex Griffith CR.1 project, with no success at all.

*   *   *

In early 1942 the War on the Home Front had changed dramatically. Hitler's invasion of the Soviet Union on 22 June 1941 had put back the threat of a German invasion of Britain. The Japanese attack on Pearl Harbor on 7 December 1941 had brought the Americans into the war. The first fight for survival, which had been won in the air, had given way to the second fight, 'The Battle of the Atlantic', now in a critical phase, in which all three operational commands of the RAF were to play an important part.

The RAF, engaged in planning the strategic air offensive, was on the verge of the greatest expansion in its history. The aviation industry, under the direction of the MAP, had overflowed into commercial factories and back-street workshops. From 'tin bashers' to furniture manufacturers the industrial muscle of the country was being diverted into building up our air forces, while the Empire Air Training Scheme was being established to provide thousands of aircrews. The RAF was, at last, about to break out of its shell and emerge on a wartime footing.

Against this background of momentous activity, Whittle's turbojet project, lurching from one crisis to another, was but a drop in the ocean. It was a tremendously vital one, all the same.

*   *   *

During February 1942, flight trials of the E.28 powered by the W.1A engine began at Edgehill in Warwickshire — about seven miles north-west of Banbury. As before, Gerry Sayer was the pilot.

Early in the tests it was found that, though the W.1A was developing more power and burning correspondingly more fuel than the W.1 at ground level, the endurance of the aeroplane was increased. This extra power gave a much more rapid climb, and so the fuel available for cruise at height was increased. This confirmed Whittle's original predictions concerning fuel consumption, which had been the subject of such speculation and adverse criticism.

Flight trials continued intermittently during February and March 1942, but were suspended temporarily when a turbine blade failed in flight. The failure occurred during a climb and at a height of about 4,000 feet. In his report, Sayer said that the first indication of trouble was a howling noise and vibration, but he found that he was able to keep the engine running at about 10,000 rpm, which was sufficient to enable him to get into position for a safe landing on the airfield. In the course of these trials a speed of 430 mph was reached at a height of 15,000 feet. This was far beyond the E.28 design speed, but handling was excellent.

Captain Eric 'Winkle' Brown RN, who was to fly the machine later on, described its handling characteristics: "It had a very simple cockpit layout with as many engine gauges as flying instruments, for this was primarily an engine testbed. The view was superb, and almost uniquely so for a single-seat aeroplane of that era.

"Taxiing was delightfully simple with the steerable nosewheel, which was probably fitted because the large fin and rudder would otherwise cause weathercocking in a cross-wind. For takeoff the engine had to be opened up slowly to prevent excessive jet-pipe temperatures, but the full 16,700 rpm could be held on the brakes. Acceleration was reasonably good, and the takeoff run without flaps was short.

"In normal flight the controls were all quite light and effective, but the ailerons heavied up with speed. There can have been few nicer aeroplanes to land than this little beauty. At 90 mph it could be glided with undercarriage down and flaps up and the engine idling, with excellent control at that speed. The flaps had to be pumped down by hand, and then speed could be reduced to 80 mph when the E.28 would virtually land itself off such an approach".

The increasing frequency of turbine blade failures was causing much concern. Unfortunately, the problem was clouded by the fact that in most cases accidental circumstances could not be ruled out. Thus, there was therefore great uncertainty about the real causes of the failures, but there was little doubt that the higher speeds and higher temperatures at which the engine was being run were important contributory factors so the need for better materials became pressing.

The RAE and the National Physical Laboratory helped with this problem, and the former recommended that fewer and stiffer blades be used. This, plus the change to the nickel-chromium alloy Nimonic 80, eventually was to make important advances possible.

On 13 March 1942 Whittle started a complete redesign of the W.2B to be known as the W.2/500. Power Jets had been unhappy with Rover's production engine, and believed that a fresh start was the best way of incorporating a number of improvements, including the increased size of turbine blades recommended by the RAE.

During April 1942 the disagreements between Power Jets and Rover, which had been fermenting for some considerable time, finally reached a crisis. Whittle suddenly discovered that the Rover Company had been secretly working on a rearrangement of the W.2B, which they later designated the B.26, without disclosing their intent and purpose. They had even had the first run of this engine some three weeks before Whittle got to hear about it! Having regard to the fact that there had been no relaxation, so far as Power Jets knew, of the MAP edict that there was to be complete and frank interchange of information between Rover and themselves, and that nothing was to be withheld at meetings of the GTCC, this was a scandalous state of affairs.

There was no justification for Rover to act in such a manner. The Company had been given increasing latitude in design, but the MAP had made it crystal clear that the two companies should hide nothing from each other. Power Jets had observed this mandate meticulously, even to the extent of having Rover engineers attached.

The chief difference between the B.26 and the W.2B was that the former had straight-through combustion chambers instead of the Power Jets' counter-flow arrangement. This kind of alteration could not be described as an 'improvement for production', so was not within Rover's province. Power Jets already had a contract for an experimental engine along these lines. Before and during the controversy, Whittle had standing on his desk a wooden model of a shaft coupling which he was proposing to use in his own straight through W.3X when he had the time and facilities to solve the problems entailed — a long shaft with extra bearings and a coupling to allow for thermal expansion. There was nothing new in the concept of straight through combustion. This had been depicted in Whittle's first patent drawing. Also the de Havilland H.1 had straight-through combustion chambers.

The fact that Rover had proceeded, without prior consultation with Power Jets, to adapt the W.2B for straight-through combustion raised other issues, apart from the morality of the exercise. Whittle pointed out that the matter was not one which really turned upon the question as to whether it was a better form of engine, but whether as a production version of the W.2B it could be produced in time to meet the laid-down airframe and engine programme and in time for the war.

Long technical arguments ensued between all concerned, but at that stage it was a general belief, shared by Air Marshal Linnell, Pye, Roxbee Cox and his deputy Watt, that the B.26 was a private venture on Rover's part. When Air Marshal Linnell discovered that this was not the case, a most astonishing situation came to light. The Rover Company's work on the B.26 had been sanctioned by the Directorate of Engine Development, but had been kept secret not only from Power Jets, but also from the Controller of Research and Development, the Director of Scientific Research and other officials intimately concerned with the project, particularly Roxbee Cox. When this became known, Linnell apologised profoundly to Power Jets.

Whittle's view was that: "In one sense the whole affair was very helpful to Power Jets, because it provided clear and welcome proof of the state of affairs at which we had hinted from time to time, namely that the Rover Company intended to go their own way, and that in this course they were receiving moral and practical support from the officials of the Directorate of Engine Development".

After compromise and some whitewashing of certain individuals, it was agreed that Rover would be allowed to proceed with the B.26, but that this should not be at the expense of the W.2B production development. In fact the W.2B development continued to suffer. Once again Establishment thinking had failed to grasp the nettle, because in the end it was the W.2B which went into active service, in spite of all that had been claimed for the B.26.

Chapter 14
Visit to America

On 26 May 1942, Whittle was given his terms of reference for a projected visit to the USA, to do whatever he could to help the Americans with their own development of his engine. After talks with Roxbee Cox he went by train to Bristol, in company with a number of VIPs, and the party was then flown by D.H. 91 Albatross to Shannon Airport.

He was wearing mufti[1] for the journey, and his passport was made out as though he were a civilian because they had to pass through neutral Eire. Strange as it may seem, Whittle, who had been in the RAF since the age of 16, had never crossed the borders of the UK. The party arrived at Shannon expecting to be leaving by flying boat almost immediately, but were told that they could not take off that day because of bad weather.

They were then driven into Limerick and accommodated in the Royal George Hotel. Whittle was on tenterhooks being firmly convinced that, if it became known that he was a serving officer, he would be interned. Not that he believed that the Irish would want to imprison him, but he imagined that the German Embassy in Dublin would undoubtedly bring pressure to bear to have him interned if they got the slightest 'whiff' of what he was doing.

Apart from that, he had a large canvas diplomatic bag, containing secret MAP papers in addition to his drawings and information, which he had to guard with his life. In the event, the party was delayed for six days. His nervousness reached its peak on his 35th birthday, 1 June 1942, when his wife sent him a birthday telegram addressed to him by rank!

Whittle could not have been going at a worse time as far as the state of the war was concerned. The Japanese were roaring unchecked through the Pacific, the Russians were at their lowest ebb, the British were retreating in the Middle East, and German U-boats were playing havoc with Atlantic convoys. The Allied situation was very grim indeed.

The Atlantic, however, was fast becoming a highway for the interchange of British and US Army Air Forces personnel. RAF

[1]Mufti — British slang for civilian clothes.

aircrew cadets were being shipped across to train in America and Canada, where they could fly without risk of enemy attack. Simultaneously, US Army Air Force personnel were arriving in Britain to prepare for daylight bombing offensives. These plans, which were gathering momentum at this time, were to have a profound effect on the air war.

Before his stay in Limerick, Whittle had been led to believe that the Irish were inherently hostile to Britain, so he was very surprised to see that the main hotel was called The Royal George. Also, to his great relief, the hotel staff were exceptionally friendly. This friendly attitude was not limited to the hotel. On one occasion, a senior civil servant in the party having agreed to look after the diplomatic bag for an hour or so, Whittle took a much-needed walk and stopped in a shop to buy cigarettes. As he entered he heard the shopkeeper refuse cigarettes to an Irishman who then left. When he said to the shopkeeper, "I don't suppose it's any use me asking for cigarettes?" "What would you like Sor?" said the man; "Do you have any Players?" "Sure, I have" and he reached under the counter and produced the goods.

After the telegram from his wife, the sight of an approaching green-uniformed policeman was a source of considerable anxiety, but all was well. The hotel staff, pleasant enough before, became especially friendly — a most unexpected result.

Whittle eventually left Ireland by Pan American Boeing 314A Clipper on the evening of 3 June 1942, and arrived at the flying boat base at La Guardia, New York, the following evening, having stopped at Botwood, Newfoundland, and Shediac, Nova Scotia. He, like the young RAF air cadets, was suddenly pitchforked from war-weary and battered Britain into a peacetime atmosphere of street lights, plentiful food, booze, and lavish hospitality. Such rationing as there was was very limited.

It was a remarkable change, after nearly four years of war, for Whittle to find himself surrounded by the good things of life. Memories of Pan Yan pickle sandwiches in the office, and frugal lunches at The Hind or Denbigh Arms in Lutterworth quickly faded when he was esconced in a special suite at the Statler Hotel in Boston, by courtesy of General Electric.

Although he may not have realised it at the time, he had walked out of the frying pan into the fire as far as pressurized meetings were concerned. Initial discussions were, of course, closely concerned with General Electric's work in progress on their 'Type I Supercharger', as their engine was called for security reasons.

His W.1X engine, which had been shipped to the USA in October 1941, had fulfilled its purpose and, having given useful experience had been dismantled. But Whittle, having been through most of the problems that the Americans were then facing, was naturally bombarded with technical questions. Furthermore, as the pioneer of the project, they wanted to extract everything out of him because he was there!

He found that the Americans were much more security conscious than the British and, though back in uniform (the tropical uniform worn by RAF officers in the USA was US Navy uniform with RAF insignia), he was expected to use an assumed name. Not being cut out for this sort of thing, he thought it better to choose a name close to his real one, so he called himself Whitely: "The trouble was that I could not remember from one day to the next how I decided to spell it. My idea in choosing it was that if I was wanted on the telephone it was sufficiently near to my real one to recognise it when being paged.

"I'm afraid I would not last long as a spy, because there were times when I quite forgot I was supposed to be using another name, and frequently signed the real one on the bills for room service. However, it didn't matter because a special waiter had been allotted who was probably a member of the FBI".

After two or three days at the Statler, Mr Reg Standerwick, GE's executive in charge of the jet engine project, invited Whittle to stay at his delightful home in the seaside town of Marblehead. There, Reg and Abbie Standerwick made him very comfortable.

GE also provided him with a secretary, who worked with him at the Standerwick home and accompanied him on visits to the Lynn factory. He was not very happy at having to use a GE employee for confidential material concerning the USAAF and other firms, but felt easier on this score when it became obvious, for some reason, that Mrs Gerry Wilkinson was very hostile to Mr Standerwick. In fact she warned Whittle that the house was bugged, in that all rooms had an intercom system by which it was possible to listen-in to anything happening in any room. From then on he decided to do his dictation out of earshot, and so he and Mrs Wilkinson would adjourn to the beach which was only a short walk from the house. These pleasant interludes led to some embarrassment for Mrs W. The weather was hot and sunny, so she began to acquire a sun tan which roused her husband's suspicions. She told Reg Standerwick that she had a problem because, having been sworn to secrecy, she couldn't explain. He suggested that she tell her husband that she was being used as a guinea pig for the testing of ultra-violet sun-tan lamps. This solved her problem.

During his frequent visits to GE's Lynn factory, about ten miles north of Boston, Whittle worked closely with the late Donald F. 'Truly' Warner, the engineer responsible for the work, and his staff of engineers and draughtsmen. He was delighted to find that his contacts with them were almost as intimate as with his own team at Power Jets. He discovered that their engine was chiefly based on the Rover drawings, but they had preferred Power Jets' practice in certain features of the mechanical design, especially bearings.

He found, as Walker of Power Jets had reported during his visit, that their engine test house was a very robust affair with concrete walls eighteen inches thick. Walker had christened it Fort Knox (after the place in Kentucky where the US Government stores its gold), and this name was now painted over the steel door. He wondered what the GE engineers would have thought if they had seen his own ramshackle set-up where he had first run his turbojet five years previously!

On 10 June Whittle visited the Bell Aircraft Corporation which was situated just outside the city of Buffalo. As usual, he was accompanied by Major Don Keirn of the USAAF and Dundas Heenan of the British Air Commission, who played a very useful part in technical discussions and whose hospitality and assistance helped to smooth his path considerably. Bell had three XP-59A Airacomets under construction, the first being well advanced and the others following closely. These twin-engined fighter prototypes were to be powered by GE Type I engines. The discussions of the 11th and 12th June were very intensive, and Whittle was able to provide a good deal of information which resulted in several modifications.

He also visited the main works of the GE at Schenectady, where a team of engineers were working on a propeller gas turbine scheme: "This engine was well beyond the preliminary design phase. Indeed, manufacture was then well advanced, but nevertheless by comparison with our work it was still very much in the embryo stage".

The work at Lynn and the two propeller gas turbine projects mentioned above, by no means represented the whole of the US effort in this field. Senior officials in Washington told Whittle that the Navy Department, for example, was sponsoring about four schemes altogether, of which the most important was a turbojet project at Westinghouse — generally similar to the RAE/Metropolitan-Vickers F.2. All these schemes were in a very preliminary stage, and none of them had yet reached the test bench. Whittle's impression was that they were all regarded as being relatively long-term projects.

On 26 June 1942, Whittle was back at GE's Lynn factory, involved in technical discussions mainly associated with their test work in progress. In the course of these discussions, it was decided that an improved version of their version of the W.2B should be built, to be known as the I-16, and that this would incorporate a number of features of the Power Jets W.2/500.

During a visit to the US Army Air Force experimental base at Wright-Patterson Field near Dayton, Ohio, Whittle had many talks with senior technical officers. From the Commanding Officer, Brigadier-General Vannaman, downwards, their enthusiasm for the jet engine was impressive, and there already existed plans for test equipment on a scale far greater than anything contemplated in Britain. A plant for testing jet engines under high-altitude conditions was, in fact, being constructed at that time.

Whittle wrote to Roxbee Cox on 7 July 1942 and recorded his general impressions up to that date:

". . . it seemed to me that I had arrived at GE at about the right time, because though they had done very well up till then, they had begun to run into a lot of trouble, much of which was of a kind that we had already met and overcome, and so I had been able to give them the benefits of our experience . . .".

And he went on to say: ". . . the enthusiasm and ability here is such that I feel that the best that can be done will be done".

In another letter of the same date to Wing Commander Watt (Roxbee Cox's deputy) he had a slight dig at certain people back home when he wrote:

"I get on very well indeed with the engineers over here, because they have both enthusiasm and ability, which is a pleasant change from some we know of, and it is a real pleasure to do all I can to help the job along and I think my efforts are appreciated . . .".

In doing everything possible to help the Americans, during the past five weeks of technical grilling, Whittle began to feel severe strain once more. He had never properly recovered from the strain which had led to his going into hospital earlier in the year, and he had become exhausted and seriously in need of a rest.

Dundas Heenan and Don Kiern sensed this, and spoke to Air Marshal Hill at the British Air Commission. Whittle was then flown west to California, ostensibly to visit and confer with the Northrop Corporation who were working on a project sponsored by the US Navy. It was a propeller gas turbine scheme which they called the Turbodyne. He was then to stay in the Los Angeles area for sun, sea and peace.

The Northrop visit was a depressing experience: "When I saw drawings of the engine and studied some of the figures and assumptions on which the design was based, I felt that they were biting off more than they could chew. The design was far too complicated, and embodied at least one major fallacy. It became clear to me, when I was shown round the plant, that the equipment was hopelessly inadequate. When the firm's President, Jack Northrop, asked me outright for my opinion, it required a great deal of moral courage to tell him what I really thought. But, apparently I hadn't given offence because the firm decided to drop the scheme a short time later".

Whittle had been booked into the very comfortable and pleasant Miramar Hotel on the Pacific coast at Santa Monica, but the sudden inactivity after the Northrop visit did not agree with him. In only a few hours he had had enough of his own company and of sun, sea, etc, and, in his depressed state, it seemed to him that the hotel occupants were mainly old ladies who had gone there to die.

He appealed to Group Captain Jimmie Adams, who was in charge of the British Air Commission office in Los Angeles, to send him back east. Adams' reaction was to say that he proposed to change the treatment, and if it didn't work he would arrange for Whittle's return. He thereupon effected a transfer to the Beverly Hills Hotel, and invited Whittle to a barbecue party at the house of Mr Edward Hillman Jr that evening.

Jimmie Adams was a house guest in Eddie Hillman's house in Beverly Hills at the time. Eddie was married to June Howard-Tripp, the well-known dancer. June, who starred in Cochran shows in London was, for a time, Lady Inverclyde.

Whittle duly turned up at the Hillman house at about 4 o'clock in the afternoon, and experienced an introduction to the bizarre life of Tinsel Town:

"It was a very surprising experience. I was greeted warmly by Eddie, who was dressed in a pair of bathing trunks, and told to relax. Not an easy thing to do — I found the situation so bewildering. There were several other people there, and I just had a confused impression that there was much coming and going for no particular reason that I could see. Meanwhile, my host, Eddie spent much of the time phoning a number of people.

"I sat in a corner drinking a dry martini and feeling quite unable to adjust myself to the bizarre situation. Eddie repeatedly told me to relax and, presumably to assist me to do so, ordered his secretary to bring me a bowl of chicken noodle soup, which I did not in the least want at that time of day. The sight of a strange RAF officer sitting in the corner sipping soup appeared to excite no surprise or comment from the new arrivals".

In the course of the party that night Whittle succeeded in relaxing to such an extent that at about 3 am he was induced to join others in the swimming pool, and ruined his wrist watch! By then he had quite abandoned his intention to go back east immediately.

So, the Adams treatment produced an immediate improvement in the patient's health, as Whittle recorded: "My diary of the remainder of my stay in California is very sketchy, and my memories of it are somewhat disjointed. I found the treatment much more congenial that the Sun, rest, etc, so much so, that after ten days, I felt the urge to return to work".

Meeting famous people and being entertained by the Hollywood set had been a unique experience for Whittle, and it certainly opened his eyes and blew some cobwebs from his mind. Having had his nose to the grindstone throughout his life he had never had the time or opportunity for gadding about, and he soon became reasonably acclimatised to late lunches and evening parties.

On one memorable evening at the well-known Mocambo night club he was made to dance the rumba — a novel performance for him at that time: "I had had a lesson from June, but had not really got the hang of it, and so I felt a complete fool while attempting to do it with Arline Judge, who was an expert and looking so attractive that I felt everybody's eyes were focussed on us. My acute self-consciousness made that ten minutes feel like ten hours! I think I might have felt a little less uncomfortable if I had not been wearing uniform".

During his last few days in Washington before returning to England, Whittle learned that GE were already planning for a production rate of 1,000 engines per month, and a full-scale test plant for the individual testing of compressors and turbines. The cost of this plant alone was estimated to be about three million dollars — about twelve times as much as Power Jets were spending on their test plant at Whetstone!

Unfortunately, Whittle had not been able to stay in the USA long enough to witness the successful flight trials of the Bell aeroplane. In spite of a very much later start, the American prototype twin-engine fighter started its flight trials on 2 October 1942, five months before the Meteor, and just one year and one day after Walker and company from Power Jets had arrived in the USA with the W.1X. This was a remarkable achievement.

Throughout his visit, Whittle had been impressed by the vitality and breadth of vision incorporated in the American system, once his project had been accepted. When touring their factories, it had given him deep satisfaction to witness the might of American aviation engineering working on a project that he had created. It made him feel good, and it showed more than ever what might have been achieved if he himself had had such backing when he ran his first turbojet way back in April 1937. The Americans generally were astounded at the parsimonious attitude of the MAP towards the work of Power Jets.

He arrived back in England on 14 August 1942, knowing that his trip had been highly successful. This was confirmed by a message from Air Marshal Hill to Air Marshal Linnell which said:

"In my opinion, Whittle's visit has been of major significance in promoting closer understanding between the two countries. It has made a direct contribution in accelerating diagnosis of the causes of a number of teething troubles experienced by the GEC. Whittle's personal relationships with all those whom he has met have been of the most cordial nature. He has won great respect from American engineers in the circle which is acquainted with this development . . .".

*   *   *

Following his trip to America, Whittle was greatly encouraged by the performance of the first W.2/500 which had started its tests on 13 September 1942, exactly six calendar months from the date on which his team had begun the drawings. After a preliminary run of only thirty minutes to make adjustments, it was run up to full speed, and complete sets of readings were obtained. A thrust of 1,750 lb was recorded at full speed, and 1,800 lb at a slight overspeed. Its performance almost exactly matched predictions, and as a result Tinling wrote to Air Marshal Linnell saying:

"For the first time we have been able to design an engine with a background of experience. You will recall that when the W.2B was designed there was no experience except the limited running with the original and pre-war WU (Whittle Unit).

"I am glad to tell you that the design predictions for the W.2/500 have been fulfilled in practice with an accuracy which seems to confirm that the design of these engines can now be regarded as almost an exact science".

Whittle had a hand in the letter because he recalls that: "I was responsible for suggesting the bit about exact science, and my engineers got a lot of pleasure in quoting it back at me on sundry occasions later when we ran into trouble!"

Things were going well on the engineering side for Power Jets in the autumn of 1942. In addition to the successful testing of the W.2/500, their W.1A had completed a 100-hour test and became the first engine ever to do so, and the new factory at Whetstone was providing much-needed facilities. The planning and building of this factory had been an achievement in itself, for which much of the credit was due to Williams, Tinling and the works manager Peasgood.

When Whittle paid his first visit to the site, with Roxbee Cox and others, he received quite a shock. It was one thing to have approved the plans, and another to see the result. The plant looked far larger than he had visualised, after being so accustomed to the small workshop at Lutterworth. He and Roxbee Cox looked at each other with somewhat uneasy expressions, thinking that somebody had put over a fast one, and that the place was far larger than had been authorized. Whittle had uncomfortable visions of an official enquiry into the expenditure of public money, but Williams assured him that the plant was in accordance with the plans approved by the Directorate of Aircraft Factories and they had not been exceeded. However, by October 1942 there were problems in manufacturing a sufficient number of engines for intensive development, because there were more machine tools at Whetstone than there were operatives to man them!

During the latter part of 1942, the sorry story of the W.2B development at Rover continued. The relative success of the

Power Jets' W.2/500, and the progress that de Havilland were making with their H.1, were the chief factors which influenced Ministry policy at this time.

Another significant factor was that the initiative in the air was gradually passing over to the Allied side. The strength of the Luftwaffe was being sapped by the demands of the Russian front, and the operational requirement for a very high-altitude interceptor fighter, which the Meteor was intended to fulfil, had become less urgent. The other operational needs of the RAF were being met by improvements in conventional fighters. The new Hawker Typhoon, for example, had recently been handed over to Squadrons, and this fast and heavily armoured aircraft was already proving itself over Northern Europe and in combating the German Fw 190 at low altitude.

According to information reaching Whittle, opinion in the MAP concerning the relative merits of the engines to power the first flight of the Meteor was sharply divided. Roxbee Cox, Watt and other officials in the Directorate of Scientific Research tended to back Power Jets, and the W.2/500 as a replacement for the W.2B. Their opposite numbers in the Directorate of Engine Development, who were by now beginning to lose faith in Rover's B.26, wanted to put their money on Halford's new de Havilland H.1 which, however, needed much larger nacelles in the Meteor than the W.2B.

The development troubles of the W.2B had already influenced the Meteor programme, in that the planned production of airframes had been cut from 80 a month to 30 a month. Since quantity production of the W.2/500 by Power Jets was out of the question, with their then-available resources, Whittle suggested to Rolls-Royce that they should consider taking on the job.

Hives visited Power Jets on 4 December 1942, and said that he had discussed Power Jets' proposal with Sir Wilfred Freeman (who had retired from the RAF and returned to the MAP as Chief Executive) and Air Marshal Linnell. He made it plain that Rolls-Royce were quite definitely entering the aircraft gas turbine field, and confirmed his interest in manufacturing the Power Jets W.2/500, but pointed out, that owing to heavy commitments on the Merlin, Rolls-Royce would require extra facilities. Hives went on to say that Freeman and Linnell had agreed that the W.2/500 was the best bet, but that its production would have to be done within existing facilities.

Whittle was then startled to hear from Hives that Freeman had suggested that Rolls-Royce should take over Whetstone for the purpose of W.2/500 production. Hives' reply had been that he could only think of such a course in complete agreement with Power Jets. Whittle argued that Whetstone was equipped for research and development only, and that it was in the national interest that it should be retained for that purpose. On the other hand, he said, there existed at Barnoldswick a plant which was both manned and tooled for the production of jet engines.

As the discussion continued, it became apparent that they were all thinking in terms of the same thing, namely that Rolls-Royce should take over the management of Barnoldswick from the Rover company.

On 11 December 1942, Whittle was summoned unexpectedly to a meeting at the MAP by Sir Wilfred Freeman. It turned out to be a most dramatic and notably brutal affair, as Whittle described:

"My health had been poor throughout the year, and this was one of my bad days. I was not feeling well when the interview began — I was feeling much worse at the end of it!

"During most of the talk I was seated, while Sir Wilfred paced back and forth speaking forcefully and rather abruptly, emphasising his remarks with vigorous arm movements. Air Marshal Linnell sat at one side of the room and said very little.

"Freeman opened by saying that every jet engine up to then was either a flop or likely to be. Three years had passed and there was little to show for it. When I protested that this was not a true representation of the facts, he admitted that he might be exaggerating slightly. He then concentrated on the W.2B situation — he laid great emphasis on what he described as the failure of the W.2B and inferred that I was primarily to blame. I said I refused to accept the blame, and that on the contrary I had repeatedly protested against the course of events which had led to the situation as it then was.

"Here was the state of affairs I had long foreseen. Though I had been deprived of any effective control of the development of the W.2B long before, I was being blamed for the results of a policy which had failed.

"Freeman said that his first impulse, when he took up his new post, was to close down the whole job. After this he had felt that the best thing would be to bring all the different firms together into one organisation, which he implied would be dominated by Rolls-Royce. Though he had been dissuaded from so sweeping a step, he had nevertheless made up his mind to bring together the resources of Rolls-Royce, Rover and Power Jets under the primary control of Rolls-Royce.

"The Rover management would cease to have anything more to do with the job. Though he did not say so explicitly, I gathered that Power Jets would cease to have an independent existence. At this point he stopped in his peregrinations and asked, abruptly, 'Well, what do you think of it?' I felt I had to gain time so I replied that I had not really grasped what he was proposing, so he went over more or less the same ground once more.

"He seemed to be antagonistic to the Board of Directors of Power Jets: he admitted that Williams and Tinling had done a good job of work in initiating the venture, but thought that they had ceased to have any useful function. He went so far as to say he would have them called up. I gathered that he proposed to include Johnson amongst those he intended to call up. I protested vigorously, and said that all the people he had referred to were still doing very important work. Williams and Tinling had done far more than initiate the venture — amongst other things they were mainly responsible for the expansion which had taken place, and in particular for the bringing into being of the Whetstone factory.

"Once more he stopped and asked me what I thought about it all, so again I stalled by saying that I had not clearly grasped what he had in mind. I was almost sure that what he really meant was that Power Jets was to be handed over to Rolls-Royce, lock, stock, and barrel, but that he could not bring himself to put it quite as bluntly as that. So once more he stalked up and down embroidering his theme.

"I told him that any proposal which disturbed the Power Jets' team as an entity would be disastrous. He replied that what he had in mind did not involve the disbanding of the team. He went on to argue that a firm like Rolls-Royce with their vast resources could obviously do much better than a small organisation like Power Jets. I asked him whether the record of the past year supported his point. I pointed out that no one had equalled, let alone beaten, the Power Jets' record in the time of manufacture of the W.2/500 or in test-running results after completion of manufacture.

"He made it clear that he had quite definitely decided to transfer Barnoldswick and Clitheroe to Rolls-Royce management. He remarked that he had yet to break the news to the Wilks brothers. I said that that at least was a feature in his proposals which had my full approval.

"I asked him who would be the effective Chief Engineer of the integrated scheme he had in mind. Sir Wilfred countered by asking whether I would prefer Sir Roy Fedden (a well-known aero-engine designer whom he knew was not likely to be acceptable to me); he presumably meant as an alternative to Rolls-Royce. I replied that I would prefer me. He said he could not very well put Rolls-Royce under my orders.

"I tried to make it clear that anything which in my view would really be for the benefit of the project would have my approval. Freeman said the Ministry fully recognised that I always did what I considered to be my duty, and was not actuated by personal motives.

"At the end of this further harangue, in which he still had not explicitly stated that Power Jets were to be handed over to Rolls-Royce, though he had again implied it, he once more asked me what I thought about it, so I told him that I was not feeling well enough to take in what he really meant. At this point Linnell intervened and asked me what was the matter: I told him very bluntly that I was tired, and sick to death of the whole business. Freeman said that they could not afford to dispense with my brain for some time yet, and asked me whether what he had said had made me feel any worse. I replied that I did not know until I understood it. This more or less brought the interview to a close".

The grilling that Whittle received at the hands of Freeman was typical of the way that the Establishment had handled his project right from the beginning. Freeman, the retired Air Chief Marshal, was never explicit about his intent, but relied on inferences to check Whittle's reaction. In the light of history, Freeman's plan to bring in Rolls-Royce and get rid of Rover was the right move, which Whittle himself had promoted during his meeting with Hives. Combining the resources of Rolls-Royce and Power Jets had Whittle's full approval, but Freeman did not come right out and tell him how it was to be done. He never came out with a practical plan for the merging of the two companies, presumably because of the complexities involved concerning the Power Jets position and Whittle's determination to control his own project.

Whittle, in the circumstances, might well have thrown down the gauntlet; but it must be remembered that he, as a Wing Commander, would have been challenging two Air Marshals!

His RAF background had had a profound influence upon his life. He had been moulded and typecast as a serving officer, which put him in a straitjacket from which there was no escape during a wartime situation. Apart from that, Whittle's circumstances were so complicated that he had no bargaining position, and he lacked the commercial experience of a wheeler and dealer.

Hives, who was a shrewd operator, had wasted no time in getting to grips with the Rover situation. He and Hooker met S. B. Wilks of Rover for dinner, and afterwards Hives asked Wilks:

"Why are you playing around with the jet engine? It's not in your line of business, you grub about on the ground, and I hear from Hooker that things are going from bad to worse with Whittle".

They were great friends, and Wilks, smilingly ignoring the jibe, replied,

"We can't get on with the fellow at all, and I would like to be shot of the whole business".

Hives then said,

"I'll tell you what I will do. You give us this jet job, and I will give you our tank engine factory at Nottingham". In as short a time as that, the deal was done. There was no talk of money, and no talk of getting Government agreement to the arrangement. Hooker suspected that Hives had already done that but, as he said, "When two such big men meet together, decisions of this magnitude can be made on the spot".

Thus, the Wilks brothers of Rover relinquished their stake in the jet engine business. It might have been a very different story for them had they kept faith with Whittle and, in retrospect, it was tragic that the Ministry allowed the Power Jets/Rover situation to get out of hand. It certainly lost Britain two whole years in jet development. Had it not been wartime, the media would have got on to the appalling situation.

The decision to bring in Rolls-Royce, which ought to have been taken at national level much earlier, brought the W.2B to life and changed the entire picture. As Hooker of Rolls-Royce said: "Instead of small teams working in holes in the corner, in one stroke nearly 2,000 men and women, and massive manufacturing facilities, were focussed on the task of getting the W.2B engine mechanically reliable and ready for RAF service. The knowledge that Rolls-Royce had taken over, and the personal pressure that Hives was able to apply to all the ancillary suppliers, galvanized everybody into top gear. And, I am glad to say, Frank Whittle was delighted. From then on, he generously gave us every possible assistance".

For Whittle, this was the crucial turning point of his long, titanic, and lone fight. He realised when Rolls-Royce first took over his engine that he would lose control, and that he could never compete against them — not with the sort of facilities they had at their disposal! He told Hooker that he would leave the final clearing up of the W.2B to them, while he concentrated on improving the breed by subsequent marks of the engine.

The immediate result of the Rolls-Royce takeover was dramatic. In January 1943 the running was nearly 400 hours — about ten times that recorded by Rover in the previous month. There could not have been a more striking demonstration of Rover incompetence and foot-dragging. Some months later, John Herriot confided to Whittle that Maurice Wilks had made it plain to him that testing was to be programmed in such a way as to favour the B.26 at the expense of the W.2B.

The next few months saw a rapid increase both in reliability and the rating of the engine until, in May 1943, a 100-hour development test at a rating of 1,600 lb thrust was completed. The work included a substantial amount of flight testing in the tail of a Wellington flying testbed, and in the second Gloster/Whittle E.28 in which, by the end of June 1943, 50 hours' flying had been completed.

There is a story, which may be apocryphal, that the Wellington came alongside a Boeing B-17 bomber, and the pilot of the Wellington cut out his two piston engines and feathered their props. He then opened up the W.2B in the tail and steamed past the B-17, the crew of which saw, as they thought, the incredible sight of a Wellington with two failed engines overtaking them!

Among the Rover engineers taken over by Rolls-Royce at Barnoldswick were Adrian Lombard and John Herriot, the latter becoming chief test engineer and the key to making the W.2B work. The Rolls-Royce technical team contained at least a dozen ex-Rover engineers, but under Rolls-Royce supervision there was a very great improvement in the atmosphere between them and Power Jets. After the conclusion of the 100-hour test at full design performance on 7 May 1943, for example, Herriot phoned Whittle to congratulate him, saying that, after stripping the engine, they found only minor defects. He emphasised that a very important contribution to this result had been the twisting of the turbine blades through an angle of 5°, which Whittle had recommended to Maurice Wilks nearly two years earlier. Wilks had replied that this would disrupt production!

Whittle responded by writing Herriot a most congratulatory letter, concluding that: "There has in the past undoubtedly been a certain amount of ill-feeling, based largely on the poor view Power Jets took of the development policy of the former management, but now that you have demonstrated that you are flat-out for rapid progress in this field, you may rest assured that as far as Power Jets is concerned not a trace of this remains".

*   *   *

Part of the flying of the second E.28 powered by the W.2B was done by the Gloster Aircraft Company at Edgehill. In April 1942 there was a display of new aeroplane types at Hatfield, and the E.28 Pioneer was included amongst the performers. On 17 April test pilot John Grierson flew the machine, accompanied by an armed escort of two Spitfire Vs and a Typhoon, the 70 miles from Edgehill to Hatfield for the demonstration. Very special security arrangements had to be made in advance, and immediately before take-off the all-clear had to be obtained from Fighter Command, to ensure that there were no 'bandits' in the vicinity.

Grierson reported that he never saw the Spitfires again for the rest of the flight, and that the Typhoon could only just keep up with him at maximum cruising power, and had to go 'through the gate' occasionally to keep abreast: "After making several circuits at Hatfield, so as to lose height and speed, I landed and found the surface rather rough. The machine was taxied straight into the special hangar. As I came out of the hangar, one of the escorting Spitfires reached the aerodrome in a power dive".

Two days later, when the cloud base at Hatfield was only 600 feet, Michael Daunt demonstrated the E.28 before the Prime Minister, Mr Winston Churchill, and a group of officers from the Air Staff. (Gerry Sayer, Gloster's former Chief Test Pilot, had been killed flying a Typhoon some months previously, and Daunt had taken over). His flight lasted for only six minutes, but in that time he completely stole the show by flying across the aerodrome at about 400 mph — some 50 mph more than any of the Spitfires or Mosquitoes could do!

Test pilot John Grierson in his book, *Jet Flight,* wrote: "The story went round that the Prime Minister, in swinging round in order to follow the course of the E.28, had to move so quickly that he very nearly spilt his whisky and soda! Mr Churchill was so impressed that he immediately wanted to know why we had not got squadrons of jet fighters, and the production of the F.9/40 (Meteor), as well as the de Havilland jet fighter (Vampire), automatically received a great boost.

Whittle was not even invited to be present on this occasion!

At Power Jets the emphasis during late 1942/3 was on testing the W.2/500. They were hoping that Rolls-Royce would produce this engine after completing 100 W.2Bs (now known as the Welland), but these hopes faded because the company showed an increasing reluctance to do so. Their attitude was understandable, in view of the rapid development of the W.2B, and the fact that the tooling at Barnoldswick was planned for it.

Rolls-Royce, in fact, were going ahead with an engine known as the B.37 (B for Barnoldswick) which was a straight through engine generally similar to Rover's B.26, but incorporating the best features of the W.2/500 design. Power Jets had not been consulted on this development, and Whittle made the point with Hives, who stressed that this was not deliberate, and was largely due to their preoccupation in taking over at Barnoldswick. Hives said that in any case the B.37 was considered to be so small a step from the B.26 as not to justify any fuss over it.

However, this Rolls-Royce version, which became the Derwent I, was competitive with the Power Jets W.2/700 (a development of the W.2/500) in that both engines were designed to give a thrust of 2,000 lb. When discussing the question of essential close collaboration between the two firms, Hives reminded Whittle that the only solution was to have a definite link-up. Hives was under the impression that when this subject had been discussed some time ago that it had been left with Power Jets to make the next move.

It transpired that there had been a complete misunderstanding between the two parties back in 1942, and Hives, who was finding MAP gas turbine policy constipated, appeared to be keen to carry on with further discussions in an attempt to find a basis for a link-up. He agreed that Power Jets had shown plenty of goodwill and willingness to co-operate, and said that he always told third parties that he got on well with Whittle and Power Jets. But, he made it abundantly clear that Rolls-Royce would not be satisfied with a position in which they had to take their orders from Power Jets. Whittle replied that he would like to see an organisation for engineering liaison set up of so intimate a nature that it would not be possible even to use such a phrase.

These differing viewpoints of previous comments by Hives and Whittle clearly illustrate the gulf between the two men when it came to setting up a commercial deal. In fact, the proposals for a commercial link-up came to nothing, and no terms of reference were ever agreed, but fortunately the technical collaboration between the two companies was unaffected: "The atmosphere was so cordial that it gave rise to firm and lasting friendships between the engineers involved. The personalities of the individuals concerned contributed much to the happy situation.

"We were fortunate indeed in having to deal with such people as Elliott, Chief Engineer, and Stanley Hooker who was in command at Barnoldswick and Clitheroe. Their policy was not to be different for the sake of being different, but to make the utmost use of any work of value shown up in the results of Power Jets. This policy bore valuable fruit".

Whittle felt that, as time went on, two factors had contributed to Hives becoming less enthusiastic for a commercial alliance with Power Jets. The first was that Hives had acquired control of Barnoldswick — making Rolls-Royce the largest firm in the jet-engine business — without having to do any financial deal for the purpose. The second concerned Whittle himself. He had been unwell for some time, and his health was progressively deteriorating. Naturally, Hives became aware that Whittle was under great strain and this must have influenced his thinking, especially when from May 1943 Whittle was posted to the RAF Staff College for the three months' War Course. There was no guarantee that he would even return to Power Jets, which greatly weakened that company's bargaining position during his absence.

*   *   *

On 29 April 1943, some three weeks before Whittle went to the Staff College, he wrote to Sir Stafford Cripps, the Minister of Aircraft Production, about the future of the gas turbine industry in Britain. During the course of this letter he argued a very strong case for the complete nationalisation of the gas turbine industry, viewed from any political standpoint. His main point was that the only private finance was that furnished by the 'B' shareholders of Power Jets; no other firm had risked a penny of their own money. His last paragraph read:

". . . the case for nationalisation seems to me to be overwhelmingly strong, so much so that the public would be entitled to raise a vigorous outcry through parliament if a few private firms are allowed to grasp for the benefit of their shareholders that which should properly be the property of the State . . ."

The letter went on to suggest steps which should be taken, and included the suggestion that private shareholders should be bought out.

This extraordinary act on Whittle's part was a calculated gamble to safeguard his child, Power Jets. As has already been explained, repeated efforts by the management of Power Jets and senior civil servants in the MAP had failed to sort out the contract position of the company, which made it virtually impossible to negotiate a commercial alliance with any other firm. Whittle was highly conscious that without such an alliance the chances of Power Jets' surviving were minimal.

Whittle's action was not governed by any materialistic motive on his part, but what he was advocating was consistent with the political beliefs he had held for many years: "Though I hasten to add that my enthusiasm for public ownership per se was severely undermined by the subsequent history of Power Jets, and nowadays I do not align myself either with those who advocate total public ownership or total private enterprise. I further deluded myself into believing that, in a nationalised gas turbine industry, the Power Jets' team would naturally be at the apex of the pyramid".

In due course Whittle was bitterly to regret writing this letter to Sir Stafford Cripps.

Whittle's bias towards socialism in those days did not, in his eyes, conflict at all with his position as a serving officer. On the contrary, as a state servant, he thought it would be a fine thing if everyone served their fellow men as state servants. He naively believed that nationalised industries would evolve an esprit-de-corps, like that of the Royal Air Force and the other fighting services and that industrial unrest would disappear to the point where a strike could be treated as mutiny.

As a result of his experience with Power Jets, he later rejected socialism to the extent that he intervened in two general elections on behalf of the Conservatives. First in May 1955, when he spoke in support of Dudley Williams standing as Conservative candidate for Exeter. Secondly in October 1964, when he wrote

On the flight deck of a British Airways Concorde in 1984: Chris Orlebar and F.W.

With Prince Charles and Sir Austin Pearce, Chairman of British Aerospace, in 1983.

Sir Frank collected his Order of Merit from HM The Queen on 23 June 1986.

With 'Tommie' (real name Hazel) and Prime Minister Margaret Thatcher in June 1986.

Looking at a 757 and an Airbus with the chairman of Esso, Archie Forster. In the background is Roy Fowkes, who joined F.W. as an apprentice in 1943 and has for many years been his 'Man Friday' in the UK.

Before leaving London for Hong Kong on a Cathay Pacific 747 on 27 September 1986: Sir Frank with his son, Captain Ian Whittle. Whatever would we have done without dad?

WHERE IT ALL HAPPENED

KEY

1. **COVENTRY**
   FW Born 1 June 1907
   Rover HQ

2. **CRANWELL**
   RAF College — 1st Flight E28

3. **HORNCHURCH**
   111 Fighter Squadron 1928

4. **WITTERING**
   Central Flying School 1929

5. **DIGBY**
   2 Flying Training School 1929

6. **HENDON**
   RAF Display — Crazy Flying

7. **FELIXSTOWE**
   Marine Aircraft Testing. 1931-2

8. **HENLOW**
   Officers' School of Engineering. 1932

9. **CAMBRIDGE**
   University (Peterhouse)

10. **RUGBY**
    BTH Works (1st Run of Jet Engine
    April 12 1937)

11. **LUTTERWORTH**
    The Ladywood Works

12. **RUGBY**
    Brownsover Hall — Design HQ

13. **WHETSTONE**
    Power Jets new factory.

14. **BRUNTINGTHORPE**
    Research & Development Test
    Flying Aerodrome
    Whittle 1st Flew Meteor I

15. **GLOUCESTER**
    Brockworth E.28 Test Flights

16. **GERRARDS CROSS**
    Staff College

17. **DERBY**
    HQ Rolls-Royce

18. **BIRMINGHAM**
    Rover HQ

19. **BARNOLDSWICK**
    Rover factory taken over by
    Rolls-Royce

20. **HARROGATE**
    MAP

21. **EDGEHILL**
    Flight Testing of E.28.

22. **MANSTON**
    Whittle Flew Meteor III
    High Speed Course — Herne Bay.

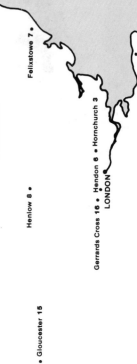

an open letter to the voters of Smethwick which was a fierce attack on the Labour candidate, Patrick Gordon-Walker.

On both occasions Whittle's views were given wide publicity by the press on the morning of election day. Gordon-Walker was the only Labour candidate to lose his seat.

*   *   *

Meanwhile, the expansion at Power Jets had been considerable; the staff had increased to over 600, and the greater part of the new Whetstone factory was in use. The output at Whetstone, however, in Whittle's opinion, "was very unsatisfactory in proportion to the manpower and equipment available, especially by comparison with the Ladywood Works". Relatively, both the quality and quantity of the work had fallen off, chiefly due to dilution by poor-quality labour. Many of the more recent employees were not voluntary recruits, and had been directed under war-time regulations. For the first time Power Jets ran up against labour unrest stirred up by a Communist shop steward.

During May 1943, Whittle was able to do some catching up with his flying. He had flown a Miles Master on 3 March 1943, but the previous entry in his log book was dated 20 May 1941 when he took Williams and Tinling for local practice flights in an Avro Tutor from Cranwell. During 1940 and 1942 he had done no flying at all!

His log book records that he flew several aircraft types during May 1943, including the Master, Magister, Mentor, Tiger Moth, Hurricane I, Hurricane II and Spitfire. But the one aircraft that he had set his heart on flying was, of course, the little E.28 Pioneer. Although he had done some taxiing trials in this little beauty the Ministry had refused permission for him to fly her. It was not because he was lacking the necessary skills: they didn't want to risk the aeroplane and its engine designer. Finally, in May 1943, the MAP gave him permission, and he was cleared to fly the machine. With Hurricane and Spitfire flying experience behind him, he was in the act of climbing into the E.28 when he was told that it had been declared unserviceable, and was likely to remain so for several days.

Balked at the last moment and naturally feeling very disappointed, Whittle retained a sense of humour about the incident, saying that: "It has since been suggested to me that the real reason was that somebody at the MAP had suddenly become nervous about my flying the aeroplane, and had phoned through instructions that I was to be prevented. Possibly someone had reported that I had fallen asleep from exhaustion after flying a Miles Master for two hours".

Whittle had certainly needed his flying to give him an uplift at this time, because on 11 May 1943 he had seen Sir Stafford Cripps regarding the nationalisation proposals he had submitted in his letter. Cripps told him that he agreed in general with the points contained therein, but his problem was ways and means, because the Government was not a Socialist one, and the law allowed him to take over firms only if they were inefficient: "At this point Cripps gave me a rather penetrating look, and said, 'Power Jets does not give me that excuse, does it?'

"I replied, 'No, Sir!' ".

Uneasy about the whole affair, on 24 May 1943 Whittle started his three months' War Course at the Staff College, during which he was promoted to temporary Group Captain. This made him the most senior officer on the course. Air Vice-Marshal Hill (later Air Chief Marshal Sir Roderic Hill) was the Commandant, and Air Commodore Fiddament (Fido) was the Assistant Commandant, and both were very understanding about Whittle's position. He was allowed to have his secretary, Mary Phillips, to help him, (she was quartered with the WAAF personnel during her visits), and he was excused certain of the less important exercises.

Whittle enjoyed the change: "From my point of view, the most interesting of the visits was to the Photographic Interpretation Unit at Medmenham. This was a key unit in the Intelligence organisation, and its function was to glean information from photographs taken by reconnaissance aircraft. One of the staff engaged on this work was a young WAAF Officer, Flight Officer Constance Babington-Smith, who was later to write several books on the subject. She was an attractive young lady who combined personal charm with an intense interest in aircraft. It was she who spotted much of the evidence betraying the work the Germans were doing on jet- and rocket-propelled aircraft, work for which she was subsequently decorated.

As soon as she realised who I was, and my connection with jet propulsion, she virtually detached me from the rest of the Staff College party, to get my views on some of her more interesting photographs, and so I spent most of the time with her poring over photographs of Peenemünde and other airfields with indications of German jet activity.

"I was particularly struck by the way scorch marks on the grass indicated that the Germans were flying twin-engined jet aircraft, though none of these aircraft actually appeared in the photographs. Other photographs, however, showed quite clearly the tailless rocket-propelled interceptor, the Me 163.

"While she and I had our heads together over the photographs, I noted that I received many envious glances from the other students, and a very amused one from Fido Fiddament. On the return journey to the Staff College, Fido pulled my leg unmercifully. I had a little of my own back when he asked what perfume she used. I replied, 'Judging from its effect on you, Sir, it must have been Air Commodore's Ruin', at which he roared with laughter".

At the end of the course Whittle was re-posted to the Special Duty List and returned to Power Jets, but this had not been intended.

The general extension of the scope of jet propulsion activity had led to certain changes of organisation in the MAP. Roxbee Cox's Deputy Directorate was made a full Directorate, and he was given the title of Director of Special Projects.

During the last six months of 1943 the development effort at Power Jets was largely transferred from the W.2/500 to the W.2/700. They failed to achieve the 2,000 lb thrust target with the W.2/700 during 1943, but managed it in early 1944. They did, however, succeed in getting over 2,000 lb thrust under overspeed conditions with a W.2/500, and two of these engines were flight-tested in one of the prototype Meteors in November 1943. During this period both Power Jets and Rolls-Royce were getting impeller failures, and this trouble was eventually solved by stiffening up the impeller blades at the expense of some loss of performance.

On 24 October 1943 Whittle saw Sir Stafford Cripps again, and was told that Power Jets was to be taken over by the State: "At the time of the interview I didn't fully grasp what Sir Stafford Cripps had in mind. However, I had understood enough to make me feel extremely uneasy, and that the Minister intended the nationalisation of Power Jets only, which was a far cry from my original proposals".

Whittle, realising that he had jumped out of the frying pan into the fire, wrote to Cripps on the following day recording his objection to the nationalisation of Power Jets alone: "It is my view that many of the civil servants in the Ministry are quite ready to do ruthless things with the young and still small Power Jets, but are too much afraid of the old-established firms to be equally firm with them . . .".

Hitherto, Whittle and some of the senior civil servants involved had made proposals that the Government should take over control of Power Jets in order to clear the complex situation in which the company found itself. But nationalisation was a very different matter, because it meant the State buying out shareholders' interests at its own price.

On 2 November 1943, Sir Stafford Cripps and Sir Harold Scott met with Sir Maurice Bonham-Carter, Williams and Tinling, and repeated much of what they had told Whittle. The price to be paid for the assets of Power Jets was vaguely discussed, with Cripps thinking of a sum somewhere between £100,000 and £250,000. Cripps went on to say that, if agreement on price was delayed, then he would take over possession of all the plant, and direct all the labour to a new Government company. This meant leaving Power Jets in possession of only its paper assets, such as patents, and nothing else.

Cripps didn't waste any time regarding his threat to put the Company into cold storage, because he wrote to Bonham-Carter on 26 November 1943 as follows:

"I have now received a report from Mr. Sam Brown as to his visit to Power Jets, and it is quite clear that there is no basis between us for acquiring the assets of the Company. I must therefore consider immediately the other alternative as we urgently need the plant for general experimental purposes".

Thus, Cripps was ready and willing to pull the trigger, and there was nothing that Power Jets could do about it except to acquiesce on price. On 1 December 1943 Cripps told the directors of Power Jets that the Treasury would not support a sum in excess of £100,000 in payment of the company's assets, and once more implied that, if some such sum was not acceptable to the shareholders, the company would be dispossessed of its personnel and premises.

How sad it was that Whittle, for all his brilliance and courageous fight in making his turbojet project a reality, should have been hoisted by his own petard. Roxbee Cox, Freeman, and many other senior officials in the Ministry sympathised with Whittle's point of view. Roxbee Cox told Whittle that he,

Freeman, and Air Marshal Sorley (who had succeeded Air Marshal Linnell) had discussed the matter with the Minister and indicated their opposition to the proposed plan. But Cripps, of course, was on solid ground, and amongst the reasons that he gave for his action was that it had been Whittle's wish in the first place. This was a gross distortion of the facts; it was very clear that Whittle was most strongly opposed to the nationalisation of Power Jets alone. The probable truth is that the Ministry had manoeuvred itself into a position impossible of solution. It was under a moral obligation to provide safeguards, and had promised to protect Power Jets' commercial interests but had completely failed to do so. Nationalisation provided a way out of their dilemma. It was a cutting of the Gordian knot.

Shortly before the end of 1943 Roxbee Cox told Whittle that, under pressure from the US Government, it had been decided that some official disclosure of Allied work on jet engines should be made. Whittle was made a Commander of the Order of the British Empire in the New Year's Honours List, but this caused no Press comment, because there was nothing unusual about the award of the CBE to a serving officer of his rank.

On the evening of 6 January 1944, a joint statement was issued by the British and US Governments for publication after 11 pm on that day. Whittle had no knowledge of this until Miss Iris Carpenter of the *Daily Herald* showed him a copy, shortly before he heard it on the midnight news of the BBC.

The next morning Whittle found himself a front-page feature throughout the national press: "I was by no means prepared for the astonishing consequences of publication. I had been too close to the job for many years to see the situation from the point of view of the average citizen. Our failures were more prominent in my mind than our successes, and so the reaction of the Press and the public had a stunning effect".

Whittle was not the sort of man to relish sudden fame and publicity. Besieged by reporters and snowed under with mail, he found himself having to answer the same old questions over and over again, 'ad nauseam'. He had never been free from acute shyness, and official cocktail parties and the like were often a severe ordeal for him: "On occasions like these, perhaps the thing I dread more than anything else is being cornered by an inventor".

The British public, who became well aware of Whittle and the brilliant achievements of Power Jets during January 1944, were more than a little surprised when only a few weeks later they learned in official announcements that Power Jets Limited was to be nationalised.

The Treasury originally would not support a sum in excess of £100,000, but Cripps had relented to some extent and said that he was prepared to offer approximately £130,000 for Power Jets' assets. On 3 January 1944 Tinling accepted the offer on behalf of the Board, but pointed out it was not considered to be fair, and was accepted only because of the Minister's threat to put the Company into 'cold storage' if it were not accepted. Tinling's letter also recorded that the Minister had even rejected the Company's proposal that the value of the assets should be submitted to arbitration.

Whittle saw the Minister on the same day, 3 January, armed with a set of notes recording his disapproval of the nationalisation of Power Jets alone, for the purpose of establishing a National Gas Turbine Establishment which was eventually formed in 1946. These notes, a copy of which was handed to Cripps, also reflected Whittle's disapproval of the manner in which it was proposed to acquire the Company: ". . . It seems to me unsatisfactory and unnecessary to impose a price with the virtual threat of extinction as an alternative. I do not understand why arbitration cannot be tried . . .".

But there was nothing that Whittle could do and, three days later, on 6 January 1944, Mr Sam Brown of the Ministry wrote to Tinling and placed formally on record the Minister's point of view:

"After due consideration, the Minister reached the definite opinion that the national interests demanded the setting up of a Government-owned centre of gas turbine technology. The present stringency of building labour and resources generally renders it quite impossible for the Government now to construct a suitable new establishment. In these circumstances the Minister was forced to the conclusion that he had no option but to exercise his rights, which are not, I think, in dispute, to re-take possession of the facilities occupied by the Company at Whetstone, but constructed wholly at the Government's expense, and which are now and always have been the property of the Crown.

"At the same time the Minister recognised that the adoption of this course would seriously prejudice the Company's future. He therefore considered it only fair to tell you and you colleagues quite frankly of his intentions, and to say that if you wish to do so, he was prepared to delay taking action while an attempt was made to see whether it was possible by negotiation to arrive at a mutually acceptable price at which the Government should buy out the Company.

"In the result a mutually acceptable price has been reached. In the Minister's opinion — as indeed in my own — it is a very full one, and one which can be justified only because of the difficult position in which the Company is placed, and the very special relationship which has existed for some years now between it and the Department".

The implication that Power Jets had willingly accepted a price of £135,563 10s, for the total purchase of its assets was, of course, quite wrong. Having been threatened with extinction, there was nothing else that the Directors could do except agree to the terms, although they regarded it as something akin to 'armed robbery'.

The circular letter to the shareholders recorded that the plant and equipment operated by Power Jets had been provided at a cost of £350,000, and that a further £950,000 had been expended by the MAP on development work at Power Jets.

So ended Power Jets Limited, the private company which had revolutionised aeronautics and in so doing had founded a great new industry. Its pioneer team was deprived of its right to build and develop jet engines, and the damage was serious — a skilled team is far more valuable than the sum of its parts. The decision was rough justice, by any standard, but if Cripps had had the political clout at the time he might well have nationalised virtually all of the aircraft industry, as did the Labour Government of 1976!

The Government Company was called Power Jets (Research & Development) Limited, and so there was some continuity in name as well as in personnel and equipment with the old Company. Roxbee Cox was appointed Chairman, and the Board included Williams and Tinling.

In early February 1944 Rolls-Royce got to hear that Power Jets was being nationalised, and the Company immediately requested and received an assurance from the MAP that the proposed Government company would not be competitive with private industry. This reaction was one which Whittle had foreseen and feared and, as events were to prove, he had very good reason.

The circumstances surrounding the nationalisation of Power Jets and the position in which Whittle found himself reveal his moral strength and his commitment to the RAF. The price paid for the assets did not include any payment to him, because he had offered to surrender his shares and rights to the MAP some time earlier. When Cripps took over the Company he asked Whittle if his offer still held good, and Whittle confirmed that it did. He did so with considerable reluctance because of his strong objection to the nationalisation of the Company, and because Cripps had said, in effect, that it would make no difference to the price which would be paid for the assets of Power Jets — it would merely have the effect of giving the other shareholders more.

The value of the shares and rights he was surrendering, according to the spurious valuation imposed by Cripps, was about £47,000, which then was a very considerable sum of money. His decision was made none the easier because certain senior officials implied it was unnecessary, and that he was taking an over-conscientious view of his duty.

Moreover, he had received a strong hint from Sir Wilfred Freeman that he was unlikely to receive promotion if he did not broaden his Service experience, because it was against Service policy for senior officers to be over-specialised. Freeman had emphasised his point by remarking that Whittle could scarcely expect to be an Air Marshal attached to Power Jets. The Air Chief Marshal had conveniently ignored the fact that Whittle had invented, developed and knew far more than anyone else, about the type of equipment that would power the RAF for decades to come!

There were personal considerations in that he wanted to be free from the need to worry about the state of his bank balance, and to ensure that his family would not suffer hardship in the event of anything happening to him.

These personal problems were paramount at this particular time. After the tremendous blast of publicity, he had begun to learn that one of the penalties of fame was an unavoidable increase of personal expenditure. Also, his health was deteriorating again and he was suffering acutely from chronic eczema, especially of the ears, and had been repeatedly told that the basic cause of his troubles was nervous strain.

During the final phases of the nationalisation transaction, and the surrender of his shares and rights, he was a patient in the RAF hospital at Halton: "The effects of the sudden and unwelcome publicity of a few weeks earlier, my resentment over the nationalisation business, and my severe internal conflict about my shares, undoubtedly played havoc with an already strained nervous system. However, while in hospital, I didn't drop my work entirely, and I received a number of official visitors".

Whittle had written to Cripps on 11 January 1944 setting out his reasons for deciding to part with all financial interest in his shareholding. His main reasons were:

"My belief that a serving officer should not be in a position to benefit from his employment in any commercial sense . . .

"In order that I could be held to be free of any taint of commercial motive, so that I should not be barred from the counsels of the Ministry especially on matters of policy . . .

"My second object has never in fact been achieved, partly no doubt because the offer of shares to the Ministry was not formally accepted and the position therefore remained ambiguous, and partly because my actions were not sufficiently known to individuals concerned. I say that I failed in this object because, in my opinion, I have not carried anything like the weight I should have done in matters of policy".

The letter then set out the personal reasons why he felt he was making a considerable sacrifice and these have previously been discussed. After a series of discussions with Sir Harold Scott and Mr Sam Brown, an agreement was concluded between Whittle and the Minister of Aircraft Production. This was dated 28 March 1944, and signed while Whittle was in hospital.

The preamble of this agreement contained the following:

"The Inventor considers that as a serving officer engaged on full-time employment on such development, it is improper for him to have or to appear to have any commercial interest in the results of the Company's operations, and that accordingly it is his duty to divest himself absolutely of his financial interest in the Company and in the commercial development of his inventions, and to rely on official awards for his rewards, and the Minister, while being of opinion that there is no legal obligation on the Inventor to dispose of such financial interest, recognises the Inventor's conception of his duty . . .

". . . The Minister has agreed to accept such transfer, on the understanding that such transfer shall not prejudice or affect any application by, or on behalf of, the Inventor for the grant of an ex gratia award in respect of the inventions, and that he shall be entitled to retain for his own benefit any award so granted to him. Also SUBJECT to the requirements of the public interest, the Minister shall afford the Inventor such facilities as he may reasonably require for the purpose of presenting and supporting his application for the grant of an ex gratia award in respect of the inventions".

Thus, Whittle's financial recompense for inventing the jet engine rested with those responsible for making awards.

After the agreement had been signed, Sir Stafford Cripps wrote a personal letter to Whittle on the following day. Cripps concluded by saying: "May I also take this opportunity of expressing my admiration of the inventive genius and hard work you have put into the development of your engine. It represents a valuable asset to the State, and the success already achieved must be as gratifying to you as it is to me".

During previous talks with Sir Wilfred Freeman, Whittle had insisted, as a condition of his surrendering his financial interests, that his interpretation of his duty as a serving officer should be endorsed by the Air Council: "I did not want to run the risk of going down in history as a fool, or to have my action used as evidence that I had gone out of my mind. I commented that it would in any case be presumptuous on my part to insist on doing what I was doing as an act of duty, if my superiors did not uphold my view". Accordingly, he wrote formally to the Air Council on 27 March 1944 inviting an official endorsement.

He did not receive the Air Council's reply until the latter end of May which contained the following:

". . . the Council accept the view, that as a general principle, a serving officer should not make a commercial profit out of his full-time employment.

". . . the application of the principle is sometimes difficult, and the cases which arise shade imperceptibly from one class of case into another. The regulations accordingly provide that exceptions may be made with the special sanction of the Air Council. Thus, in your case, the award of a percentage of commercial profits was made to you with proper authority; and you were free to act on your own judgement either to retain your financial interest in the company or to surrender it. The Council, however, appreciate the high motives which have led you to adopt the second alternative, and consider that your action was in accordance with the best traditions of the Service".

This Air Council letter was sent with a personal letter from Air Marshal Sorley who said: "I feel sure that this letter, together with the one which the Minister sent you on 29 March, should be sufficient to ensure your position when the time comes for you to go to the Royal Commission" (The Royal Commission for Awards).

In his reply to Air Marshal Sir Ralph Sorley's letter, Whittle, who was in hospital, wrote, ". . . As for ensuring my position when the time comes for me to go to the Royal Commission, I hope that it may never be necessary for me to have to 'ask', though I may be driven to it for the sake of my family. It would be extremely distasteful to me to have to do so, and I feel that I should never need to do so — the State should look after its own . . .".

At this time, when Whittle was in hospital in very poor health, it is understandable that he should have written in that vein. They had given him nothing positive to go on, and he was left with assurances that all would be well when he went before the Royal Commission. But, in the event, he had to wait for *four more years* before he was relieved of his anxieties and the need to worry about his financial position.

Whittle was in hospital from the end of March 1944 for six months and, for a few days in the middle of July, his condition deteriorated so much that the doctor placed a complete ban on visitors. However, he recovered sufficiently to be allowed out occasionally, and he was discharged at the end of August.

Two days after leaving hospital, he learned that he had been promoted to temporary Air Commodore with effect from 1 July 1944: "This was very welcome news, in view of the indications I had received that promotion was unlikely until my Service experience had covered a wider field".

*   *   *

While Whittle was in hospital, the Allied landings in Normandy had taken place on 6 June 1944, and Allied air supremacy in the West was to be maintained throughout the remainder of the war and ensured that victory was inevitable.

Whittle's personal challenge from the outset had been his desire to give the RAF a jet fighter, and for him it had been a race against time. But, due to engine problems and the unnecessary political factors described in previous chapters, it was not until May 1944 that the first Meteor Is powered by Rolls-Royce Wellands (ie, the production W.2B) were delivered to the RAF. A unit known as the CRD Flight had been formed at RAE under the command of Wing Commander H. J. Wilson. By June 1944 this Flight had received six Meteors, and were putting in a considerable amount of flying time. A few weeks later these aircraft were transferred to 616 Squadron at Manston, and began operations against the V.1 flying bomb on 27 July 1944.

The year 1944 was one of great activity in the turbojet field in Germany also. The Germans were desperately in need of high-performance fighters. The Allied bombing offensive, both by day and night, had reached a devastating intensity and the enemy was thrown more and more on the defensive. This acted as a great spur to their production of both turbojet and rocket-propelled aircraft. Soon, the Me 262A powered by two Junkers Jumo 004B turbojet engines, and the rocket-propelled Me 163B, began to be a serious menace, especially to the daylight bombing operations of the US Army Air Force. The effectiveness of the Me 262, which had the speed to evade the escorts and the firepower to knock down the bombers, was well illustrated on one occasion when the Americans lost 32 out of a formation of 36 Flying Fortresses.

For this reason the British Meteors were temporarily withdrawn from combat operations (the V.1 attack had in any case almost ceased, because of the advance of the Allied armies through France and the RAF's bombing attacks on the launching sites) and used in tactical trials with British-based American bomber and fighter formations in an effort to evolve defensive tactics against the Me 262 during daylight bombing operations. Lockheed P-80s and Bell P-59As were used for similar tactical trials in the USA.

In his report on the British trials, Wing Commander Wilson commented:

"Results of these trials must have proved very depressing to the Americans with their existing aircraft, as it would appear that Meteors could sail in as and when they pleased, each destroying two or three Forts and pull away without the escorting fighters (even Mustangs) being able to do very much about it".

He concluded that the only answer to the enemy jet aircraft was a long-range escort jet fighter.

For policy reasons the Meteor was not involved in any air-to-air combat clashes during World War 2, and there were no jet-versus-jet battles. However, apart from V.1 operations, Meteors carried out patrols and air-to-ground straffing, and proved to be a very reliable machine with good handling characteristics. The Me 262 had a better performance, but was not nearly as strong, and it had severe operational problems. Generally speaking, the engine was unreliable, and the Luftwaffe lost well over 200 pilots in training accidents alone. However, the Allies had nothing to match it in terms of speed and firepower.

The Germans had three jet aircraft which went into combat during the Second World War; the Messerschmitt Me 262, the Arado Ar 234B, and also the rocket-propelled Messerschmitt Me 163B. In comparison, the Allies had a range of four jet machines powered by fully developed and reliable engines, but the Meteor was the only Allied jet to go into operation. The German Jumo 004 engine had a 'life' of about 25 hours. It had the dangerous characteristic that it could not be 'opened up' rapidly; any attempt to do so resulted in stalling of the compressor and total loss of power.

The range of Allied jets consisted of the Gloster Meteor, the de Havilland Vampire, the Lockheed P-80 Shooting Star and the Bell P-59A Airacomet. This state of affairs was brought about by Frank Whittle alone, who pioneered the turbojet on both sides of the Atlantic.

Chapter 15
The Government Company

Whittle came out of hospital at the end of August 1944, still in poor health, to find that after three months of stagnation in Northern France the tide of war had changed in favour of the Allies. They had broken through German defences and, having total command of the air, were advancing across the Low Countries.

During his absence, the personnel and plant of the old Power Jets and of the Gas Turbine Section of the RAE at Pyestock had been amalgamated under Power Jets R & D Limited. Roxbee Cox remained Chairman, Constant, formerly the head of Pyestock, became the Chief of the Engineering Division of the whole organisation, and Whittle's position was Chief Technical Advisor to the Board.

He returned to the fray to find himself once again in an atmosphere of argument and discontent: "This was probably aggravated by a sharp cleavage between those, like Constant and the Pyestock team of engineers, who were content to regard the organisation primarily as a research establishment, and others, like myself and the pioneer team which I had recruited, who still hoped that the government company would retain its dominant position as engine designers. It was a great pity that Constant and I, who had worked in harmony for so many years, should find ourselves at variance when we had to work together in the same organisation".

For the first time Whittle had doubts about his usefulness within the organisation. He felt that it was virtually coming to an end, but he took no steps to make a break at that time, because he was fairly sure that any such move would be followed by the resignation of a number of other engineers, and he did not wish to expose himself to the charge of breaking up the government company.

It was galling for him that this state of affairs should have come about, at a time when the hesitation and doubt which had hampered his work in the earlier years was rapidly dissipating.

There was abundant evidence that the revolution which he had brought about in the aero-engine industry was at last rapidly becoming fact. Hives had decided that Rolls-Royce would definitely switch over from piston engines to gas turbines, and that future development work on piston engines would be very limited, if not stopped altogether. The Chief of the Air Staff had also indicated that the RAF would be going over almost entirely to jet-engine fighters.

These events may not sound very dramatic in the light of present-day development in space, but at that time when the Second World War was in its closing stages they were of great significance, as millions of us who now jet around the globe will appreciate.

In January 1945, Whittle accepted a directorship of Power Jets (R & D) with the sanction of the Air Council. He did so in the hope that he would regain some of his former influence on engineering policy, and this hope was shared by Roxbee Cox and other members of the Board.

The Minister had appointed an Advisory Committee whose function was to advise the Board of Power Jets and the Ministry on the activities of the Company, and to ensure the co-ordination of the Company's work with other gas turbine work in Britain. This was known as the Gas Turbine Technical Advisory and Co-ordinating Committee (GTTACC), and its members included representatives from the aircraft industry, the MAP and the Admiralty. Whittle missed the first two meetings because he was in hospital, and he returned to find that he had also been co-opted onto an internal committee dealing with technical policy.

Things went well for a time, and it seemed that Whittle might have his way, even to the point of obtaining a substantial expansion of capacity to enable the Company to make sufficient numbers of engines to provide a feed for the development of production methods.

Proposals along these lines were approved by the Technical Policy Committee and subsequently by the Board, and were submitted to the MAP. It seemed, for a while, that the Ministry would authorize this extension of capacity. But, at a meeting of the GTTACC on 18 April 1945, Hives and others from industry made it quite clear that, in their view, it should be no part of the Company's function to design and build even prototype engines, and that there must be no competition with industry whatsoever. These gentlemen had, apparently, conveniently forgotten that at the dawn of the aircraft industry during World War I, many companies were virtually given a blank cheque.

It became apparent during the meeting that pressure groups had been at work to reach agreement and take concerted action. The degree to which these members wished to restrict the activities of Power Jets was most clearly shown when Halford (de Havilland) asked if Power Jets, acting as consultants, would design an engine for a firm if requested to do so. Roxbee Cox, the Chairman, replied that if pressure of other work did not preclude it, the Company would be prepared to furnish a general arrangement drawing. Several members then indicated that in their view any such action would be competitive. Lockspeiser, the Chief Scientist of the MAP, put it to these members: "Your case is that if Power Jets make a complete engine they are in competition?" Halford replied, "Yes".

When it became clear that MAP officials were back-tracking on the provision of capacity issue, and tending to side with the industry, Whittle resigned from the committee, seeing that "the writing on the wall was painfully plain". At this point, disgusted with the course of events, he had lost all desire to remain associated with the government company, and made this clear to Roxbee Cox and other members of the Board.

This was a very hard time for Whittle. Now that the industry was expanding rapidly, with Rolls-Royce in the forefront, people had forgotten about the crucial times when the same companies had shown no interest: "When every morning there was a new part to draw, a new part to be machined into hardware". Without Whittle, these parts of the world's first turbojets would never even have been designed. It was Frank Whittle himself who had to tell everyone how to create them, often using very special alloys, and it was very hard for him to tolerate a situation in which those who had founded a new industry were deprived of the right to design and make even experimental engines.

It was obvious to Whittle that people of the calibre of Walker, Cheshire, McLeod, Feilden, Ogston, Voysey, Bone and many other members of the original team, would not remain much longer with a government company which was destroying their initiative and failing to utilise their unique talents as pioneers who had launched the aircraft gas turbine. Upon his return after six months in hospital, Whittle sensed that the spirit and drive which had formerly characterised the work of the Power Jets team was diminishing, and he thought that there was little doubt that nationalisation had caused a serious drop in morale throughout.

The spark, the euphoria and the dedication, which had characterised the atmosphere in the old days at the Ladywood Works, had evaporated because the challenge was missing. Dr G. B. R. Feilden, who had joined Power Jets in the summer of 1940, together with R. D. van Millingen, remembered that magical atmosphere:

"We had all been very closely concerned with work on the E.28 engine and the question arose which of us should be given the task of installing the engine for the taxiing trials. I remember vividly that, as we stood in the corner of the workshop, Whittle produced some straws which he held behind his back and I was lucky enough to pick the one to install the taxiing engine; Geoffrey Bone had the job of installing the flight engine.

"We took our engine down from Lutterworth to Gloucester, all very secretly, in the height of the war, and I remember for the first time I had sleepless nights over my work, waking up in a cold sweat. Had we put the split pin in the centre of the turbine shaft? Of course we had, but this indicated the pressure we all felt to do the best possible job.

"One evening, fairly late, we had finished everything and the aircraft was taken out on to the grass airfield and the engine was run up. It started very nicely and we got it up to 13,500 rpm, at which we hoped the aircraft would roll quite smoothly and we could do a little trundle round the airfield and see that all was well. It barely moved on the water-sodden grass in early April 1941. We went away disconsolate. However, the following day we ran the engine up to a rather higher speed and the aircraft luckily moved. Finally, we got it up to 16,500 rpm and the aircraft did a short hop. For me, that was one of the most marvellous moments of my life".

Whittle experienced one of those moments in October 1945 — five months after the War in Europe was over. He flew a jet aeroplane for the first time himself, a Meteor I powered by two Power Jets W.2/700 engines. "Strictly speaking, I should not have done so without CRD's permission and, in fact, I did not intend to do so when I climbed into the cockpit — or at least I don't think I did!

"On the morning of 19 October I went to our airfield at

228

Bruntingthorpe to make one of my periodic visits of inspection. I felt a sudden urge to do some taxiing tests in the Meteor. After some twenty minutes of this I returned to Whetstone, but returned to Bruntingthorpe after lunch. After two flights in a Tiger Moth, I decided to do some more taxiing tests. By this time I had acquired a familiarity with the cockpit layout and with the feel of the aeroplane up to take-off speed, and so I yielded to an irresistible urge to take off. I landed after a few minutes at very modest speeds.

"I derived intense satisfaction from the experience, partly because, having had only about two hours' flying practice on elementary training types during the preceding twelve months, I had found myself much more at home in the aeroplane than I had expected, and partly because this particular Meteor was powered by W.2/700 engines designed and made by Power Jets. The occasion when an engine designer has piloted an aeroplane powered by his own engines must have been very few since the Wright Brothers' first flights in 1903.

"Three days later I flew the Meteor again. This time the duration of the flight was 45 minutes, and I essayed much greater speeds and heights than on the first occasion. I was very much impressed with the simplicity of the controls, the complete absence of vibration, and the excellent visibility from the cockpit, in which respect it was far superior to anything I had previously flown.

"I had an even more exhilarating experience a few days later while I was at Herne Bay in connection with the attempt on the World Speed Record. At the request of a public relations officer of the Ministry of Supply, I flew a Meteor III up and down the High-Speed Course. At the time this request was made, I was suffering from the effects of a Rolls-Royce party at Margate the evening before, so I agreed with some misgiving and with the mental reservation that I might cancel at the last moment, but by the time I reached the airfield at Manston, I felt completely recovered and took off.

"The High-Speed Course was clearly marked by a line of buoys spaced a few hundred yards from the low cliffs which border the Thames estuary east of Herne Bay. Herne Bay marked the western end of the course.

"Approaching from the eastern end, I dived down to the beginning of the course from a height of about 1,500 feet, pushing the throttles wide open as I did so. I levelled out at a height of about 50 feet and covered the three kilometres in about fifteen seconds. I then climbed, did a wide turn, and repeated the procedure from the opposite direction. Visibility was extremely good and I felt only slight bumps as I made my two runs, and I was therefore rather puzzled as to why a decision had been made not to attempt a record on that day. I never knew what my speed was, because at that height I deemed it unwise to do other than to use my eyes to see where I was going, but I assume that it must have been about 450 mph, as this was the maximum speed at sea level of the Meteor III with Derwent I engines.

When I returned home a few days later I failed to impress my younger son, then nearly eleven. When he asked me "What speed did you do Daddy?" and I replied "About 450 mph I should think", his disappointed comment was "What! only 450!" The day following he told a friend of the family: "He only did 450 you know, and they will do 600 — he must be out of practice!" In fact the 600-mph Meteors had much more powerful Derwent V engines.

During 1945, Whittle was called upon to give many lectures, attend public functions and make speeches. He had become a famous man and spoke to packed audiences wherever he went. The most important lecture he delivered at this time was the First James Clayton Lecture of the Institution of Mechanical Engineers, entitled 'The early History of the Whittle Jet Propulsion Gas Turbine' and an address to the Royal Institution. He was subsequently awarded the Clayton Prize of the 'Mechanicals' of £1,000 in recognition of the pioneer work described in the paper.

Earlier in the year, on 5 April 1945, he had received an interim award of £10,000, from the Ministry of Aircraft Production, pending his case which would be brought before the Royal Commission on Awards to Inventors at some future date. This was conveyed in a letter from Sir Harold Scott, Secretary of the Ministry of Supply, who concluded by saying:

"The Minister desires me to take this opportunity of expressing his appreciation of the valuable service you have rendered to the Air Forces, and to aviation and engineering generally, and of the sense of public duty which has marked all the steps you have taken".

During 1945 there had been clear signs that the break-up of the Power Jets team was inevitable. Two key members of the original team had left in October, and these had been followed by three others a short time after. Whittle had foreseen this, and stayed put only because he didn't want to be accused of breaking up the government company. Ultimately, when he lost all hope that the Company would retain the right to design and develop any engines and to continue development of production methods, he decided to resign from the Board. On 22 January 1946, he sent in his letter of resignation, addressed to Roxbee Cox. This was a long and detailed document covering Power Jets' problems, during the course of which he said:

"The primary factor in the whole unfortunate situation is that the Power Jets' engineering team is largely built up of engineers who have an intense interest in doing a practical job of work, who desire to see their products used, who are only interested in research as a necessary ancillary to development and not as an end in itself, and who require the stimulus of a succession of fruitful short-term objectives. In short, the team is not suited to the present function of the company. It is the right crew in the wrong ship . . .".

Clarifying his own position, he explained that:

"I find myself in sympathy with the views of the majority of the engineers, and therefore do not regard myself as suited to head the engineering team of a research and development organisation of the type Power Jets is supposed to be. My forte is to direct a few large-scale projects towards a neat and worthwhile objective. I cannot arouse much interest in a myriad of small-scale and relatively unrelated experiments which end merely in a mass of reports".

On 24 January 1946 he wrote to Air Marshal Sir Alec Coryton, who had succeeded Air Marshal Sir Ralph Sorley as Controller of Research and Development, and enclosed a copy of his letter of resignation. In conclusion, he told Coryton he felt that the time had come for him to move on to a broader stage, and that he had already endured a subordinate role in this field for too long.

*   *   *

The break-up which Whittle had foreseen occurred a week or two later. Some sixteen key members of the original pioneer team resigned en bloc, leaving only Wing Commander Lees and one or two others of those who had formed the backbone of Power Jets since 1940. In the event, Power Jets (R & D) remained in being as a small patent-holding Company, while the manufacturing and experimental resources of Whetstone and Pyestock and the Flight Testing Unit at Bruntingthorpe were taken over by the newly constituted National Gas Turbine Establishment.

When the break-up occurred the members of the old pioneer team formed an association known as 'The Reactionaries', which until 1985 met annually at a dinner held on the Saturday nearest to May 15 — the anniversary of the first flight of the E.28/39 in 1941. This was remarkable proof of the strength of the team spirit, and of the nostalgia which the majority of Whittle's former colleagues feel for the old Power Jets' days.

There was no doubt that powerful forces had operated against the Power Jets team from 1940 onwards: "Many individuals contributed to what happened — they included Government officials and influential individuals in industry — and for many different motives. There were those who definitely desired the suppression of Power Jets for commercial reasons; there were those who wanted Power Jets only as a research organisation; there were those who wanted to discredit the principle of a government company for political reasons; but their actions, whether for good or bad motives, all contributed to the same end".

Power Jets would certainly have gone under many years earlier if the company had not proved its technical excellence, despite severe handicaps. It was leading the field in manufacturing methods, particularly in sheet metal work, the broaching of turbine discs, and so on, and it also produced a machine for profiling turbine blades (as the Director of Engine Production said: "If anyone wants to know how to make these things he only has to come here" — ie, to PJ). In the four years which had elapsed since the W.1 did its flight trials, Power Jets had nearly trebled the thrust without any increase in size and only about 70 per cent increase in weight, and all this was accompanied by a very great improvement in the specific fuel consumption.

The Company also held the technical lead in the field of gas turbine technology until 1944, although Rolls-Royce were catching up fast, and made some striking contributions to progress during 1945.

At the time of the break-up, it was quite remarkable that only Rolls-Royce and de Havilland had put more jet engines into the air than Power Jets. Indeed, no other firm had yet equalled Power

Jets' record for the number of types of engine which had powered experimental aircraft (W.1, W.1A, W.2B, W.2/500 and W.2/700).

Following his resignation, Whittle made a short lecture tour in Holland and Belgium, and on his return he was informed that his post had been disestablished. He was not the only one to find himself without a job. Williams and Tinling were in the same boat. Johnson, by virture of his extensive patent knowledge, became Managing Director of what was left of Power Jets (R&D).

Whittle was concerned and sorry for his two old RAF colleagues, Williams and Tinling, who "After ten years, suddenly found themselves deprived of their chief interest in life. There is not a shadow of doubt that, but for their initiative in 1935, my work would never have taken practical shape. There is equally no doubt that they were primarily responsible for bringing into being the Whetstone factory. They also carried the greater part of the administration throughout the time during which Power Jets expanded from nothing to an organisation of about 1,300 strong. I sincerely hope that, if this record does nothing else, it will make clear the magnitude of the debt which the nation owes to these two men".

When the Minister, Mr John Wilmot, learned that Whittle was out of a job he immediately offered him the post of Technical Adviser on Engine Design and Production to the Controller of Supplies (Air) as an Acting Air Commodore, which Whittle accepted, not wishing to be an unemployed Group Captain!

After a long gruelling lecture tour in the USA and in Europe during the latter part of 1946, he agreed to a second visit to America primarily to receive the US Legion of Merit and the Daniel Guggenheim Medal, with a lecture tour tacked on. During this visit his health broke down before he had completed the programme. This was his third and most severe breakdown, and resulted in hospitalisation at the US Naval Hospital in Bethesda, Maryland, in January 1947 and two further periods of treatment in London in late 1947 and 1948, after which he was obliged to retire from the RAF on 13 April: "In a friendly talk with the Chief of the Air Staff, Lord Tedder, we agreed that retirement was the best course in the circumstances".

So, having joined the RAF as an apprentice in September 1923, Whittle was placed on the retired list on medical grounds after twenty-five years in the Service. He retired with the rank of Air Commodore. The Ministry of Supply proposed that on his retirement he should take a post as a temporary civil servant at a salary which, together with his RAF pension, would leave his financial position unchanged. The purpose of this gesture was to free him from money worries while he made up his mind what he was going to do.

Fortunately, he was at last relieved from these worries when, in May 1948, the Ministry of Supply and the Treasury accepted a recommendation of the Royal Commission on Awards to Inventors that he should receive an ex gratia award of £100,000 free of tax (this to include the £10,000 awarded earlier).

Whittle emphasised that he was not a claimant before the Royal Commission. Having decided that a further award to Whittle was to be made, the Ministry of Supply formally requested the Royal Commission to go outside their terms of reference as such, examine his case, and make a recommendation. Lord Justice Cohen, the Chairman agreed, and the case was prepared on Whittle's behalf by the late E. L. Pickles and other Ministry officials.

This sudden turn of events came as a very welcome surprise to Whittle, but it was not until he attended a brief before the Commission that he learned of some of the steps which led up to it. One of these was a letter written by Roxbee Cox, to the Royal Commission, dated 2 October 1947, which had a very considerable influence, and this is reproduced herewith as a fitting tribute to a very great man:

"You have asked me for an appraisal of the work of Frank Whittle. It seems to me a little strange that in this year of Grace after so many people, including myself, have defined the major contribution to progress which Whittle has made, and after so many learned and professional bodies have given him their major awards, any appraisal is necessary. However, I will do my best to sum up the Whittle achievement once again.

"I think you are aware that jet propulsion is one of the most direct illustrations of a fundamental law of nature — Newton's Third Law — and has been recognised by man since at least 150 BC, when an engineer with the somewhat flamboyant name of Hero made proposals for its employment in an engine.

"The gas turbine also is not new. The first design recognisable as a gas turbine was patented by John Barber in 1791. Thereafter there was only very slow progress in gas turbine technology until the present century. It is generally accepted that progress was delayed by the lack of material suitable for continuous operation at high temperatures with appreciable stress.

"Whittle's contribution was the association of jet propulsion and the gas turbine. Before him the gas turbine had been regarded, like other turbines, as a machine for supplying shaft power. Whittle recognised it as the ideal means of providing jet propulsion for aircraft.

"His patent embodying this idea is dated January 1930. His subsequent difficulties in getting his idea taken up and exploited are too well known for recapitulation here. Finally, with the aid of two men whose contribution has been too often overlooked, J. C. B. Tinling and R. D. Williams, a jet propulsion gas turbine engine to Whittle's ideas was designed, constructed and, in 1937, tested.

"It is one thing to have an idea. It is another to have the technical and executive ability to give it flesh. It is still another to have the tenacity of purpose to drive through to success unshaken in confidence, in the face of discouraging opposition. Whittle, whose name in the annals of engineering comes after those of Watt, Stephenson and Parsons only for reasons of chronology or alphabetical order, had these things.

"It is, I think, generally admitted that without Whittle's determination to turn his idea into reality we should not have begun to think about the jet-propelled aeroplane (whatever thoughts we might have slowly developed about the propeller gas turbine aeroplane) until the idea had been forced upon us by the exploits of the enemy with their jet-propelled machines. In the closing stages of the war, however, we had in fact developed, on the basis of Whittle's efforts, a new fighting weapon in the form of the Meteor aircraft: now we are well on the way towards a jet-propelled air force, and the gas turbine engined civil air fleet is being developed.

"It may be said that without Whittle the jet propulsion engine and the other applications of the gas turbine would have come just the same. They would. But they would have come much later. Whittle's work gave this country a technical lead in aircraft gas turbines of at least two years. Properly exploited and maintained, this lead should mean that this country can sell its aircraft gas turbines abroad for years to come. You know better than I do the extent to which Rolls-Royce and de Havilland are producing income for the country. The first of these firms is achieving this with engines which are the direct descendants of the Whittle engine. The second is achieving its contribution with an engine which would not have been designed but for the stimulus and information provided by the early Whittle successes.

"The success which Whittle achieved reacted rapidly upon the work of others in the gas turbine field, notably the RAE team working in association with Metropolitan-Vickers Limited. They had been concentrating on a propeller engine with an axial compressor, in contrast to Whittle's jet propulsion engine with a centrifugal compressor. Whittle's work inspired them to swing over to axial compressor jet propulsion, and to that extent he is the stepfather, so to speak, of that class of engine, the first example of which in this country was the Metropolitan-Vickers F.2.

"The notable success scored by the British aircraft engine industry in the aircraft gas turbine field, a success due in part directly to Whittle, and as for the rest, directly stimulated by him, naturally attracted attention in other fields. The successful application of the gas turbine in the difficult aeronautical field begat endeavour in the land and the sea applications of the gas turbine. The knowledge gained through research and development for the aircraft application was largely applicable in these other directions. Here again, if the chance is grasped there is a wonderful opportunity to build a great industry and, if our technical lead is properly exploited, one which will provide us with considerable national income. If and when this comes to pass, some of the credit will be Whittle's.

"So far the gas turbine in Great Britain has been generally regarded as a means of propulsion of fighting aircraft. I think posterity, looking at its achievements on land and sea as well as in the air, will see it rather as a great commercial asset — presuming that we today do our duty in exploiting it. They will see too that the initiative in its development came from aeronautical technologists, and at the head of these they will see Whittle".

A few days after receiving his award he was made a Knight Commander of the Order of the British Empire (KBE) in the Birthday Honours List, and was subsequently knighted by King George VI at an investiture during July 1948:

"As the King touched me on each shoulder with the sword, I became the first Old Cranwellian to receive the honour of Knighthood. The satisfaction which this gave me was overshadowed by my regret that I was leaving the Service in which I had served since the age of sixteen, and which had given me the training which made possible the jet engine".

Chapter 16
Sir Frank Whittle,
OM, KBE, CB

In June 1986 Sir Frank and Lady Whittle flew from Washington to London on a trip which proved to be one of the highlights of his remarkable life. He was received by the Queen, from whom he received the insignia of the Order of Merit, and in the afternoon he had tea with her.

He also attended a reception of the Order of the Bath in Westminster Abbey, and had a lengthy talk with the Prime Minister at Number 10. During his visit, he was guest of honour at several important functions concerning the aviation industry and in particular the RAF, which is always close to his heart.

Returning to RAF Cranwell as a guest of the Commandant for the Graduation Parade of the 93rd Officers Initial Training Course brought back many mixed memories of sixty-four years previously, when he was there as an apprentice and as a cadet. Later, he was Guest of Honour at the Old Cranwellians' reunion dinner.

For a man of 79 his diary of appointments covering the visit was formidable, and would have exhausted most men of half his age, but throughout he was in good form, spritely and full of humour. Undoubtedly, he had mellowed with the years but the eye, keen as ever, missed nothing.

During Whittle's next visit to the UK, in September 1986, the author attended a lecture he delivered to aeronautical engineers at Speedbird House, Heathrow, London. The auditorium was packed and overflowing with technical people who had come to hear the great man. The hall was darkened and a reading lamp illuminated the small, stocky figure of Whittle, dressed in a dark, well-cut suit with waistcoat, white shirt and Concorde tie, his white hair contrasting with his deep brown eyes and rimmed spectacles. A great burst of applause greeted him as he stood erect on the dais with hands gently resting on the ledge of the lectern. His talented and technical audience was immediately captivated as Whittle began telling the story of the creation, birth and development of his turbojet engine.

His listeners, aware that they were in the company of one of the greatest engineers of all time, quickly responded to his humour which, like his photographic slides, punctuated the flow of his dialogue in dramatic and amusing fashion. Having delivered countless lectures over many years in numerous parts of the world, Whittle gave a masterly performance, which was reflected in his timing and his great ability to carry his audience throughout.

He spoke for just over an hour and then answered a bombardment of highly technical questions with polished ease, sometimes having to take care not to divulge confidential information. Being Whittle, he explained the reasons why he was unable to provide such information, usually ending with a quip or a joke to avoid any sign of pomposity.

Having been in Whittle's company for over an hour and a half, everybody was conscious on leaving the hall that they had been privileged to meet a great Englishman. His refreshing cocktail of technical brilliance, laced with bubbly humour, had been an unforgettable experience.

Sir Frank Whittle, eighty on 1 June 1987, saw the year which marks the fiftieth anniversary of the first test run of his turbojet engine on 12 April 1937. Celebratory functions were arranged on both sides of the Atlantic. The first at the Smithsonian Institution in Washington DC, USA, on 12 April to be followed by an anniversary dinner in London attended by the Duke of Edinburgh.

When, in 1948, Whittle was retired from the RAF on grounds of ill-health, some people at that time regarded him as a spent force who had burnt himself out and would probably vanish from the scene, content to spend the rest of his life in gentlemanly retirement. But this was far from the case.

His biographical notes in the appendix reveal his fascinating and eventful life to date, together with the honours and awards that the world has bestowed upon him. There was a rather special event in October 1986. The Hong Kong chapter of the Royal Aeronautical Society invited him to give the address at their main annual event. He was flown out to Hong Kong on a non-stop flight (on Rolls-Royce engines) after the Farnborough Air Show by his son Ian Whittle, a senior captain of Cathay Pacific Airways. Ian recalls that just before the descent: "As we overflew

Canton in southern China, father reappeared on the flight deck and settled himself in for the approach and landing.

"Now the approach into Kai Tak Airport, Hong Kong, coming in to land on runway 'One Three' is, to put it mildly, rather unusual. All seems quite normal until the aircraft crosses the coast at one thousand feet heading toward the hills that form a backdrop to the urban area of Kowloon, the mainland part of this colourful city. From this point, a sustained descending right turn has to be made over the built-up area to line up with the runway about thirty seconds before the touch-down.

"Unfortunately, I had not thought to brief my father about the nature of this final approach, and was unaware of his consternation when he observed the flight path apparently taking us to certain destruction amongst the craggy hills. To his credit, he said nothing. Or perhaps he was speechless? Anyway, he was delighted to see the runway appear in his field of vision in the final stage of this demanding approach.

"We touched down smoothly, and I heard father joke with the flight engineer saying, 'I couldn't have done it better myself!' This was an occasion of great pride to me and I was a happy pilot".

The supreme moment of Whittle's life was when, at the age of twenty nine, he first ran his turbojet and smelt the kerosene and heard the thunder of the engine he had created. The event became the great turning point in aviation history, and firmly established his name throughout the world for generations to come. The saddest time for him was to see the break-up of his pioneer team: "One consequence was the cancellation of important projects, notably the LR.1 which should have been the world's first turbofan. It was half complete when stopped. And then the power plant for the M.52 (the Miles supersonic aircraft) went down the drain — also nearing completion".

Whittle's story is one of triumph over adversity. The adversity should have been caused by recalcitrant droplets of fuel, and the absence of high-temperature alloys. Instead the worst difficulties were created by purely political factors. Perhaps we can ease the path for Whittles of the future!

Appendix 1

Career, honours and awards

Born 1 June 1907, in Coventry, eldest child of Moses and Sara Alice Whittle.

Educated Earlsdon and Milverton Council Schools and at Leamington College.

1923-26 Aircraft Apprentice, No 4 Apprentices' Wing, RAF Cranwell.

1926-28 Flight Cadet, RAF College, Cranwell.

1928-29 Pilot Officer, No 111 Fighter Squadron, RAF Hornchurch.

1929 Flying Instructor's Course, Central Flying School, RAF Wittering. In 1930 married Dorothy Mary Lee (two sons). Crazy flying event, RAF Pageant. Instructor at No 2 Flying Training School, RAF Digby; also lecturer in Theory of Flight. Filed patent for turbojet.

1931-32 Test pilot at Marine Aircraft Experimental Establishment, RAF Felixstowe. Turbojet patent granted and published.

1932 Officers' School of Engineering, RAF Henlow. Officer i/c Engine Test Section, RAF Henlow.

1934-36 University of Cambridge (Peterhouse) Mechanical Sciences Tripos.

1935 Became Senior Scholar of Peterhouse.

1936 Formation of Power Jets Ltd. Graduated with 1st Class Honours. Granted postgraduate year, during which arrangements were made to build the WU engine.

1937 WU first run on 12 April.

1937-46 Appointed by RAF to Special Duty List.

1939 Air Ministry contracts for W.1 flight engine and Gloster E.28/39 aircraft.

1941 First flight of E.28/39 on 15 May. Full information handed to USA in October.

1943 War Course, RAF Staff College.

1943 After prolonged delays Rolls-Royce took over engine development and put W.2B through official Type Test at full design performance. Limited production of this engine as Welland I.

1944 Meteor I, powered by two Wellands, became operational and initially used for shooting down flying bombs. Power Jets nationalised.

1946 Appointed Advisor to Ministry of Supply; lecture tours.

1946 Power Jets (R & D) converted to NGTE, and deprived of the right to design and develop engines. Whittle and many colleagues resign.

1948 Invalided out of RAF and knighted. Received an award of £100,000 on recommendation of Royal Commission.

1948-52 Honorary Technical Advisor to BOAC.

1952-53 Wrote "Jet".

1953-57 Mechanical engineering specialist to BPM, main operating company of the Shell Group.

1957-59 Technical Advisor, Shell Research.

1959-61 Consultant and lecturer.

1961-69 Technical Advisor to Bristol Siddeley Engines (later Rolls-Royce) on design and development of Whittle Turbodrill. Also expert witness for defendants in Rateau v Rolls-Royce patent action.

1974 Freelance study of SST propulsion.

1976 Emigrated to USA and married second wife, Hazel S. Hall.

1977- Navair Research Professor, and from 1979 Adjunct Research Professor, US Naval Academy, Annapolis. Wrote textbook on gas-turbine design (*Gas Turbine Aero-Thermodynamics*).

Orders

1944 Commander of the Order of the British Empire (CBE).

1946 US Legion of Merit, Degree of Commander.

1947 Companion of the Order of the Bath (CB).

1948 Knight Commander of the Order of the British Empire (KBE).

1986 Order of Merit (OM).

Honorary doctorates

ScD, Cambridge	DSc, Leicester	DSc, Exeter
DSc, Oxford	DSc, Warwick	LLD, Edinburgh
DSc, Manchester	DSc, Bath	DTech, Trondheim

DSc, Cranfield
DTech, University of Technology (Loughborough)

Learned societies
UK
Royal Society, Fellow
Fellowship of Engineering, Fellow
Royal Aeronautical Society, Hon Fellow
Institution of Mechanical Engineers, Hon Fellow
Society of Engineers, Hon Fellow

USA
National Academy of Engineering, Foreign Associate
American Academy of Arts and Sciences, Foreign Member
Franklin Institute, Hon Life Member
American Institute of Aeronautics and Astronautics, Hon
Fellow

Belgium
Société des Ingenieurs, Hon Member

Canada
Engineering Institute of Canada, Hon Member

Medals
UK
Gold Medal of the Royal Aeronautical Society, 1944
James Alfred Ewing Medal, 1945
Reginald Mitchell Memorial Medal, Stoke-on-Trent Society of
Engineers, 1946
Kelvin Medal of the Institutions of Civil and Mechanical
Engineers, 1947
Rumford Medal of the Royal Society, 1950
Albert Medal of the Royal Society of Arts, 1952
Churchill Medal of the Society of Engineers, 1952
Melchett Medal of the Institute of Fuel, 1949
Award of Merit of the City of Coventry, 1966

USA
Daniel Guggenheim Medal, 1946
Benjamin Franklin Medal of the Franklin Institute, 1956
Goddard Award and Medal of the AIAA, 1965
US Department of Transportation Award for Extraordinary
Service, 1978

International
Gold Medal of the Fédération Aéronautique Internationale, 1957
John Scott Award of Philadelphia, 1957
International Communications Prize with Columbus Medal, Genoa, 1966
James Watt International Gold Medal, Institution of Mechanical Engineers, 1977

Professional honours
UK
Peterhouse College, Cambridge, Hon Fellow
Institution of Mechanical Engineers, James Clayton Prize
Central Flying School Association, Hon Member
Guild of Air Pilots and Air Navigators, Member of Livery
Royal Designer for Industry

USA
Society of Experimental Test Pilots, Hon Fellow
American Society of Mechanical Engineers, R. Tom Sawyer Award
Tony Jannus Award
Member of International Hall of Fame, San Diego
Member of Travel Hall of Fame, American Society of Travel Agents
Engineering Hall of Fame (General Electric)
USAF Academy, Member of Mess
Distinguished Achievement Award, Wings Club
National Air & Space Museum Award

Civic Honours
UK
Hon Freeman of Royal Leamington Spa

USA
Hon Citizen of Oklahoma; Key of City of Tulsa

Whittle patents (abridged listing)

Priority date	No.	Subject
16 January 1930	347206	Turbojet
	347766	Rotating intake guide vanes for centrifugal compressor

23 July 1931	375105	(Joint with J. H. McC. Reynolds) Supercharging of piston engines
	451972	Variable-ratio electrical transmission
16 May 1935	456976	Double-sided centrifugal compressor
18 May 1935	456980	Turbojet with double-sided compressor (WU first edition)
25 July 1935	461887	Gas turbine with both single-stage and two-stage double-sided compressor
4 March 1936	471368	Bypass jet or turbofan engine
15 December 1937	511278	Vortex flow design for turbine and compressor
25 February 1938	512064	Engine intakes arranged to swallow boundary layer
9 December 1939	577971	General arrangement of W.1
9 December 1939	577972	Vaporizers for combustion
19 December 1939	583022	Air-cooled turbine disc
2 March 1940	577132	Equalizing flow in multiple ducts
2 March 1940	583111	Aft fan (No 1 Thrust Augmentor)
2 March 1940	583112	Aft fan plus supercharging rotors
2 March 1940	584126	Compressor intake with swirl vanes and guide chutes
1 December 1941	593403	Turbofan with multiple gas generators
2 February 1942	582978	Exhaust cone construction
7 April 1942	587511	Ducts for oil etc passing through diffuser blades
13 May 1942	587512	Jet pipe support
17 November 1942	588084	Thrust boosting by ammonia injection
	588918	Aft fan (No 2 Thrust Augmentor)
	588085	Aft fan (No 3 Thrust Augmentor)

28 July 1947	629143	Installation of turboprop
1 March 1949	677835	Prewhirl rotor ahead of centrifugal compressor
5 August 1949	641062	Smelting and casting in atmosphere of nitrogen

Technical Appendix 1
The Stern Report

When Frank Whittle's proposal for a turbojet came to the notice of the Air Ministry the obvious course for the officials to take was to look up what was known on the subject. This amounted to a slim file, in which the most authoritative document was a report dated September 1920 by Dr. W. J. Stern, of the Air Ministry's own laboratory in South Kensington. The title of this report was ARC (Aeronautical Research Committee) Engine Subcommittee Report No 54, entitled "The Internal Combustion Turbine" — price two shillings (10p).

Stern failed to consider what might be attainable in the future, in such matters as blade efficiency or high-temperature materials. When it is realised that he considered bronzes as turbine rotor materials, and concluded that the best material for the combustion chamber was cast iron we can see how the dice were loaded against the IC turbine in reaching his conclusions. Even his estimates of component efficiency, while doubtless reflecting his best assessment in 1920, were far below what Whittle's calculations suggested should be possible. For example, he studied available types of rotary compressor and concluded that: "Moreover, the compression efficiency of 60 to 65 per cent can only be obtained for slow speed and thus very bulky rotors . . . A compression efficiency of 70 per cent . . . is thus only realisable in the case of large plants with well-designed intercooling between the stages . . .".

Stern's thinking was directed entirely towards heavy and complicated plant designed to drive a propeller. His overall conclusion was: "In a submitted design for aircraft, the weight of a 1,000 hp set comes out to something of the order of 10 lb per hp, the fuel consumption being 1.5 lb oil per bhp hour".

All this was good news to the established makers of piston engines. It suggested that the IC turbine was so uncompetitive as to be unworthy of the slightest consideration. So when a junior RAF officer suddenly proposed not only a totally new engine, the turbojet, but also one with high component efficiencies and extremely light in weight, it was hard to take the proposal seriously.

Technical Appendix 2
The Turbojet

The engine today known as a turbojet — but named by Whittle as a Gyrone — is one of the simplest and purest forms of heat engine. Air is drawn in at an inlet or intake and compressed in a compressor. Whittle wisely chose a single-stage centrifugal compressor, but in order to handle double the airflow he made it double-sided, each half being a mirror image of the other. The air, heated by compression, is fed into one or more combustion chambers or combustors; in Whittle's first experimental WU engine he used a single large chamber to avoid the problem of chambers not all lighting together. Here a liquid fuel is injected and steadily burned. The type of fuel is not critical; Whittle used diesel oil, later replacing this by kerosene. From the combustion chamber hot gas is delivered to the turbine which drives the compressor. Ideally the gas is uniform all over the inlet to the turbine, but in Whittle's earliest engines this was far from being achieved. In the original WU engine the gas was delivered to a vortex scroll upstream of the turbine rotor, but in all later engines the gas passes through a ring of nozzle guide vanes or stator blades which direct it on to the turbine rotor. The latter could have been an inwards radial wheel but even in the original WU Whittle chose an axial-flow unit with a peripheral ring of blades set into a central disc. The blades on the turbine disc deflect the high-speed gases flowing through them, and this provides the driving torque. Downstream of the turbine the gas flow was led to a propelling nozzle where as much of its energy as possible was converted into speed — kinetic energy — in its expansion back to the pressure of the surrounding atmosphere.

This form of heat engine is known as a constant-pressure gas turbine. The heat is added in the combustion chamber at constant pressure, and the vital unit which makes the prime mover self-sustaining is the turbine turned by the flow of hot gas. In all previous gas turbines the turbine had been designed to extract as much shaft power as possible, leaving the smallest possible energy in the flow of hot gas. In Whittle's engine the reverse was the case. Only just enough energy was extracted to drive the compressor. All the rest provided the energy of the propulsive jet.

Technical Appendix 3
The Whittle engines

The first patent

Filed on 16 January 1930, British Patent No 347,206 was the first in the world to describe a practical turbojet. The proposed engine had an annular inlet (2) to a two-stage axial compressor (4) followed by a single-stage centrifugal compressor (7). After passing through a diffuser (9) and right-angle elbows with cascade vanes the compressed air entered a series of parallel combustion chambers (10) into which fuel was injected (11). The hot gas was then guided through an axial-flow turbine with two stages (14) on one disc (13), with a ring of stator vanes (15) between the rotor stages. The turbine drove the compressor via shaft (16). Finally the hot gas was expanded and accelerated through a divergent nozzle ring (17).

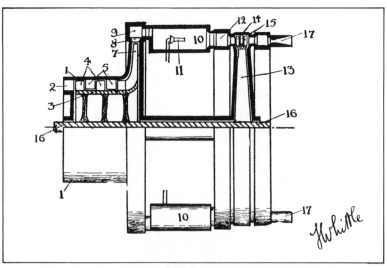

Reproduction of drawing, illustrating British Patent No. 347,206, filed 16th January 1930

The WU

Though entirely practical, the arrangement depicted in the patent drawing differed considerably from the first experimental

Whittle Unit (WU) actually built. The latter had no upstream axial compressor stages, but used a large centrifugal compressor, and this was made symmetrically double-sided to obtain the greatest airflow from a given size, and thereby reducing skin-friction losses. The impeller was given the greatest number of vanes (30) that manufacturing limitations allowed, to reduce blade loading and avoid stalling at the impeller inlet. Surrounding the impeller was a scroll-type volute leading into a vertical expanding diffuser pipe containing a honeycomb of divergent channels. At the top of the diffuser the compressed air was turned through 90° by a cascade of seven vanes in an elbow before entering the single combustion chamber having a single burner. This delivered hot gas via a large curving pipe into a nozzle scroll shaped to discharge the gas through its annular exit facing the turbine with constant angular momentum. No turbine nozzle guide vanes were fitted. The turbine itself was a single axial rotor, made like the compressor from a single forged disc, the two being linked by the shortest possible tubular shaft. The turbine was overhung, a bearing downstream being difficult to arrange, and the turbine disc was cooled by water jackets in close proximity.

The design assumptions for the WU — some of which were to prove slightly optimistic — were: compressor efficiency 80%; turbine efficiency 70%; axial velocity at turbine exhaust 800 ft/s (14% of heat drop); efficiency of final expansion 97%; air mass flow 26 lb/s; fuel flow 0.3635 lb/h (= about 168 Imp gal/h); power to drive compressor 3,010 hp; static thrust 1,389 lb. The assumed PV (pressure/volume) diagram had the following points: A start of compression, 14.7 lb/in^2, 288°K; B compressor delivery, 64.6 lb/in^2, 439.5°K; D, delivery from combustion chamber, 64.6 lb/in^2, 1,052°K; E/F turbine nozzle mouth, 23.45 lb/in^2, E 795.8°K, F after reheat 836.7°K; G, jet nozzle, 14.7 lb/in^2, 737°K, 1,720 ft/s.

Note: at that time "turbine efficiency" meant shaft power divided by heat drop to the static pressure at exhaust, the leaving velocity being treated as a loss. Today, turbine efficiency is taken to mean shaft power divided by the heat drop to total pressure at exhaust, leaving velocity not being treated as a loss. In the light of events, only the WU compressor efficiency was assumed over-optimistically. Assumptions for turbine and exhaust efficiencies were conservative.

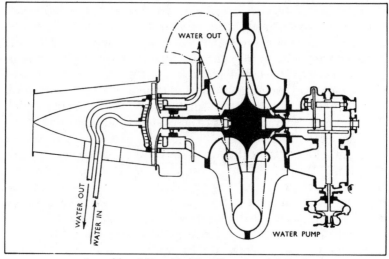

Assembly of First Model of Experimental Engine

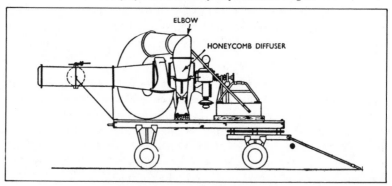

Test Assembly of First Model of Experimental Engine

WU reconstructed

When testing stopped on 23 August 1937 Whittle reluctantly decided on a major reconstruction, and the WU Model 2 did not make its first run until 16 April 1938. In retrospect the design appears clumsy and complicated, but it satisfied several new objectives: to burn in a straight chamber, to improve the compressor diffuser system and to make the engine axisymmetric. Instead of delivering into a scroll volute the impeller delivered into ten curved pipes connected to the front of a long cylindrical casing. This carried the air to the rear of the engine where it entered the single large combustion chamber arranged in the reverse direction, the air and flame travelling forwards. At the front this chamber delivered into a nozzle ring and reverse-flow turbine, the blade angles of which conformed to flow having constant angular momentum (which Whittle had incorrectly assumed to be normal turbine design practice). Downstream of the turbine the gas flow was split into ten, turned through 180° and delivered aft through ten jetpipes. Heat exchange between the compressed air and hot gas was a deliberate objective.

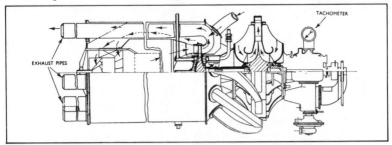

Assembly of Second Model of Experimental Engine

The design assumptions for the reconstructed WU were realistic, being based on experience of actual running: compressor efficiency 70% (still far better than anything achieved previously); turbine efficiency 70%; efficiency of final expansion 90%; mass flow 26 lb/s; fuel flow 0.3635 lb/s; static thrust 1,240 lb (not attained because of turbine failure).

WU Model 3

A second major reconstruction took place between 6 May 1938 and the start of a new test programme on 26 October 1938. During the interim extensive testing took place on vaporizing burners, but (as briefly related in the text) two heartbreaking years were spent trying to achieve acceptable combustion. In the third model of the WU there were features borrowed from both its predecessors, but the big change was that there were ten combustion chambers. These were of the reverse-flow layout. The compelling reason for this was that it was the only way that the sheet-metal work could be adapted to the rotor and other expensive parts. Other advantages were that the outer casings were kept cool, thermal expansion and assembly problems were minor, and (a vital factor in view of subsequent experience) it was possible to make quick modifications to the burners and other "innards". Because of its cost the original compressor impeller was retained, though the cracked buttress ribs had to be machined away and the vanes were made thinner. The turbine was unchanged except that its flow direction was reversed to the "normal" direction, the gas finally escaping through the jetpipe used in the original 1937 engine. The one thing that had worried Whittle, namely simultaneous lightup of all ten chambers, was ensured by interconnecting tubes linking the air casings and flame tubes.

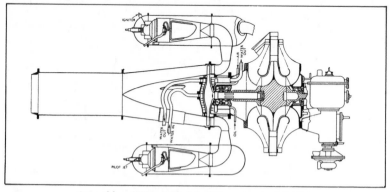

Assembly of Third Model of Experimental Engine

The agonizing failure to obtain good combustion with 31 different vaporizers, and many dozens of minor modifications, was due to small disturbances in the chamber aerodynamics which could not be reproduced on the test rigs. At last, on 9 October 1940 the Model 3 engine was run with Lubbock (Shell type) burners which instead of vaporizing the fuel used high pressure atomization. This was the beginning of light at the end of the tunnel. Among many other modifications found to be beneficial were the addition of curved guide-vane rings in the inlet to the compressor, a change from the old De Laval bulb-root type of turbine blade attachment to the new fir-tree root, and the possibility of eliminating the turbine water jackets.

W.1

On 30 June 1939 the DSR (Director of Scientific Research) visited Ladywood Works, witnessed a run at 16,500 rpm and immediately decided contracts should be placed for a flight turbojet and for a jet aircraft powered by it. Design began forthwith on the W.1. This differed only in fairly minor ways from the WU third model. The most important changes were:

construction was much lighter; the auxiliary gearbox was much smaller and lighter; the compressor impeller had 29 blades instead of 30 (as originally planned for the WU Model 3) to avoid resonant coupling with the ten combustion chambers; the number of turbine blades was increased from 66 to 72, each secured by a fir-tree root; and the compressor casing was provided with four mountings picking up the tubular structure of the E.28/39.

While the W.1 was being made some major parts were finally considered to be unairworthy, and instead of scrapping these it was decided to combine them with various spare components made for the WU and thus create an additional non-flying engine, the W.1X. This was delivered, loosely assembled, in November 1940, and was first run on 14 December. It was suspended by swinging links from the roof of the new test house at Ladywood Works, thrust being measured by spring balance and later by a hydraulic thrust-meter. It was sent to US General Electric after completing 132 hours' running. Dr Harry Ricardo assisted in development of the fuel and control system, which in later engines included a top-speed governor and a barostatic valve which progressively reduced fuel pressure as a function of altitude.

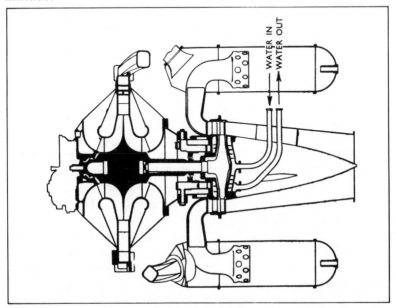

Assembly of W.1 engine (combustion chamber details not shown)

The W.1 itself owed a great deal to experience with the W.1X. It was first run on 12 April 1941, and over the next 46 days the W.1 was run up to full design speed, cleared for flight in a 25-hour Special Category Test at 850 lb thrust at 16,500 rpm, installed and checked out in the aircraft and put through the first 10 hours of flight trials!

The W.1(T) was a modified W.1 constructed from spares and used for bench development. It was first run in October 1941. The W.1(3) was also a modified W.1, tested during 1942.

The Specification for the W.1 was remarkably similar to that for the original build of the WU as run in April 1937; figures asterisked were unchanged: compressor impeller tip diameter 19 in*; impeller tip width 2 in*; outer diameter of eye 10.75 in*; inner diameter of eye 5.5 in*; number of blades 29; material Hiduminium RR.59 (1937 alloy was RR.56); compressor casing magnesium alloy 299 to DTD.350; turbine blade mean diameter 14 in*; blade length 2.4 in*; blade material Firth-Vickers Rex 78 (1937, Stayblade); blade chord 0.8 in*; number of blades 72 (1937, 66); disc material Firth-Vickers Stayblade*; maximum speed 17,750 rpm. Maximum achieved speed was 17,000 rpm, at which the mass flow was about 22 lb/s at 36 lb/sq in gauge, exhaust (jetpipe) temperature 870°K, thrust 950 lb and specific fuel consumption about 1.37.

W.1A

This engine was based on the W.1 but incorporated several of the major new features planned for the W.2 which it was desired to test in advance. The chief new features were found in the compressor inlet, which had stationary guide vanes giving the air a pre-whirl in the direction of rotation. Another major change was that the turbine was cooled only by air, the vanes of the cooling fan being machined integral with the disc and rotating immediately inside a peripheral ring of radial stator exit vanes on the front and rear of the disc. Initial testing, in May 1941, was very disappointing, the chief reason being poor turbine performance. The turbine had been designed for much too high an exhaust velocity; moreover, on the advice of the RAE, aerofoil blading had been used. When the turbine was rebladed in accordance with Whittle's previous practice of designing the blade profiles to conform with the inter-blade channels, and the cooling airflow for the rear of the disc had been omitted, the

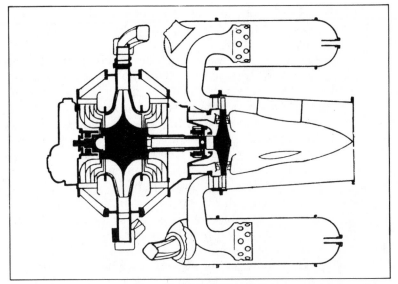

Assembly of the W.1A engine

W.1A came near its design rating of 1,450 lb, actual thrust being 1,340 lb. The elimination of the cooling airflow from the rear of the turbine stopped the injection of relatively stagnant air immediately downstream of the turbine which had caused choking in the exhaust annulus and thus resulted in a wholly new phenomenon, surging of the compressor. As modified, the W.1A showed a marked improvement in sfc (specific fuel consumption) over all previous engines, and powered the E.28/39 aircraft.

W.2

This engine was planned in 1939 as the second-generation turbojet, significantly more advanced than the W.1, and it was ordered in 1940 and built mainly by Rover. As constructed, it differed from the Power Jets design in certain mechanical features. The Power Jets team carried out more detailed calculations and these showed that in some respects the engine was very critical. If the assumptions of component efficiency were not realized, the penalties were likely to be very severe, and from the first run it was clear that this was, in fact, the case. The most serious shortcoming was that the turbine had been designed for exit velocity too near the speed of sound. Thus, as the design component efficiencies were not realized, exhaust velocity reached the critical value at well below design full speed. As a result, compressor surging and high jpt (jetpipe temperature) prohibited running at above 75% rpm.

Accordingly Power Jets spent much of 1940 designing a less critical engine, the W.2B, and this was planned as the engine of the F.9/40 (later Meteor) twin-engined fighter. Complete sets of Power Jets W.2B drawings were passed to the several companies involved in manufacture, though the first two engines to be tested were made by Rover and again differed from the Power Jets design. Meanwhile, in 1941 Power Jets and BTH jointly built the W.2 Mk IV, or W.2/4, which was a W.2 modified in stages to bring it nearer to W.2B standard. Most unfortunately, this was totally wrecked at about 9,000 rpm on its first run with a new impeller, though none of the four people inside the test chamber was seriously injured. The reason was a previously undetected crack across the impeller forging almost across a diameter.

The W.2B development proved to be troublesome and very protracted. Difficulties included surging, high jpt, turbine blade failures and many other kinds of mechanical failure. Whittle advised Rover that he was convinced the 1,600 lb design thrust would be reached with a 5° twist of the turbine blades, but the advice was ignored. Rover's own (secret from Power Jets) "development" was a disaster, being stuck at around 1,000 lb. Eventually Whittle was forced to the conclusion that Rover's grip on the W.2B had precluded proper development. Accordingly, on 2 March 1942 design began on a complete redesign, the W.2/500. It was the first engine built mainly by Power Jets, and the design, construction and initial testing were all completed in six months, full design rpm being reached on 2 September 1942. Much of the success of the W.2/500 was due to improvement in turbine blade material, notably the development by Mond Nickel of the nickel-chromium alloy Nimonic 80. The results achieved with the W.2B/500 plotted so exactly on the design curves that Whittle was misled into declaring "jet engine design has become an exact science". So it did later become, but Power Jets still had to endure a 1942 punctuated by every kind of disappointment, including random failures of W.1A turbine blades (caused by a thermocouple downstream) and an epidemic of failures of the W.2/500 impeller (caused by resonance at around 14,000 rpm). In 1943 the W.2/500 flew in the Meteor and E.28/39, while Rolls-Royce at last twisted the turbine blades of the W.2B through the 5° which Whittle had requested *two years earlier,* and sailed

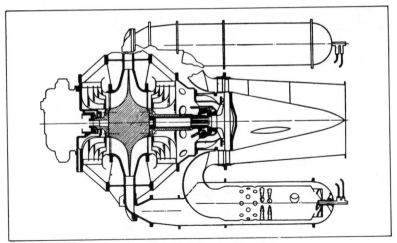

Assembly of the W.2B engine

through a 100-hour type test at the design rating of 1,600 lb. The engine very quickly went into production as the Rolls-Royce Welland I, power unit of the Meteor I.

In 1944 Power Jets made limited numbers of the W.2/700, the last of Whittle's own designs to be built and the last with reverse-flow combustion chambers. Lest any should think there was anything mistaken about the reverse-flow chamber, it is a feature of the majority of smaller turbofan, turboprop and turboshaft engines today, and will continue to be used. The W.2/700 was rated at up to 2,500 lb, but the Rolls-Royce Derwent with straight-through chambers was picked instead to power the Meteor III as used in action late in the war.

Technical Appendix 4
Subsequent Patents

In March 1936 Whittle filed UK Patent No 471,368, for a bypass jet engine or ducted fan (today called a turbofan). Not only did this describe the turbofan completely, and explain its advantages, but the patent even envisaged the addition of afterburning (reheat) for takeoff and supersonic flight. D. L. 'Don' Brown, who worked on the supersonic Miles M.52 (which was to have been powered by a W.2/700 with afterburning in both the jet and in a surrounding bypass flow), wrote an article for *The Aeroplane* in March 1959 describing Whittle's many ducted fan and related ideas and expressed astonishment at the fact that, at that date, not one turbofan was in service anywhere. Later Brown became Principal of the (Power Jets) School of Gas Turbine Technology; he died in 1987.

In March 1940 Whittle applied for patents covering two forms of turbofan, which he called Thrust Augmentors. The first was similar to today's front-fan engines, in that the fan was upstream of the engine. It differed in that there were two stages which contra-rotated. The other scheme, adopted in order to save time and give the concept a chance of actually being built, was to add an aft fan downstream of the engine. The jetpipe led to a two-stage turbine whose rotor carried double-deck blades, the inner part of each blade being a turbine driven by the hot gas and the outer part being a fan blade working in fresh air from a peripheral ram inlet. The fact that drawings of this scheme were given to General Electric in 1942 is not mentioned in the company history-book *Seven Decades of Progress* despite the fact that precisely the same scheme was adopted in General Electric's first production turbofan in 1961!

A 1941 patent described an arrangement in which multiple Whittle turbojets were arranged as gas generators to discharge through a single large turbine driving a fan supercharging the core engines. In other schemes the multiple turbojets were geared to single or tandem fans upstream, the tandem fans comprising a large LP unit pressurizing the engines and a bypass duct and a smaller medium-pressure fan pressurizing just the core engines.

PENDIX 4   259

Yet another engine, the LR.1 (Long Range 1), was triggered off in 1943 by Whittle's appreciation at the RAF Staff College of the need for long-range bombers for the Far East. In one form the LR.1 comprised a turboprop with an eight-stage axial compressor followed by an HP centrifugal compressor, as later built by Rolls-Royce in the Clyde. In another version it was a turbofan with a two-stage axial LP fan, of 2.5 bypass ratio, followed by the same eight-stage axial compressor and centrifugal in the core engine. Weighing an estimated 2,770 lb, this impressive engine was calculated to give 2,860 horsepower, for a fuel consumption at sea level of 1,890 lb/h. Specific fuel consumption of the turboprop was estimated at 0.41.

All these engines were eminently practical. None was built, and it was to be more than ten years before anything resembling them was actually to be developed.

Whittle's last major patents, dating from 1956, were for the basic principle of the Turbodrill, and for its control ram. As described in Technical Appendix 5 this yet again was a brilliant idea.

Technical Appendix 5
The Turbodrill

While advising BOAC Sir Frank visited a Bahrein oilfield. He soon decided there simply had to be a better method of drilling than to apply the torque at the top of hundreds of sections of drill string, which frequently broke and whose stored torsional energy had to be "unwound" every time an extra section was attached. He calculated it was similar to trying to rotate a needle on the end of a human hair 2ft (0.6 m) long or more!

In 1953 his appointment as Mechanical Engineering Specialist to BPM, main operating company of the Shell Group, enabled him to study the problem in detail. He quickly decided it was more sensible to apply the drive at the bottom of the drill string, using the drilling mud as working fluid for a hydraulic turbine. He was aware that a long direct-drive turbine having 100 stators and 100 rotors was in use in the Soviet Union. Sir Frank decided that a much smaller and simpler drive ought to be possible. He started on the design with the help of a project group of two draughtsmen seconded from Stanlow refinery and an engineer from Shell Oil of the USA.

By 1957 the design had been completed of a turbodrill having a five-stage contra-rotating turbine comprising a high-speed rotor turning at 3,000 rpm in one direction with a low-speed rotor rotating in the opposite direction at 500 rpm, the two rotors being coupled through an epicyclic gearbox. The low-speed rotor was directly coupled to the bit shaft. This arrangement was much more compact than the Russian type, but it was against Shell policy to get directly involved in making drilling equipment.

In 1959 Dr (later Sir) Stanley Hooker, Technical Director of the newly formed Bristol Siddeley Engines Ltd (BSEL), invited Sir Frank to Bristol and became interested in the project. The result was that BSEL embarked on the development of the Turbodrill. Following initial tests at BP's Eakring Field, Notts, and Plungar Field in Leicestershire, full-scale trials took place on Severnside. In one test at Eakring 600 ft (183 m) of Bunter sandstone was drilled in one hour. Later, in limited commercial operation, a hole was deviated from the vertical to a final inclination of 40° in 2,000 ft (610 m) in ten hours, an operation which would have taken days with conventional methods.

Each complete Turbodrill had 70 parts and cost £3,000 at 1970 prices. Drilling costs over years of testing averaged US$1.50 per foot, compared with about $3.50 by conventional methods. Altogether 32 Turbodrills were made, and they achieved their design targets fully. A special company, Bristol Siddeley Whittle Tools (BSWT), was formed to exploit the Turbodrill, but in 1966 BSEL was bought by Rolls-Royce, which went bankrupt because of the RB.211 turbofan engine in 1971. BSWT's work was terminated along with many other subsidiaries.

Technical Appendix 6

A Brief Summary of Power Jets' Work on Turbofans

by Sir Frank Whittle, OM, KBE, CB

The overall efficiency of a jet engine is the product of the thermal efficiency and the propulsive efficiency.

The engine may be thought of as an 'energiser' within a duct — it 'inhales' air through the intake at the front of the duct and expels it (plus combustion products) rearwards through a nozzle with much increased velocity and increased temperature. The thermal efficiency is the increase of kinetic energy (proportional to the square of the velocity) induced divided by the chemical energy of the fuel consumed.

The propulsive efficiency is the product of the thrust and forward speed (ie the 'rate of doing work') divided by the increase of kinetic energy.

The thrust is proportional to the product of the rate of airflow through the engine times the increase of velocity induced, ie the difference between the jet speed and the flight speed. Thus thrust is a function of jet velocity, whereas the kinetic energy increase is a function of the square of the jet velocity, so the higher the jet velocity the greater the thrust per unit of mass flow, but the lower the propulsion efficiency because of the greater amount of kinetic energy wasted in the wake. For example, if the jet velocity is three times the flight speed (ie the difference between jet velocity and flight speed is twice the latter) the propulsive efficiency is 50%, whereas if the jet velocity is only twice the flight speed (ie the difference is equal to the flight speed) the propulsive efficiency is 66.7%, but for this the rate of airflow (the 'mass flow') would have to be doubled to give the same thrust.

From the earliest days of my work on the jet engine I realised that for speeds of the order of 500 mph the propulsive efficiency would be only about 50% as compared with about 80% for a propeller at much lower speeds, so I cast around for ways to improve on this; I wanted to 'gear down the jet', ie to convert a low-mass high-velocity jet into a high-mass low-velocity jet. The obvious way to do this was to use an additional turbine to extract energy from the jet and use this energy to drive a low pressure compressor or fan capable of 'breathing' far more air than the jet engine itself and forcing this additional air rearwards as a 'cold jet'. It was clearly desirable to arrange for part of the output of the fan to 'supercharge' the main engine (usually referred to as the 'core engine' or gas generator). The complete system is known as a 'turbofan'.

I filed a patent application for this arrangement in March 1936 at the same time that Power Jets was formed.

The turbofan concept was, of course, too ambitious a project to embark on with the available finance and before a simple jet engine had been demonstrated, so the scheme, of necessity, 'remained on ice' for a few years.

Once the jet engine had proved itself, I sought a simpler temporary means of improving the propulsive efficiency. I wanted something one could 'tack on' to the simple jet engine and so conceived the 'aft fan' in which an additional turbine in the exhaust of the main engine also carries fan blades as 'extensions' of the turbine blades.

The first embodiment of the idea we called the No 1 Thrust Augmentor. This was a very simple concept — two oppositely running rotors — but it had to be abandoned when preliminary design showed that practicable blade angles and speeds were not possible.

Then followed the No 2 Augmentor — a more conventional two-stage arrangement also with fan blades as extensions of, ie external to, the turbine blades.

The No 2 Augmentor did not proceed beyond the design stage at Power Jets because it was superseded by the No 3 Augmentor, but the drawings were sent to GE in the USA in 1942 where it was developed in later years to become part of the power plants of the Convair 990. A smaller version was used in the Falcon Fanjet.

The No 3 Augmentor had the turbine blades outside the fan blades. This arrangement came to be known as a 'tip turbine'. This basic arrangement was very attractive because the fact that the turbine blades had a much higher speed than the fan blades (by virtue of the greater diameter) made a single rotor possible. Unfortunately a major disadvantage of this arrangement was the ducting. The exhaust from the main engine had to be led to the tip turbine through a series of ducts which passed through, and interfered with, the flow into the fan blades.

The No 3 Augmentor was built and tested, but though it did give a substantial increase in static thrust, this increase was much less than it should have been because of the loss of fan efficiency due to the flow interference mentioned above. The heat picked up by the fan flow further reduced the efficiency. There is no doubt that much could have been done to improve matters — by streamlining and lagging the ducts to the tip turbine, but Power Jets was then too overloaded to spare the time and effort.

Some time later we embarked on the No 4 Augmentor which was generally similar to No 2. In combination with a W2/700, it was to have been the power plant of the Miles 52 supersonic aeroplane. A particular feature of the M.52 power plant was that the power was further augmented by burning additional fuel both before and after the fan turbine.

Unfortunately the contract for the M.52 was cancelled as also was that for its power plant as a consequence of the conversion of Power Jets (R & D) into the National Gas Turbine Establishment.

The first attempt at the turbofan proper, ie having the fan ahead of and supercharging the core engine, was the LR1 intended as the power plant of a four-engined bomber for operations in the Pacific. The mass flow through the fan of the LR1 was to have been 3-4 times that through the core engine, ie the 'bypass ratio' was 2-3.

The LR1 was the most serious 'casualty' of the policy resulting from the formation of the NGTE. It was cancelled when about half built. Had it been completed it would have been the world's first turbofan. As it was, several years were lost before turbofans began to supersede straight jets for subsonic aircraft.

The main turbofan patent 471368 would have expired in 1952 but, at a hearing in the High Court of Chancery, Mr Justice Lloyd Jacob gave it the maximum extension of 10 years on the ground of exceptional merit and that unfortunate circumstances had prevented its exploitation. Even so, it still expired just as turbofans became 'fashionable'.

Bibliography

Jet by Sir Frank Whittle, Frederick Mueller, 1953.
The 1945 Clayton Memorial Lecture, Sir Frank Whittle, Institution of Mechanical Engineers.
The Beginnings of Jet Propulsion by Lord Kings Norton, The Royal Society of Arts, Trueman Wood Lecture, 27 March 1985.
Not Much of an Engineer, biography of Sir Stanley Hooker, Airlife, 1985.
Development of Aircraft Engines and Fuels by R. Schlaifer and S. D. Heron, Harvard Graduate Business School, 1950.
Government History of the Second World War, Design and Development of Weapons, Gas Turbines and Jet Propulsion, 1964, HMSO and Longmans.
Seven Decades of Progress, General Electric Co, Aero Publishers Inc, 1979.
World Encyclopaedia of Aero Engines, Bill Gunston, Patrick Stephens, 1986.
The Jet Age: Forty Years of Jet Aviation, Walter J. Boyne and Donald S. Lopez, editors, Smithsonian Institution Press, 1979.
Jet Flight by John Grierson, Sampson Low, Marston, 1945.
Journal of the Royal Aeronautical Society, Centenary Edition, 1966.
I Kept No Diary, Air Commodore F. R. ('Rod') Banks, Airlife, 1983.

Index